PUT MONEY IN THY PURSE

Micheál Mac Liammóir, actor, designer and playwright, was already appearing on stage by the age of thirteen. In 1928 with Hilton Edwards he established the Dublin Gate Theatre, where he has acted in over 300 productions. He has also played frequently in London and abroad, and in 1949–50 took the part of Iago in Orson Welles' film OTHELLO, described in this book. As well as plays, poems, stories and essays in Irish, Micheál Mac Liammóir's books include the autobiographical ALL FOR HECUBA (1946), EACH ACTOR ON HIS ASS (1960) and AN OSCAR OF NO IMPORTANCE (1968), and the plays ILL MET BY MOONLIGHT (1957) and WHERE STARS WALK (1961). He also compiled the one-man entertainment THE IMPORTANCE OF BEING OSCAR (published 1963), which he has performed throughout the world.

MICHEÁL MAC LIAMMÓIR

PUT MONEY IN THY PURSE

The Filming of Orson Welles'
Othello

WITH A PREFACE BY ORSON WELLES

EYRE METHUEN
LONDON

First published in 1952
by Methuen & Co. Ltd
Second, revised edition 1976
by Eyre Methuen Ltd
11 New Fetter Lane, London EC4P 4EE
Copyright © 1952, 1976 by Micheál Mac Liammóir

Printed in Great Britain
by Fletcher & Son Ltd, Norwich

ISBN 0 413 31890 7 (Hardback)
ISBN 0 413 36740 1 (Paperback)

PREFACE

by

ORSON WELLES

WHY is it, I wonder, that most of us who are Micheál Mac Liammóir's friends—having never been his victims—are so very certain that at any minute we might be?

'O that Micheál——!' we say, with a knowing, a vaguely apprehensive sort of leer.

What do we think we mean? In company, 'that Micheál' of ours doesn't slash or slaughter, or even prick, but lavishly spreads about him, instead, the pleasant oils and balms of good humour. He is an entertainer rather than a conquistador, a good companion, who could certainly scratch, but who prefers to purr. If he must be excluded from the full title of wit, his lack is ruthlessness and his only fault a preference for being kind.

Why, then, do we think of him as so fatal a swordsman among conversationalists, so perilous a man to meet over a martini? I now reveal his true, his darkest secret. It is simple almost to the point of squalor: he keeps a diary!

The diarist, having arranged a sort of rendezvous with posterity, moves, for all his good manners, in a solid aura of menace. Most of Micheál's acquaintances don't know why, but this is what makes them so jumpy in his presence. Some of us, of course, have long had our suspicions. For, as a contraction of the pupil is said to betray the dope fiend, so we are warned by a certain glitter, a cold glint of appraisal in the eye of the abandoned wretch who has given himself over to the keeping of a private journal.

I have had diaries myself. But, then, I have known how to leave them alone: an entry or two just for the thrill of it, and then back to normalcy. I count myself lucky. The addiction to diaries, the habitual keeping of a journal, a secret vice like the eating of hashish, degrades the diarist himself to something very like the moral status of a drama critic and, unlike drugs, destroys not only the character of the user but of his friends.

Having exposed Mac Liammóir for what he is, an explanation of this book requires that I make full confession of being myself an inveterate, an incurable snoop.

My friends, such as remain to me, are about evenly divided between those who do not believe that I would stoop to steaming open their most intimate correspondence, and those who, having caught me in the act, have decided to forgive me.

Knowing my curiosity to be such that I am perfectly capable of learning Gaelic in order to read it, Micheál (who not only keeps his daily journal under lock and key, but writes it in the Irish language) has guarded it with such exquisite caution that at long last I was forced into the desperate manœuvre of begging him to publish it. This book is the result.

I would have preferred to have been the only reader. Indeed, my portrait emerges from the Mac Liammóir journal as a rather unpalatable cocktail of Caliban, Pistol and Bottom, with an acrid whiff here and there of Coriolanus. I am to be found (the dialogue being rendered in a peculiarly quaint version of Americanese) railing and raging against its author, a veritable force of bad nature, a withering blast from off my own Middle Western prairies.

I must defend myself against this, because the truth is

that Micheál's ears, during almost every moment of our daily work together, rang with highly merited praise. A nice reticence witheld him from keeping any record of this success. The rare exceptions, for comic effect, are elaborately dwelt upon. Permit me to insist that if there is an impression that my administrative tactics are just a trifle more thorough-going than Captain Bligh's, only Micheál's modesty is to blame.

It is reported that I addressed him as 'harp'. I ask the reader to believe that I do not use or approve of that special level of slang ('kraut' for German, 'hunky' for Hungarian, 'limey' for Englishman, etc. etc.). For the benefit of those who share my loathing for even the mildest shades of chauvinism, I must explain a joke whose point was in deliberate bad taste:

'Harp', you see, brings to mind that improbable figure, the Irish-American of St. Patrick's Day parades, complete with budget-sized shamrock and souvenir shillelagh, and Micheál is something else again. His far-wandering spirit has chosen never to travel without a plush knapsack, plum-coloured and chock-full of the more attractive Edwardian airs and continental graces, but no shamrocks at all. Indeed Micheál, who does really look a bit like something Beardsley would have drawn if they'd taken away his pencil-sharpener, is the very last Irishman on the broad face of the earth to be called 'harp'.

So much for that. As they say at banquets, Micheál Mac Liammóir needs no introduction. He has proven himself in every one of the numerous mediums of his choice, and has done so again and again.

Well, then, here is a book of his about a film we made together. I have nothing significant to add to the first of these projects, which you are evidently about to read, except to say that I hope it won't keep you from seeing *Othello* for yourself.

I don't think even Micheál would mind.

ILLUSTRATIONS
between pages 132 and 133

The Chief Characters in this Chronicle :

ORSON WELLES — A Movie Star and Director, Conjuror, Viveur and Philosopher of determination, playing Othello

HILTON EDWARDS — A Director of the Gate Theatre in Dublin, a Restoration character in appearance and temper, playing Brabantio. Partner to

MICHEÁL MAC LIAMMÓIR — An Actor, the chronicler of this Tale, playing Iago

RACHEL — A Royal Siamese Lady (feline)

CORALIE CARMICHAEL — A Tall Dark actress at the Gate Theatre

ARTHUR — A Factotum

RITA RIBOLLA — A Tall Dark Viennese lady, Secretary to Orson Welles

LEA PADOVANI — An Italian actress of tempestuous Beauty

TRAUNER — A Scenic Artist, Philosopher, and seasoned Francophil

BOB COOTE — A British movie actor of Integrity, playing Roderigo

CÉCILE AUBRY — A young French actress with a Smile

LEE KRESSEL — A New Yorker at work in Europe

SIGNOR FACCHINI — Roman businessman with a hoarse voice

DR. MIHAIL WASCHINSKY	A Polish director of Unusual Distinction, assistant to Orson Welles
JULIEN DERODE	A handsome French manager inclined to diplomatic Charm
JEAN DAVIS	A Parisian distributor with a Babylonian profile
FAY COMPTON	A lovely Actress, accompanied by Angels and Demons, with musical instruments, playing Emilia
GOUZY	A Swiss Script Girl, Linguist and Gourmet,
NICHOLAS BRUCE	An Anglo-Russian actor of charm, playing Ludovico
SUZANNE CLOUTIER	A Beautiful Girl from Ottawa via Paris, known as Schnucks, and playing Desdemona
MICHAEL LAURENCE	An Irish actor of distinction, playing Cassio
GIORGIO PAPPI	An Italian of Many Parts, his Astral Body that of a harassed Stag
MARY ALCAIDE	A Middle West Girl, Secretary to Orson Welles, young Italophil of great charm and forbearance

Camera-Men, Extras, Movie Stars, Fans, Hotel Managers, Arabs, Jews, *Femmes* and *Valets de Chambre*, Servants, Friends, Poets, Politicians, Caids, Society Ladies, Relations, Pimps, etc.

PART I

January 27th to March 29th, 1949

EVERYTHING happens in sevens, or on the seventh, the seventeenth or the twenty-seventh. Wire arrived for me from Paris this morning and was brought to my sick-bed by Hilton, who as my partner in the Gate Theatre wanted to know was it of professional import, and as old and exceedingly tried friend was anxious that I, in convalescent stage following nervous breakdown (still don't believe I had one but was possessed by evil spirits; however, Breakdown following Influenza was what doctors called and still call it), should not be upset.

Wire was from Orson, and said, 'Dearest Micheál enthusiastically repeat offer made by me to Hilton you play Iago with me in Othello film stop can you come to Paris to arrange things stop when can you come stop I will try to come to Dublin if you can't come to Paris stop love to you both Orson.'

H. explained he hadn't said anything about it all last week as I was too ill to listen to reason, but that Orson had been twice on the phone, and that in spite of his (H.'s) lurid description of my fast departing youth (departing! feel I never had any) and of present borderline condition (set about with medical advice of menacing character), he, O., still wanted me to make a test, American associates insisting on this as they didn't know my film work (not surprising). He had wired to say please would I consent to making test, as if I would there could be no longer any possible doubt about my playing. This seems gratifying, if impulsive, summing-up of my filmic possibilities.

As breakdown had compelled me to step out of Christmas show at the Gate which was, and still is, I am disgusted to say, running to crowded houses without me, I don't see how I can go to Paris and start work on film tests. To utter amazement, H. informed me that medical advice considered it would be a good thing to do, that my health would probably burgeon again as result of change of scene, and that it was only Brain Fag I must avoid. This throws lurid light on medical opinion about films and acting in general: probably they are right.

Suddenly as I write I conceive all this as not too subtle plot of H. and doctors not merely to get me out of bed but out of their sight, and have a good mind not to stir. The only thing that propels me at all is the fact that dry rot has been discovered in house and we live almost entirely in dining-room: study, sitting-room, office, and large portion of the stairs are dismantled by gangs of workmen and give forlorn appearance of set for *King Lear* by Salvador Dali.

JANUARY 29TH

Orson on the phone: voice not changed at all. He said the same of me: we expressed emotion and revived memories of last farewell on quay-side at New York fifteen years ago. Said I was very ill; he said the trip and the sight of him would cure me. Said I was very old; he said so was he. (Forgot to point out that Othello was supposed to be.) Said I'd never played Iago, he said he'd never played Othello. Said I had put on weight; he said so had he, and that we'd be two Chubby Tragedians together and that he was going right out to buy yards of cheese-cloth. Said I didn't think I'd be any good on movies; he said I was born for them. (Good God!) Said I didn't see myself as villain, he said unmentionable word and that I was patently villainous in all eyes but my own and Hilton's. All this confusing but intriguing. Finally rang off and turned to H. saying I didn't think I could go.

H. no support at all. Pointed out that *Drunkard* was doing very nicely without me and that I wasn't wanted in the new Strindberg production anyhow. (*Father* going on when *Drunkard* run is over.) He also added that my attitude was nauseatingly *coy*, that in my heart I not only wanted to do it but had already decided I would, and that if anything held me back it was my own conceit that would prefer not trying to not succeeding. (Nearly capped this by saying 'Like the poor cat i' the adage' but superstitious dread of ill-luck following quotation from *Macbeth* prevented me.)

Can all this be true? Have crawled back to bed with Siamese cat Rachel and am brooding.

Later. Still brooding.

Still later. Darling Coralie came to supper and said obviously I must go. Pointed out that in any case it was only for test, and she and H., speaking together as if they'd learnt it—most probably they had—said, 'That's the best part of it,' explaining, separately, that if test didn't like me or I didn't like test I could come home and be exactly where I now was, wherever that may be. Lot of gibberish followed about glories of part of Iago and how I would reproach myself if I neglected offer.

Clearly I shall go, driven from home and from small but, in the main, approving Irish public by dearest friends.

FEBRUARY 1ST

Mass movement to get me away continues and is even joined by Arthur, our Man, who has taken to hovering near the door of my room wearing Protestant expression and asking when he should begin to pack, and will I want dinner jacket, tails, or both?

I reply that my party days are over and that if Paris sees me this month all I am likely to require is a bed jacket.

Orson again on the phone and suggests my going on the seventh (of course); also that scene he suggests for the test is the one with Roderigo beginning 'First I must tell thee this: Desdemona is directly in love with him,' and repeats jocular statement about our both being shot through yards of cheese-cloth.

Presume it must be remnants of illness that make me dread stepping out of the house, let alone into aeroplane, as doctors remain firm in conviction that the change will do me good. What if I get dizzy again, I ask? Doctors point out it's no worse getting dizzy in Paris than in Dublin, especially as even if I *do* fall over in the streets at least I know the city well and can speak French. Can't see what this has to do with it, and suspect Freudian association in insular mind between French language and act of Falling, but H., lighting third cigar before lunch, and looking boisterously healthy in grey double-breasted suit and polka-dot tie, said I must allow someone to know better than myself about something.

FEBRUARY 4TH

Loathesome weather. Old Pal Johnny Sheridan arrived and walked me to doctor's house, where I was assured I was twice the man I was. Quelled with difficulty all sorts of sub-acid witticisms that came welling up in reply to this ridiculous sally, but must admit that I now remain calm at sight of clouds blowing over the sky, child playing at open doorway on corner of canal, Hilton turning from Sartre to Spenser with remote contented sigh, rain coming down from the mountains, tabby-kitten running stiff-tailed across the street, and that these and other innocent spectacles no longer fill me with panic-stricken desire to die and go to heaven, hell, or wherever it is one is sent.

At door of our house Johnny departed and I walked round blackened garden through the damp, dream-soggy air muttering lines for test (definitely decided by dear friends and self that I go to Paris): 'First I must tell thee this: Desdemona is directly in love with him.'

Hilton, smoking gigantic cigar, said film acting will be good for me as I'll be forced to *think* rather than *frame about*, a phrase I do not find in good taste.

Drove to my old aunt Craven's to say goodbye. She

remarked with truth that we are now an excessively scattered family, what with Mac, beloved brother-in-law, and Mana, beloved sister, on Australian tour, and other sisters in England and Ceylon. Mac's daughter, Mary Rose, the only one of us left at home. I point out that I am only going for a week and only to Paris, where I go at least once every year; Aunt C. looked prophetic and said she didn't fancy all this travelling by air. Came away feeling apprehensive.

FEBRUARY 6TH

Arthur, looking determined, has begun to pack. Hilton inserts bottle of Power's Whiskey for Orson between suits and loads me with messages. Winnie Menary and her two boys to supper: feel depressed saying goodbye, but Winnie, H., and entire army of friends combine to remind me how lucky I am to leave Dublin for delirious week in Paris. Have never thought of film test as delirious experience but am doubtless wrong.

PARIS. FEBRUARY 7TH

Direct flight Dublin–Paris allowed no glimpse but vast ectoplasmic blanket of fog which occasionally gave nauseous heaving movement as though the earth below were turning from side to side in uneasy sleep. Fog slowly gave way to dim landscape seemingly miles below and peppered with snow, but could judge from slim oblongs of fields that France had been achieved.

Sat next to bony Australian gentleman, who said in tones of echoing corrugated iron that he admired my acting but couldn't remember what the plays he'd seen it in were called. Asked me whether like himself I was an internationalist, and went on to say he couldn't speak French or any other foreign tongue as he didn't like foreigners and failed to see why everyone couldn't speak the same way. Felt more convinced than ever that internationalism exists only as fancy-dress disguise for uniformity, and that chiefly in the minds of those who are familiar with one nation only and with language and mode of thought of that nation. Also that probabilities of friendship between nations speaking same language are slight. Alliance perfectly feasible, friendship unlikely, as they are bound to pronounce words in a manner not merely different but irritating to each other's taste; one set calling it *Luv* and the other *Laav*, whereas if one of them calls it *Love* and the other *Amour* all is well. They then seem neither popinjays nor outsiders, merely intriguingly incomprehensible.

Aer Lingus crew very friendly and had drinks with them on arrival at Le Bourget with immediate results of dizziness. No one to meet me but suddenly heard my name announced followed by request to repair to telephone.

This found to be situated in remote wooden tower, approached by rickety wooden ladder swaying in heavy gale and filled with bickering officials who gave brief business-like smile, politely indicated telephone, and proceeded with bickering. Long silence punctuated with baritone buzzings finally gave way to unknown (female) voice with apparently Viennese accent that said Was I Me? Said, after brief hesitation, Yes, and was asked in agitated tone was I *sure* of this? Said Absolutely in spite of sudden hideous doubt (owing to memories of N.B-D.) and voice cried 'Gott sei Dank!', and would I wait until she could contact the sheep's-head of a chauffeur at airport of Orly where he had insisted I was to alight. Said Yes again and repaired to bar.

All this had taken a long time and friends from Aer Lingus had now vanished. Sat alone and read *Invitation au Château* in great contentment, and after an hour and a half was collected by small man in leather coat and beret with strong Belgian accent and driven to the Hotel Lancaster in the Rue de Berri. Tall sprays of lilac in the hall, groups of apéritif drinkers, and a glowing warmth, and I found myself suddenly confronted by tall and striking lady, very smart, black hair-do, wearing horn-rimmed glasses and harassed expression and speaking effortless English. Viennese accent, so remarkable on the phone, only detectable in certain words. She introduced herself as Mme Rita Ribolla, 'the secretary of Mr. Velles,' she added, then sneezed violently and muttered 'Pfui Teufel'. I said 'Gesundheit' and she 'Danke' as the lift took us to sixth floor, and there was Orson in the doorway, huge, expansive, round-headed, almond-eyed, clad apparently in dungarees, and miraculously unchanged.

Indulged in much hugging and dancing round discreet olive-green and dull-gold suite, then settled down to some *fine à l'eau* by log fire. No bridging of the years seemed necessary: exactly as he used to be, perhaps larger and more, as it were, tropically Byzantine still, but essentially the same old darkly waltzing *tree*, half banyan, half oak, the Jungle and the Forest lazily pawing each other for mastery. I said incredulously that most people changed some way or another as life flowed by, and he said that only applied to *nice* people, and that lousers like us never changed at all whether it was 1934 or 1949 or Dublin or Chicago or Paris.

Room filled with people: I can only remember Lou Lindsay, an American who Cuts, and Maurice Bessi, a Frenchman who Edits and Publicises; both agreeable. Where should we all dine? Felt dizzy at the very thought, arranged to meet O. for lunch the next day, and am going to eat in my room, which is in red and white and has colossal jar of parrot tulips to welcome me.

FEBRUARY 8TH

No work to-day as O., looking profoundly Baronial, said I ought to relax. So we relaxed together at Méditerranée in Place de l'Odéon for lunch, relaxed in the car all afternoon (driver as Belgian as ever and the Bois superbly arranged in seven hundred shades of grey at lowest estimate), relaxed alone for tea in red and white room, where O.'s doctor visited me and relaxed me more than ever by putting me on a diet of all the things I like best, also on much air, not too much exercise, and massage once daily.

Masseur recommended duly arrived, an uncommunicative giant with an obliterated nose, hands like muffins, and the name of Moïse; I now feel equal to, if not anxious for, several rounds of boxing if only I knew the rules: can this be correct state of affairs from relaxation viewpoint?

Charlie Lederer turned up at seven, known to the world and to Hollywood in particular as Wit and Scriptwriter, Champion of his Race, and Practical Joker. Found him entirely sympathetic and was struck by intense almost dazzling blueness of eyes not as a rule associated with Jewish faces: Lou Lindsay made vigorous reappearance, and atmosphere of relaxation continued with sense of stimulus and well-being, a combination one meets occasionally but rarely except among Americans and which is one of their greatest achievements. Dinner, which was at Tour d'Argent, hilarious. Claude Térrail, the genius of the place, and forever associated in the mind with its dimly coloured impeccability, panelled lift, perfume of wine-dabbled rose-leaves and sour cream, curving glass wall with panorama of Paris reclining at one's feet, Claude Térrail, in spite of sleek and burnished appearance as of ambiguous hero in some *madrigal de Provence*, proves in conversation full of humanity and has a store of curious stories reflecting—is it unconsciously?—great plainness and sincerity of temperament. This, with Lou's blond, bluff blackguardism, Charles's sympathetic skipping-rope form of wit, and Orson's thunderous chortling, made a good party. Orson contributed mood of thirteenth-century pirate (if there were any in the thirteenth century) and entire Renaissance was dealt with and practically exploded by him before coffee was reached.

No reaction of dizziness followed, but was promptly replaced, on return to red and white room, by unsuitable and morbid pangs of homesickness.

FEBRUARY 9TH

We did some scenes to-day, 'First I must tell thee this' and some others; O. sitting with a script in his hand against a window past which rain fell in slanting sheets, and self alternately sitting and pacing up and down past log fire. Overhead some workmen hammered fitfully at something or other. Not relaxed at all. O., however, enthusiastic at intervals that grew shorter and proclaimed loudly that he would now not hear of my making test, as he knew definitely already that Iago and I were just made for each other, and waxed so prophetic of triumph that my mind, grown suspicious through long years spent, however brokenly, in native land, thought this was probably tactful if roundabout way of getting me back to Dublin. Contract, however, immediately discussed in detail, and small army of business men summoned for cocktails and duly warned I was to be treated with care.

Rita Ribolla, summoned from her lair where she spends her days and nights, she tells me, either in waiting for Mr. Velles to ring her or in telling others who *do* ring her that he, Mr. Velles, is not at home, arrived in smart grey slacks, and, armed with note-book, took down impressive particulars on separate piece of paper, looking patient as she did it. Slacks and patient expression did not escape critical comment from O.

Discovered during the evening that certain scenes of proposed *Othello* film had already been shot in Venice last September with Lea Padovani as Desdemona, and another Italian artist as Iago. Name, though he was found unsuitable, escapes me (Freud? Probably). Remember Padovani—a beautiful creature—very well in Italian part in English film made two years ago at Taormina in which Hilton played with her, John Clements and Kay Hammond, but could not recall that she spoke any English. Nor, said O., did she, but she was learning it with great application, and had, moreover, dyed her superb dark hair to required Venetian blond.

But could she learn enough English to play Desdemona in time for film? If not, said O., she could be dubbed (this indeed a revelation, though on second thoughts I must have known that such a process would be possible).

Fell to brooding on Padovani's English and on time required for all there was to do if I really was going to make the film with him, and put some leading questions to O., reminding him that Hilton and I wanted to re-open in Dublin in October; that illness and film combined had kept me out of present season, and that if I was to be of any use to my partner or to our theatre——

Nothing easier, cried O., as film undoubtedly over by August at latest, which would give me time not only for Irish season but for short holiday with himself beforehand. Felt delightfully reassured.

FEBRUARY 11TH

Relaxation treatment continues in the guise of frantic whirl of luncheon and dinner parties with Charlie Lederer and Lou Lindsay, also with dear Virginia, Orson's first wife, who has skipped through Paris like a gay little thrush *en route* for somewhere else, Orson presiding over these feasts with dark and cataclysmic gaiety that suggests old English word, now regrettably fallen into disuse, Wassail, Wassail.

Also there are repeated rehearsals of various passages concerning Othello and Iago (Orson still apparently pleased) interspersed with lengthy discussions with Trauner, who is doing the sets.

Trauner is a stocky Hungarian-Parisian of sober yet twinkling intelligence and charm, whose pale auburn hair and skin and pale, restless eyes make him look as if he were carved out of fresh gingerbread, also as if he had a moustache, though he is clean-shaven. Cannot explain these impressions, but there they are. He made the décor for *Enfants du Paradis* and many other good things; I find his designs for *Othello* impressively virile and evocative.

All is to be Carpaccio, says Orson, lumbering round the room and waving his arms about. (Why do directors always walk about rooms? Is this their only way of getting exercise, or do they expect, on principle of African witch doctor, to find solution hidden somewhere in the furniture? Hilton also has this distracting habit, but he pounds up and down and O. floats, though lumberingly, round and round.) Carpaccio; which means hair falling wispishly to shoulders, small round hats of plummy red felt (though film not to be in colour), very short belted jackets, undershirt pulled in puffs through apertures in sleeves laced with ribbons and leather thongs, long hose, and laced boots. Females also laced, bunched, puffed, slashed, and ribboned and with rather calculating curly hair-do; they won't like any of this if I know them, but like true actresses will, I am convinced, endeavour to look as unlike period as possible and brilliantly succeed.

Shooting, they think, will be in Rome, Venice, and Nice; this will be pleasant, I imagine, though a more adventurous nature might hanker after regions less familiar, but I'm feeling battered and am content with people and places I know.

Had tea to-day with Seán Murphy, our Minister in Paris, and with his wife, both of them charming to me, and a lovely house. Missed for a moment the car driven by Belgian, who had changed parking position while waiting for me, and, overcome by sudden dizziness, fell flat on my back in middle of the Rue Georges V (so glad it wasn't Place Blanche). Explained to officer and wife who assisted me with great helpfulness to my feet that I wasn't drunk, merely *surmené*, which did not however appear to impress Madame, who gave the national chortle and said 'Ah sans blague,' which might have meant anything and probably did.

Orson, perturbed at my vivid recounting of this incident, made me lie flat (this time on olive-green sofa) while he diverted me with stories of his first arrival in Galway on his way to act with us at the Gate in 1930: this also revived unpleasing memories of my portrait of him in my autobiography *All for Hecuba*, at which he nearly lost control and admitted to having read the book with pleasure until reaching the Ghastly Parody of himself, at which he had thrown it several times across the room (presumably to and fro, or would it be in same direction on different occasions?).

I made stirring defence, thus banishing last remains of dizziness, and mentioned that everyone I knew had felt the same, from Lady Headfort to my sister Mana, all agreeing that everyone but themselves was painted with sympathy and even skill, and it was only when I got to *them* that I showed a disappointing lack of perception, even of common decency; and O. then said the truth was that I was sweet to my acquaintances and mean to my friends.

Some desultory brooding over this ever since has led me to think it may be true.

FEBRUARY 13TH

Sunday. Pearl-grey morning, all the colours dimmed and blurred; one of those French Sundays to be interpreted only by Seurat or Debussy. Walked alone to Cité and wandered through bird and flower markets; indescribably delicate light. Best of all on return was sight of elderly gentleman in black bicycling slowly round Place de l'Étoile through mother-of-pearl atmosphere with basket on the front handles containing beautifully shaved French poodle, its paws on front of the basket and a large Heliotrope Bow round its neck. Orson says I made up the Heliotrope Bow but I didn't.

Well-known English actor called Robert Coote suddenly appeared to-night, having flown from Hollywood in order to play Roderigo, for which O. says he should be perfect. Long

session began; we read through many scenes and I perceived
O.'s judgement to be right. Coote very agreeable, with that
mixture of jumpy seriousness and abrupt good humour that
makes the English so different from all other people; also
first-rate comedy sense. He vanished however as suddenly
as he had arrived, leaving O. pleased with the cast so far.
Found myself alone with Rita and Orson in olive-green suite
illumined by leaping flames from log fire. Rain, still audible,
now invisible owing to darkness having fallen. O. began to
dab away at picture-book written and illustrated by him for
his daughter Christopher, while I continued reading of enchanting book by Colette called *Prisons et Paradis*.

Rita filed her nails pensively and sighed, and the workmen
began again to hammer at something overhead.

O., still dabbing brilliantly but looking disturbed, said
those workmen followed him all over the world and had
disturbed him in places as far apart as Brazil, Austria,
Great Britain, and U.S.A. He was sure they were the same
ones.

Rita, muttering *fantastisch, fantastisch!*, continued with her
nails.

O. said would she shut up and throw that file out of the
window, she sounded like a chipmunk having lunch.

Rita put away file into discreet grey and gold bag and sat
demurely with folded hands.

O. asked her severely, Had she no amusing anecdotes to
relate?

Rita said No; amusing things seldom happened to those
whose lot in life was to sit in a small room waiting for der
telephone to ring.

O., moistening brush and eyeing her with abstract scientific
interest, said why, in that case, not get herself a larger room?

Rita, with faultless logic, said she could not see how a larger
room would necessarily supply her mit amusing anecdotes.

Was he, Orson, to take it then that, she, Rita, was not

contented with her lot in life? (Sullen are you, Mme Ribolla? Eh? Mutinous are you, eh, Madam Glum?)

Ach, not at all, Mr. Velles.

Then why was she wearing expression of second contralto in minor operatic work? And why did she always have to carry that God-awful note-book around?

To make notes in, said Rita.

Then who, said O., as she was so clever, was expected to arrive that night?

No von at all, except a Dutchman who vished to play Roderigo, said Rita, after elaborate glance at book.

What about Miss Padovani, said O., throwing down his brush.

That was for to-morrow night, Mr. Velles.

What! wasn't to-day Monday?

No, Mr. Velles, to-day we are Sunday.

In that case what was she, Mme Ribolla, thinking of to appear in slacks?

Na wirklich, Mr. Velles, what is then wrong mit the Schlacks?

It is *Sunday*, Mme Ribolla. Perhaps you don't quite realise what *Sunday* means to us plain folks from the Middle West? No? Well, that's just too bad. But one of the things it *doesn't* mean is mutinous women in slacks.

Madam Glum and self then invited by O. to dine at the Taillevent in the Rue St. Georges. (What about der Dutchman? said Madam G. Der Dutchman, said O., could come another time, and added that she, Rebellious Rita, must leave word mit dem porter. At any rate, Roderigo, like Iago, was now cast.)

Talked during dinner (Rebellious Rita's slacks now replaced by irreproachable black skirt) about Othello, New England, the Bible, Al. Jolson, and the Inequality of Woman, latter topic directed entirely by O., who reveals himself as implacable reactionary and says they can't even cook. (Faint protests from Rita quelled by his popping lumps of lobster into her mouth.)

On return to hotel we were confronted by spectacle of der Dutchman, immensely lanky youth with flapping overcoat, flowing scarf, fluttering tie, and flying blond locks, who, in spite of porter's suggestions, had waited for audition for four hours, much of that time it would appear having been spent in the bar. Rita flew to her room.

Dutchman, in spite of Orson's Ivan the Terrible expression and brief stop-press mode of address, pursued us to suite, and endless reading of Roderigo scenes ensued. Dutchman (looking like Jane, Jane tall as a Crane) now began to fly unsteadily round the room throwing cushions and books about, tearing off his tie and opening his shirt to ensure what he called 'den batter breading, esn't et?' He then announced in hearty Rotterdam accent that his conception of Roderigo was, perhaps, unorthodox (could he please heff en liddle drink, *ja*, en liddle, diny visky?) but if Mr. Velles would listen for en moment he would see: (ah! tankoo, Mr. Velles, glug, glug, glug). Now! Lazzen to thass, Mr. Velles,

> Vot en full fortune dott de tack-laps owe
> Eff he can cahrry et dhoos!

Ha ha ha! You understand now, I tank, esn't et? Sach en fool, this poor Roderigo—as Iago has explicked of him, one Poor Trash of Vaynice. And mit den eyes, when he tries to be intalligent, exprassion somesing *so*. (Demonstration of demented smile and of violent squint now offered as *pièce de résistance*.) For en Close Up, esn't it? Wery amusing! Ow yes, dear Chappies! *dess* wass how he *feels* it must be! So has somesing already to his anspiration spoke, and Lazzen!

A good deal more then followed, interspersed with more liddle diny viskies, language growing less and less easy to understand and more and more reminiscent of Beowulf.

He left us at unidentified hour—my watch had stopped and

O. never wears one—but loud crowing of cocks would undoubtedly have accompanied his tottering exit had we been
in the country—and after this O. lay flat on his back in front
of (now lifeless) remains of log fire and said that admittedly
we had been in the presence of genius but probably *talent*
was what was required for the part of Roderigo, and he still
thought Coote was good.

Morning now creeps greyly over Champs-Élysées and rain
still patters down. Unearthly energy, which invades and
deserts me at alternate and unsuitable moments, would easily
enable me to continue writing this blather from now till
Doomsday, but one must sleep sometimes.

FEBRUARY 14TH

Arrival of Lea Padovani after long and apparently perilous
flight from Rome. Paris fog-bound, and the plane, bearing
Padovani, circled for hours, depositing her at last hundreds
of kilometres from spot where landing originally intended
and causing Orson, driven by Belgian, to scurry half over
France before tracking her. Effective entrance through white
doors into olive-green room made at last, Padovani also in
olive-green (darker than room) augmented by heavy gold
bangles and notes of astrakhan and surmounted by gilded
coiffure *à la grecque* which made her eyes appear as two
luminous and faintly reproachful black grapes: what a pretty
creature she is. Manner completely *en suite* with appearance,
warm and impulsively glowing, and we had a tumultuous
dinner in Montmartre.

Night-clubs successfully avoided, Padovani and I both
expressing our respectively Mediterranean and Atlantic distaste for what P. called 'these frightful necked lady, who
dances together very close to table where one drinks so bad
champagne ah Dio mio! for me I find this very disgusting my
dear, *no no no no no per carità!*' and we parted fairly early.

Rita, severely referred to by Orson as Vienna's Answer to

the Travel Problem, as he seems to blame her for the delay of Padovani's plane, met me in the lift in gloomy mood and said she thought P.'s hair a triumph and that she, too, would not mind being a blonde for a while if she felt sure that the comments of Mr. Velles would not be couched in a style unfit for human ears, and added that she personally was fond of night-clubs, but that no one outside of Rome or Vienna seemed to go to them (Ach, Vienna! when Mr. Velles was making *Third Man* mit Carol Reed what *Fun* she had had mit all the old friends), and that she was now about to pass a few more sleepless hours in her room waiting for der Telephone to ring.

Have decided to go home on Wednesday: Rita says she will arrange flight for me.

FEBRUARY 15TH

Long day of working and eating with Orson and Padovani. She is fascinating and doesn't seem to like Desdemona at all.

DUBLIN. FEBRUARY 16TH

Home again. Luminous grey weather with buds appearing faintly on the trees. Hilton in fine form came to meet me at Collinstown with Raymond Percy, our manager, and they both said the doctors were right and that I looked a thousand times healthier.

It's grand to be home. Found our typist Beryl immersed in *World of Girls*, old and beloved children's school book by L. T. Meade which recounts the doings of Annie Forest, impulsive gipsy-like heroine, caught in a maelstrom of passion-drenched girlish adventures. Had thought nobody but myself and Betty Chancellor was fascinated by such trivia, and enchanted to find Beryl and our Arthur at grips as to who shall finish it first.

Workmen still flood the house and soon we will be able to

leave the dining-room without danger, but I suppose by that time I shall be far away. The thought of this, combined with the sight of Hilton working at his desk on *The Father* and of Rachel sitting with folded paws regarding me with slightly squinting turquoise eyes, still makes me wish to do nothing but wait for next season and watch the spring come back to Ireland.

No time now to write as theatre in upheaval of dress rehearsals for *Father*. Carl Bonn's set good, though I find it too light in colour, Hilton horrifyingly good, so is Coralie in Acts 1 and 3; in her scenes with the Doctor she hasn't got it yet. Mary Rose is playing Bertha: revolting and enormous dog has bitten her erstwhile Botticelli nose causing necessity for invisible (how are you) strap: this gives her a false Roman-Jewish profile and looks like clumsy attempt to convince audience that she really is the daughter of Hilton and Coralie, both of whom have Conks.

I admire and loathe the whole thing and find the last act, with H. and C. at top of their form, insupportable.

FEBRUARY 24TH

Newspapers full of praise for *The Father*: agony of the first night having passed over, we are all left in cataleptic condition of flatness. Cast played extremely well, so well I could hardly sit in my seat. In fact didn't sit in it all the time. Denis Brennan played Pastor with much skill: I think he's going to be an important Irish actor if he sticks the pace and does not (like self, according to H.), get into ruts.

Drinks with Lennox Robinson and others at intervals; immediate dizziness resulted, so turned to coffee.

Poor devils to-day start first rehearsals of *To Live in Peace*. I sit mainly at home (at medical advice) gently entertaining old pals Johnny and Tiger at intervals of making desultory notes for new comedy (not at medical advice).

No word from Orson, and wonder is my film career at

an end. Cannot make up my mind if joy or sorrow would
ensue if it were.

FEBRUARY 25TH

Choice between joy and sorrow not called into question
as contract arrived to-day. Contract totally inexplicable to me,
as agents' stipulations have rendered it like Chinese puzzle,
but Hilton and Manager Raymond Percy (former puffing
with remote and puzzled expression at cigar which has
extinguished itself unobserved, latter passionately biting
nails) assure me all is well, and that Orson and our own
agents most fair.

I'm to return to Paris for a month's rehearsal on—need
I say?—March 7th. After that Rome.

MARCH 3RD

Daffodils, having already made refined début among
potted hyacinths in the shop windows, now surge into the
Dublin streets along with primroses, catkins, and sheaths of
tulips; the sellers in their black shawls stand red-nosed in the
sweeping winds at every corner and croon or bellow their
witticisms: the Strindberg centenary pleasingly swells our
audience, and now poor Hilton is suffering from laryngitis
and has had to leave the cast. This sort of thing, himself and
myself absent from our own season, so typical of joyful
spring: roaring winds, frost-nipped buds, frayed nerves, fruit
salts, and aching throats inevitably associated with the
Awakening of the Year.

Thank God for Hilton's Oldest Pal and a White Man
if Ever There Was One: Reginald Jarman has crossed the sea,
sprung with two days' panic-stricken rehearsal into the
breach, and is now playing H.'s part. Furious audience
surged into the theatre in mood of mockery, then surged out
again full of praise. Reginald himself in almost perpetual
condition of Salvini-esque frenzy—he has broken several

pieces of stage furniture and is bruised from head to toe; and Dorothy Casey as the Nurse has also sustained minor injuries—Reginald sups with us every night after the show and bellows away at Hilton, who croaks back with undiminished enthusiasm, thus undoing all the good that silent day had wrought.

Wild weather, wild plans for the future, wild wind-blown drives to Howth with whispered conversation, wild teas with Mary Rose in semi-abandoned cottage on the edge of the cliffs, all echoing to memories of Mac and Mana, who send wild news from time to time of their Australian tour: this for me is one of those vividly unreal periods in which one seems imprisoned in a wind-tossed and totally isolated present, the past a shadow, the future as blank as a strip of virgin celluloid (which I suppose is fairly accurate, indeed almost literal image of my own immediate destiny).

MARCH 5TH

Tea with Madam Gonne MacBride. This ceremony, however frequent, has invariable effect on me of romantic pleasure. Her heroic and now cavernous beauty, made sombre by the customary black draperies she wears, is also illumined by an increasing gentleness and humour; she has now what seems a faint far-away amusement at life. Although she will die a partisan, with the inescapable background to her splendour of years passed alternately in revolutionary conspiracy and in long terms of imprisonment, that portion of her mind which Yeats described as 'all but turned to stone' is somehow delicately perceived by herself and as delicately passed by, as one passes in time of peace by a monument celebrating the tragedy of war.

Of course one can't be with her for five minutes without her conjuring up, though she has never spoken of them, all his images. I sit and watch that fragile body bent with age, the restless hands, the smiling head held a little to one side, the gold-flecked eyes that grow alternately dim and brilliant as she talks, and I think: There before my eyes she sits: the 'phoenix' who 'lived in storm and strife', she who was 'beautiful and fierce, sudden and laughing'; there is 'the dim heavy hair' that's 'streaked with grey', the 'eagle look', the lips 'with all their mournful pride'; and I am faintly surprised to find that the 'one flaw' that he had celebrated more beautifully than any of her perfections seemed to me untrue. He wrote:

> Your small hands were not beautiful,
> And I am afraid that you will run
> And paddle to the wrist
> In that mysterious, always brimming lake
> Where those that have obeyed the holy law
> Paddle and are perfect; leave unchanged
> The hands that I have kissed
> For old sake's sake.

Well, to me her hands are beautiful.

She is perhaps the only person in the world now who is as wonderful as the poems that were made for her, and they are the best of her generation. No one so single-minded has ever lived, I think. When she asked me what Hilton and I were doing and I told her about the *Othello* film she said, 'How splendid—perhaps you and he can learn about films and make them for Ireland one day.'

She likes sherry, tea, cigarettes, and the society of her son Seán and of his wife; she likes poor people, wild birds, speculative ideas, and a horizon beyond her windows that is ragged with mountains; and when one goes away she comes smiling and very slowly to the door to wave goodbye.

PARIS. MARCH 7TH

Woke up with a thump too early for the early call, and the morning smelt of rain. Arthur came in with the coffee, opened curtains on faint morning darkness lifting over naked garden, then switched on lamps revealing room littered with (in the main packed) luggage, also Rachel uncoiling herself from foot of bed, opening bluebell eyes and yawning in Siamese. Coffee was followed by desolate bath gleaming grey as a cloud. I lay there and thought liverishly of eternity until situation of actualities crept slowly back to mind.

Clouds rolled over Howth (could see, in spite of them, Mac's cottage distinctly, and I visualised Mary Rose asleep inside, wearing Roman-Jewish plaster as Amy March wore clothes-peg) and more densely still over Wicklow mountains. Then it was fog all the way, and the French fields were still sprinkled with snow. All the passengers looked hideous as they read their Irish *Digests* and drank their last Jamesons, and one little girl, travelling alone to school in Paris, said she loved the Gate and would I draw something (unintelligible word drowned by roar of machinery) in her album?

Obligingly drew sea-monster of loathsome aspect, and she said she didn't think it did me justice, but that all the same she would show it to the other girls. Roundabout conversation which followed revealed that she had asked me for sketch of self-portrait and thought that I'd done it. Still, in fact, thinks it, I suppose, as I had no heart, energy, or will to tell her otherwise. Left me at French Customs with dubious glances between my face and portrait in the album. Cannot feel convinced that the other girls will flock to see me as Iago on strength of contribution.

Rita waiting for me at the barrier, looking smart, handsome, and pale as a witch, with new hair-style; she explained, as Belgian drove us away from Le Bourget, that all plans were in the melting-pot. No one yet decided on for cast except Orson, Coote, and self, and if Emilia was not soon forthcoming, she said, O. would go quite mad. In fact, we would all go quite mad, please take a cigarette.

Mentioned that I had heard names of at least a dozen London actresses already associated with the playing of this part but Rita said No, not one of them had been engaged by der Velles (this a new and interesting version of Mr.) and that as for the amount of Desdemonas—*fantastisch, fantastisch!*

Traffic block in the Champs-Élysées coupled with volleys of abuse and cynical chortles of highly national flavour put an end to the discussion as the Belgian turned with hair-breadth skill and speed into the Rue de Berri.

Orson, dressed in what appeared to be white serge pyjamas and felt boots, gave me heart-warming welcome in the olive-green suite, and executed superb dance to accompanying song composed by himself at the age of fourteen which goes:

> Everyone loves the fellow who is smiling
> He brightens the day and lightens the way for you—
> He's always making other people happy
> Looking rosy when you're feeling awful blue. . . .

Then changed to dark suit and vanished to conference with financiers. I lunched with Rita and Dr. Giorgio Pappi, the Italian *direttore di produzione*, who has the air of a rosy-cheeked and very startled *stag* and is friendly. Conversation mainly in Italian, which Rita speaks as fluently as English, French, and German, and with even more vigour, having learned it from Italian husband. Find that I speak it even worse than I thought, mixing it all up with Spanish, but that I understand easily enough, and Giorgio P. so gloomy about finding a cast or anything else with which to proceed with film, I almost wish I didn't.

Later. Dinner presided over by Orson (very excitable) in hotel dining-room (also green and gold, but olive gives place to jade). Table set about with young ladies, English, American and French, all of them seemingly convinced they were going to play Desdemona. Orson, rolling his almond eyes hypnotically round the table, explained, in English, his ideas about Cassio, of whom he has a poor opinion, pointing out snobbish attitude to Iago and insufferable treatment of poor Bianca.

'And a nice girl too,' he said, 'a nice, good girl: now you *know* she was good,' and he rolled his eyes more than ever, so all the young ladies hastily assumed expression of Tarts with Golden Hearts in case the quest for Desdemona might prove in vain.

Iago, he went on to say (had heard him on this on last visit and was in agreement), was in his opinion impotent; this secret malady was, in fact, to be the keystone of the actor's approach. Realised, as the talk grew more serious, that I was more in agreement than ever, but felt no necessity to assume appropriate expression so just sat there looking pleasant. (Sudden hideous thought: maybe pleasant, slightly doped expression, habitual with me during meals, *is* the appropriate one for suggestion of impotence and this is why O., who has watched me consume several meals, thinks me so made for the part? Must remember to sound him on this and prove him mistaken.)

'Impotent,' he roared in (surely somewhat forced) rich bass baritone, 'that's why he hates life so much—they always do,' continued he (voice by this time way down in boots). He then gobbled up some sturgeon, ordered some more, and went on to talk about the costumes, which are to be made in Rome.

Later still. Worked alone together on jealousy scene all the rest of the day and was reassured by O. about my peculiar suitability for Iago. Not what I feared at all.

Have suggested name of yet another well-known London actress as possible Emilia, as the one O. would like is unavailable. My suggestion made with diffidence as (*a*) he thought the Irish actor I'd cited for Cassio too young and too sympathetic for his conception—he met him in London last week—and (*b*) he doesn't want markedly English people in the cast as they'd clash, he says, with himself and me.

Also, he says, they say 'Saouldier' for 'Soldier' and keep on drinking *tea*.

However, well-known actress arrives on Thursday.

MARCH 9TH

Rehearsals continue in earnest: we live plunged in atmosphere of violence and alternate settings of Venice and Cyprus in heyday of Carpaccio. Find myself almost entirely in agreement with O.'s ideas of our characters: no single trace of the Mephistophelean Iago is to be used: no conscious villainy; a common man, clever as a waggonload of monkeys, his thought never on the present moment but always on the move after the move after next: a business man dealing in destruction with neatness, method, and a proper pleasure in his work: the honest honest Iago reputation is accepted because it has become almost the truth.

. . . 'And out of her own goodness make the net that shall enmesh them all': to be spoken simply, happily, and logically. One must feel as the cat does with the mouse: think of Rachel—what to her is evil about killing a mouse? And Cyprus is full of mice.

Later. Did bits of jealousy scene all the evening. Careful that this smooth logic doesn't make for monotony. I know Hilton might be afraid of this. O. doesn't seem to think so. Any tendency to passion, even the expression of the onlooker's delight at the spectacle of disaster, makes for open villainy and must be crushed. He must say to Roderigo in discussing the disposal of Cassio, 'Why, by making him incapable of his place . . .' Roderigo looks bland, and Iago continues with a pleasant smile as though explaining to a child why it should brush its teeth, 'Knocking out his brains.'

Monotony may perhaps be avoided by remembering the underlying sickness of the mind, the immemorial hatred of life, the secret isolation of impotence under the soldier's muscles, the flabby solitude gnawing at the groins, the eye's

untiring calculation. I like Orson's design for the growing
dependence of Othello on Iago's presence, the merging of the
two men into one murderous image like a pattern of loving
shadows welded. He is speaking many of the lines, especially
those in the Emilia cross-examination and in the 'What, to
kiss in public?' scenes, with a queer breathless rapidity: this
treatment, with his great bulk and power, gives an extra-
ordinary feeling of loss, of withering, diminishing, crumbling, toppling over, of a vanishing equilibrium; quite wonderful. Only thing that depresses me is the camera's inability
—or unwillingness—to cope with the great organ-stop
speeches, the 'Othello's occupation's gone' one, for example,
which he delivers so far with caution as if afraid of shattering
the sound-track. I feel at this apparently inevitable hush-
hush and tactful dealing with the matter a return of all my
old conviction that Shakespeare, had he written for the
screen, would have ·done his work differently; this feeling
accompanied by a longing to see Orson himself, or Gielgud,
or Hilton, or any other fine speaker of verse stand up on an
honest wooden stage and let us have the stuff from the wild
lungs and in the manner intended. This I know Orson tried
at various moments in his film *Macbeth* and people didn't like
it, a verdict possibly shared by the camera, so there maybe
is the answer.

With myself this doesn't apply so much, as he is, for perfectly sound movie reasons, cutting all Iago's explanatory
soliloquies and most of the rest is quiet, colloquial, and
credible even to the twentieth-century public.

Arrival of well-known actress to see about Emilia. As
things turned out O. had been dancing fandangos about the
British all the morning and continued without a pause all
through lunch. He really is very like Hilton in some ways,
though not in his attitude to the British. Undeniably the
greatest race on earth, also the most tiresome: this was their
sentence. Pronunciation of vowel sounds, love of draughty

rooms, tendency to say 'Sorry old man' or 'oh, why?' at intervals commented on with scorn; also predilection for whimsy abbreviations such as Comfy, Hanky, Undies, Daffs, etc. (especially Daffs), decided on by us both as marks of nauseating cerebral effeminacy. Tea-drinking habits above all referred to slightingly by O. Fearlessly pleaded guilty myself about tea, defiantly adding that in my opinion it is a superb drink and that tea-time, even more than tea itself, is one of England's great magical inventions. Added that Irish people drink it even more than English, also reminded him of Chinese and Russians. Oh, but in the proper way, *without milk*, said O.

In Ireland, I continue, we drink it a lot at night, and frequently use it as a reminder to people inclined to linger that the party is now over.

Not so bad as a method of driving friends away from one's door, said O., but added that he didn't see that made things any better. Also observed that we in Ireland, in addition to my own confession, were hypocritical as far as hospitality was concerned, also notoriously imitative, and that we had only picked up the dreary vice since the English conquest. (Don't see how we could conceivably have picked it up before.) And that if we *really* wanted to be free of their influence we would pitch every grain of tea out of the country. (I'd like to see effect of this suggestion on Irish nation.)

After lunch he went to sleep—and well-known actress arrived, looking ravishing. Joined her in her room and told her O. would soon be down.

What's he like? says she.

Grand, says I.

But how does one deal with him, I mean what sort of *approach*? says she.

Just natural, says I.

But people say he's so *alarming*, says she, and so *rude*.

Not at all, says I.

So just be one*self*, you think that's it, do you?

Just *oneself*, says I.

Divine to be in Paris, says she, looking relieved, but my God, what a journey. I'm famished, says she, what's the time?

Nearly five, says I.

Then what about some delicious *tea*, says she, and we order it and drink it together.

This room is frightfully hot, says she, sipping away. Let's have some air. So *stuffy*.

In comes the wind, and we sit pouring in lashings of milk and having a perfectly splendid time, when the door flies open, causing draught that blows things all over the room, and there stands O. dressed in pitch-black and looking like overseas edition of Elizabeth Barrett's Dad.

He closes door with severe expression, and brief sketch of formalities is dealt with.

I am hoping so much you may be shooting *Othello* in England, begins Well-Known Actress.

Why? says Dad.

Because, says she, well . . . I mean it's—sort of nearer *home*, isn't it?

Your home I suppose, says Dad.

Well yes, says W.-K.A. You see I've just bought a tiny, tiny, Elizabethan cottage. In the country.

Not in town? says Dad pleasantly.

No, no. The country. And the garden, I wish you could see the garden. Just now, in March, it's getting simply smothered in——

Daffs? says Dad suspiciously.

Hundreds, says she.

Oh, says Dad, and the daffs all seemed to troop hastily out of the room.

Chintz curtains?

Oh yes. Just the bedrooms, you know.

All blowing in like this, I suppose? Giving everyone pleurisy? And does the Vicar come to tea?

He has called, I think. I was in town. And the dog! A poppet!

I see. Well, says Dad after a pause, looking at me much as Hamlet's mother looked at the Ghost. Well, says he, when you Islanders have finished your—whatever it is you're both drinking, maybe we could go upstairs and read a little Shakespeare.

She read it beautifully, and then she and O. began to differ about Emilia's character. Then they read it again.

A trollop, says O.

A good-natured woman, says W.-K.A. firmly.

Frequently same thing, says O., but Emilia not invariably good-natured either, look at her treatment of Bianca ('Foh foh, fie upon thee!' etc.).

Then W.-K.A. said she saw what he *meant*. Then she *explained* what he meant. Then he said he didn't mean it *at all*. Then she said would he say what he *did* mean. Then he did. Then they read it again. Then she said she still saw what *he* meant and went on to say what *she* meant. Then it began to dawn that *she* didn't mean what *he* meant, neither did *he*. Not quite that way anyway. Then he said what about reading it all over *again*. Then she said did he really *think* so?

Finally he said, Let's dine at the Tour d'Argent, I'm getting hungry, and ambled curvingly into his bathroom humming 'Everyone loves the Fellow who is Smiling' in minor key.

So then she and I stole out together and drank Pernod, and then we had some more delicious *tea*, and after that we all dined and had caviare and bliny, and Orson said the only way to understand Shakespeare was by eating lots and lots of caviare and bliny and drinking plenty of champagne.

So after that we went and drank more champagne chez Eve on Place Pigalle and were entertained by *les girls* led by a really alarming *girl* who towered in bony nudity above all the others and sang:

'Ai don' want 'air; you ken 'ev 'air, she's too fett forh me —*Ai!* She's too fett forh me—*Ai!* She's too fett forh me!— *Houp-là!*'

And W.-K.A. said, really the French were so magnificent about age, it just didn't seem to make any difference to anyone at all in France, did it? and then she said the décor was very amusing but good *heavens* wasn't it airless, my *dear!* And then she found her *gloves* were missing, also her *hanky*, and then she began to wonder how the *daffs* were looking in the garden of her *tiny* Elizabethan *cottage*.

So now she's deciding to go back to England to-morrow, and she and I and all of us are wondering *who the hell is going to play Emilia?*

MARCH 10TH

Rehearsal all day. News comes through, not of Emilia, but of Desdemona. Have already seen three put through many of the lines but all of them wrong, and Orson is developing blood-shot eyes, always with him a sign of worry. Have a feeling I could suggest Mary Rose, who has many of the qualities, also gentle, dreaming Botticelli face; but am almost superstitiously loath to recommend relatives. This, if I examine it, is no high-souled principle, merely selfish dread of witnessing possible débâcle if my judgement proves wrong. Anyway M.R. is up to her eyes in *The Father* in Dublin and rehearsing with Hilton for next show *To Live in Peace*. Anyway, also, definite news comes through about discovery of French wonder-girl of whom vague rumours have long been reaching our ears.

MARCH 11TH

Maurice Bessi turned up (very spring-like and smart, dove-grey butterfly tie) with French Desdemona. Exquisite childish creature, mouth too large, but exquisite. Accent very French, (Dub?). Orson enchanted. Says yes, possibly Dub, but that she's so quick she'll probably speak English perfectly in a month's time. To this end, American script director, apparently speaking faultless English, is to arrive from Rome at any moment.

Desdemona's name is Cécile Aubry. Has already made a success in French film *Manon*.

Small, delicate, long hair like pale sunshine, looks about sixteen, irrepressible and heart-breaking smile. Obviously not a dry seat in the house when Othello starts knocking her about. Also she is clearly in the deathless traditions of the true ingénue, and represents type known to my youth as A Little Devil.

Rehearsed with her all day. Thought more and more as work proceeded what a gulf yawns between stage and film acting, and think separate names should be decided on to distinguish between them. Aubry shows to my mind no sign of any single quality essential for the stage: voice, projection, breath control, consistency of design, sustaining-power, continuity of mood, not one: she has a series of unpredictable flashes, of moments so delicious that if you could string them together, as it were, behind her back, you could make from them all of the three dresses that shone like sun, moon, and stars and were folded into a nutshell, and that, I suppose, is precisely what the camera will do. At any rate, Orson's blood-shot eyes are clearing visibly.

Arrival from Rome of script director who is to act as English professor for Aubry: his name is Lee Kressel. Stocky, luxuriant and cat-eyed, to my eyes he has stepped straight out of Ritz bar-ish drawing in the *New Yorker* but O. says No, I've got him all wrong, and mentions some other publication I don't know. Anyway, he is agreeable and amusing and works hard with Aubry all the morning and most of the afternoon. Our rehearsals with her are held at the oddest hours of the night, so she's not having a holiday. She has taken to calling up her Maman on the telephone every ten minutes to say she will soon be home and continues to mutter her lines in English during Maman's responses and enquiries, so it's rather this:

'Oui, Maman, ça va toujours, oui, je répète toujours avec M. Welles. . . . '*Why I should fearh Ai know nawt, seence guilt-ee-nayss Ai know nawt——*' '

'No, honey, "know *not*",' says Lee.

'Never mind the Not, it's the rhythm,' says Orson. ' "*Guilt*iness", chicken-pie, not "guilt-ee-*nayss*".'

'Mais pas du tout, Maman, tout va très bien . . . "*guilt-ee-nayss Ai know nott!*" . . . sank you. . . . Oui, Maman. Oui. Non, j'arrive aussitôt que possible—"*Ay know nawt—nott*" bon, bon, je ferai mon mieux, "*Ow now my Lord*"—bon, bon, faut pas m'attendre; allez-vous coucher, Maman. . . . "*Some bloudy passion shecks your very fraime*"—Comment? Non, chérie, je n'ai rien dit . . . au revoir, au revoir, Maman.'

So we live, but no Emilia yet.

MARCH 13TH

Havoc caused by Aubry who, having worked all day, announced she had signed for another film, and after scene which revealed admirable restraint on part of Orson, left him, Lee K., and me staring at each other in quivering silence.

Silence, however, speedily shattered by sort of whispered litany, conducted chiefly by self and Lee; this in turn shattered by O.'s suddenly bellowing: 'No contract: why did she have no contract?' Thoughts immediately dart towards Rita, who is summoned by O. in following terms: 'Let's get Miss Mud down and twist her arm for her.'

Rita duly appeared and very, very painful interlude followed.

MARCH 16TH

Quest for Desdemona continues (Emilia totally forgotten for the moment). Orson and I spend our time being escorted from one movie show to another to observe processions of dazzlingly lovely females, all of them under twenty-three and all of them wrong. Two more auditions for the part are held in olive and gold suite and include monumentally depressing French dreep who says she is *enrhumée*, and to prove it, loudly blows her nose between each line, also minute but brisk English Piece (perfect for minor role in very short very *brave* Noel Coward sketch), with a face like a golf-ball. In the intervals we rehearse scenes together, taking bitter pleasure in such lines as 'Oh the pity of it, Iago', and 'That we can call these delicate creatures ours and not their appetites', and 'Marry patience! or I shall say you're all in all in spleen and nothing of a man', and a score of others.

Rita now totally reinstated but retains name of Miss Mud, now used as term of jocular affection. Fiendish joke on her devised by Lee, who phoned her disguising his voice in bogus Mexican accent and invited her to dine, giving name of member of Spanish ex-royal family and describing himself as 'great admirer in the distance', was rather crushed by her haughty refusal over the wire, and still more by her not even bothering to mention the incident to us afterwards (as if lascivious designs on her by ex-royalty perfectly normal occurrence in life of Miss Mud).

Later. National fervour, so natural on the eve of the national feast (several emerald-green boxes of shamrock have arrived to the astonished delight of the staff: 'Encore une petite boîte de salade pour Monsieur'), is stressed by advent of Irish actor from London who says he is an Old Pal of mine from Dublin (my only memory of him is of swift meeting at tea-party in the depths of Bayswater where I thought he was from Wyoming or thereabouts) and wants to play Montano.

Orson says part already cast. Report this to Dear Old Pal [*sic*] whom I also invite to lunch (Why?) and when that is over see him no more until two a.m. when he pounces on me as I attempt to enter hotel on my way to bed and, merrily laughing, pushes me with great muscular determination into subterranean night-club about four feet square containing crowd of American-Polish friends celebrating St. Patrick in company with deafening Brazilian band in flamingo-coloured dusk. Band is composed of hordes of coloured gentlemen with sleeves like drawers worn by female dancers in a design by Toulouse-Lautrec, packed very tight over three-quarters of the room, and all rattling, buzzing, bashing, hissing, and screaming. We in turn all shriek conversationally at each other for half an hour, after which I invent business appointment in my room in order to get home to bed. As it is now nearly three this is greeted with oily winks and assurances that 'she'll wait for me'. Get home round about four and am just in bed when door flies open and Old Pal falls headlong into room festooned with shamrock and menacingly says it is well known in London that *Othello* will never be made at all, and he only wants, as an Old Pal, to warn me, so I suppose he's not going to play Montano.

MARCH 17TH

Festive tea at the Legation. Had no idea there were so many Irish people in Paris. Room a bower of whiskey, shamrock, champagne-cocktails, and silver tea-pots. Have decided to tell Orson nothing about last-mentioned feature of the celebration.

No sign of Old Pal: has he returned to London?

MARCH 18TH

Saw two tests made by prospective Desdemonas. One of them, in course of dialogue, said wistfully in vast close-up:

'They tell me I shall never act!' To which Orson shouted loudly, 'And whoever they are they're right, honey.'

Drove home past long queues waiting to see *Manon* (featuring Aubry) and shook our fists at them, Orson shouting out of the window, 'Hey! Don't go in there, folks, don't go in there!'

So Emilia and Desdemona problem remains acute as ever and O.'s eyes are again bloodshot.

MARCH 20TH

New plan conceived by Orson and arising out of conversation at Véfour's in the Palais Royal, where we dined and where I told him about our Balkan Tour in '39. A World Tour, says O., the moment *Othello* is finished: say September. It has been lying at the back of his head for a long time, some scheme like this, ever since he started with us in Dublin in '31 in fact, so obviously we ought to do it together. My own idea that the actor's art was too cluttered with the immovable business organisation of a large city had started it off again. We should be able to spread a carpet anywhere and do our work, that is how it appears to me, and the fit-up form was on the right lines but rendered sordid by the fact of having become an attempt to do in makeshift what was no better than an imitation of the static theatre's function without its advantages of well-built, well-painted scenery: that was the chief snare of the travelling player, and a small circle of provincial theatres all copying something better done in the capitals. One could work on the principle of the circus which travelled with the essentials of its function and appeared wherever the fancy led it. Why not?

A World Tour then. A World Tour with six plays, three of them directed by him and three by Hilton. We all play. No scenery, just the blank empty stage with tremendous lighting and accompaniment of Philharmonic orchestras picked up in the cities visited, and a carefully chosen cast of the best artists in England and America. All journeys to be made by plane and the repertory, which is to cover classic and modern ground, will include, possibly, *Moby Dick*, *Salomé*, *Richard II*, *The Provok'd Wife*, *The Duchess of Malfi*, and one or two bits and pieces by, say, Sartre, Tennessee Williams, Claudel, and O'Casey. We might open near home —say Dublin or Paris—and make slowly for Buenos Aires, or we might open in Shanghai or Bombay and move around until we hit Sydney or London or New York. Anyway, we'd travel lightly, owing to our No Scenery principles.

Crazy as this notion sounds I am moved by it, and we have talked of nothing else all day. Rehearsals for *Othello* are shoved into the background as we embark mentally on our chartered plane and storm the theatres of Europe, Asia, and America with our actors, our hampers of wonderful clothes, our headdresses and masks, our master electrician and our musical director. Long talk on the phone to Hilton (*To Live in Peace*, strange title under the circumstances, went on last week) revealed him as inflammatory to the idea of new adventures as ever, though a certain desire to know more detail was also put forward, and Orson talks of flying to Dublin to discuss things with him. I think he will too.

Appearance of Lee K. with script to cue our lines for the film seemed like a visitation from another world. O. sent him away and then drove with me to Versailles, where we continued discussion of World Tour.

Mud-splashed walk through le Hameau met with absent-minded disapproval ('Do you really feel you *want* to drag me around this gimcrack, phoney, dolled-up toy village? No, I just don't want to look at any trout in a stream. No, they don't mean a thing to me. No, I don't care if Marie Antoinette did churn her own butter: I am convinced she was no goddam good at it anyway. Dearest Micheál, where do you get these Hiking Instincts from?')

I thought it was all beautiful, the willow-bushes and the

violets and the chestnut buds, and the light lying like a dove's wing on the water; so when we had decided to open with the *Duchess of Malfi* (who? Bergner?) in Bombay before the autumn, we drove to le Coq Hardy and had gin (O.) and tea (me). ('Dearest Micheál, how can you?')

Then we went to the Ritz for more gin and tea, and were suddenly confronted with spectacle of Gabriel Pascal who, descending a long marble staircase with outstretched arms and looking like a demoniac Prince Charming in a Balkan operetta, slapped us both on the cheek and said, 'Didn't I tell you *he*,' digging me in the chest, 'would be your Iago?' After brief but fiery conversation, during which we learned of his plans for the next five years or so, he disappeared with Mephistophelean chuckles to the bar, and was replaced by Anatole Litvak, who drank something with us and said he thought he might know of a Desdemona, and would we like to see some reels of his new picture *Snake Pit* next day as she was playing important though speechless part in it.

Have seen no shows in Paris but Pierre Blanchard in play about the occupation, *Le Silence de la Mer*, which I found deeply moving, and pursued usual habit of wondering how it would translate, but think on reflection it could only move people who loved France and would fall flat on the ears of those who didn't happen to. Apart from this, nothing but snatches of films featuring unlikely Emilias and Desdemonas.

MARCH 21ST

Possible Desdemona glimpsed to-day in company with Litvak. Her name is Betsy Blair: longish lovely face crowned with light hair, and a performance full of gentleness and understanding. O. likes her.

MARCH 22ND

A day off at Fontainebleau. Lee came too and took photographs of us at ridiculous moments and all angles.

MARCH 23RD

Orson worried about money; eyes so bloodshot as to be almost invisible and give him appearance of a bull in the arena just before the kill. I, in turn, worried about Orson, also, I suppose, about *Othello*. Would hate it not to happen now; but Fatalism, which has probably ruined but certainly cheered my life, remains invincibly with me as ever in regard to matters of this sort, and cannot help feeling that if *Othello* is meant to be done it certainly will be.

Also, worry about money takes peculiarly diverting form with poor old Wounded Bull of riotous living: we never move from the hotel without the car, still driven by Belgian or, at intervals, by Belgian's understudy, and we eat nowhere but in gilded palaces in Paris or exclusive haunts by trout-streams in the country.

Rita prophesies a none too distant future in the *Vorkhouse*, but says that for herself she is used to hardship, having lived through the war in Italy, where it appears she was under grave suspicion by all parties, creeds, and nationalities, and frequently found herself in appalling situations as everyone with whom she came in contact seemed to think she was spying for the opposition.

O. and self discuss the nineteenth century, the Fratellinis, war, America, infant prodigies, Othello, the Gaelic revival, Colette, the Bhagavad Gita, Spanish cooking, the Ten Commandments, our forthcoming departure for Rome, and pistachio ice-cream. ('Ah! ils causent fantaisie!' whispered a tactful mother at lunch to-day in order to prevent her daughter asking for O.'s autograph; actually we were talking of Rita Hayworth.)

When these topics fade into abstractions and the abstractions into silence we start off again about the World Tour, and O. to-day decided that in order to get it, and indeed *Othello*, really going, he'd have to get some money, and said he was thinking of going to London to find some. Immediately saw him in my mind's eye as dark, stout, purposeful father-bird saying to squeaking occupants of the nest he had been rash enough to build: 'Now you wait here while I fly over to a little English lawn I happen to know where there are some great big worms hanging around just asking to be picked up.

MARCH 25TH

Mi-Carême, and Rita doing a Walkürenritt because she can't go out and dance. Why can't she, I ask, and am informed: 'Der Telefon.'

Rehearsals have been resumed. O. seems to have forgotten all about the quest for the English worms, also, momentarily, the World Tour. Ran through the 'Villain, be sure thou prove my love a whore' sequence in the Bois to-day (when are we going to shoot? Oh when?). Belgian sat at respectful distance reading translation of Agatha Christie, and Lee, script in hand, squatted on minute log at our feet like a benevolent Jewish Leprechaun. Moves, puzzling anyway (as I never know where camera is supposed to be or at which moment in the scene each take is supposed to begin or end), are quite impossible here as we keep stumbling over tussocks of grass and falling into rabbit holes. O., darting with mad agility from tree to tree between the stumbles, got *Mad*, in his own words, with the Leprechaun and started yelling at him: 'Come on, you monumental log of immovability! Hey! This is where the camera pans around! Come on, follow us, follow us—What the hell's the use of your sitting there with that Gioconda smile on your mug? Join the party, Baby! That's better: here we go again, "Villain, be sure thou prove my love a whore . . ." hey, what's happened to you, dear Micheál?'

This time it was no rabbit hole but a bunker hidden by bracken into which I had disappeared from view. Climbed out unscathed and rehearsal continued its wild way until we observed large audience collecting behind the trees and observing us with cool scientific interest and muttering *'formidable'* at intervals. Broke it up and were driven home.

Great excitement in the lobby owing to arrival of Merle Oberon. Still greater turmoil in olive-green suite at preparation for departure to Rome of Lee Kressel.

MARCH 27TH

Rehearsals continued. Went to the Circus to-night to see the Fratellinis. Wonderful, surpassing all expectations—I had never seen them—and defiant of all description. Drinks with them afterwards; the world they live in seems to me apart, dilated, enclosed and brilliant as a child's first Christmas party.

MARCH 29TH

Orson has vanished to London after tumultuous day with Rita, mainly concerned with things To Pack or Not To Pack. From M. Wolf, the proprietor, whose suave features become a philosophic mask of benevolence whenever he catches a glimpse of us, down to bevy of chambermaids and *chasseurs*, entire hotel personnel has been involved in wild scenes of rushing up and down in the lift, telephones ringing, telegrams arriving, messages, clothes, money, and passports mislaid. Finally we were borne away together by the Belgian; Rita, in frenzy of opening and closing suitcases and of minute instructions in French embroidered with despairing commentary in German, English, and Italian, whirled off to execute commissions in a taxi, full of intentions to join him in London, as she vaguely described, later.

On the way to Bourget he explained reasons of sudden departure. First, he would find a cast more easily in London, also he would find some money for *Othello*, to say nothing of World Tour, even if it meant making another film. One of these, already in the making with Tyrone Power, was, so to speak, on the carpet and he'd probably do it. Morocco was the seat of location and his work would only take a couple of months. That is, if he decided to do it. Meanwhile, he wanted me to go to Rome, *en route* (in event of his doing the film in Morocco) for Dublin (this surely puzzling from point of view of geography?), adding that while in Rome I could live at Frascati in a villa he had there and he would join me swiftly, probably accompanied, if he were free, by Hilton. Meanwhile, did I think Hilton would consider playing Brabantio in the picture when his Irish season was over? He was joining me for holidays in any case, wasn't he? Well, would he play Brabantio?

Car at this moment nearly collided with deeply unattractive black van which darted out of side street and was inscribed *Pompes Funèbres*, and both of us too upset to continue conversation. When we had recovered we had arrived at Bourget and there was only time for me to say yes, I thought H. would probably play Brabantio, and to ask what hadn't really occurred to me before: why, by the way, did O. want me to go to Rome?

Explosion followed:

Oh dear God! Oh Heavenly Powers! (*what else, and must he couple hell?*) hadn't I grasped even that? Oh, dearest Micheál—oh no! It just wasn't humanly possible to be such a cretin—— No, *really*—how did Hilton manage to get through life with such a moronic partner? Why, he wanted me to be fitted for my *Iago Clothes*, that was why. And anyway, didn't I *like* Rome? Wouldn't I be *happy* there? And then he himself would be back with entire contracted company (including Hilton-Brabantio), and we'd all rehearse on the terrace or under the olives, and we'd have no end of fun; or, on the other hand, Hilton and I might join him in Morocco (still on my way to Dublin, I wondered?) which would be superb setting for further rehearsals, and—no, *really no*, he couldn't believe I hadn't understood!

By this time he had whirled through the barrier and I was alone. Returned to the car and was driven back to the hotel pondering deeply on hotch-potch situation which included a voyage home by a route that made Hamlet's journey from Denmark to England via Poland seem a crow's flight in comparison, and wondering whether it wouldn't be simpler to take a plane to Cuba and wait for developments.

Consoled myself by dining in Montparnasse with la famille Jéanne, my oldest friends in Paris. News of my activities, or attempts to unravel and describe them, appeared more like Chinese puzzle than ever. Then spent evening of dazzling pleasure watching Carmen Amaya dancing at A.B.C. Found letters from Hilton, Craven, and Jim Neylin, also one from Mana in Australia, waiting for me on return to the Rue de Berri; also plane ticket for Rome dated 30th March. (Feel I was probably told of this but hadn't registered fact.) Realised that journey will therefore be to-morrow morning and have packed—I'm sure ruinously—all my things. Am now writing in bed.

PART II

March 30th to June 8th, 1949

PLANE, in which I now sit, delayed this morning by fog and we didn't leave Paris until 3 p.m.

Sitting close to me as I write is tall, bearded, and be-spectacled man dressed (excepting the spectacles) as Jesus Christ, and accompanied, it would appear, by Our Lady. Both of them in long and very beautiful Biblical clothes rather disconcertingly furnished with zip fasteners. All very strange. Their sudden appearance at airport of Orly heralded by blinding flashes of light (turned out not to be from heaven as I fancied at first but from press-photographers) caused mixed emotions among mainly French travellers; national chortle distinctly audible in places, also several remarks of Voltairean nature.

All the same they both have kind faces and hands, Ameri-can voices of the low restful kind, and gentle manners, and are very friendly to anyone who speaks to them. Lunch baskets now going round and they are served (I suppose not unnaturally) first.

Later. A ray of light hitting the eyes like a blow makes me glance up from Ernest Raymond's *Steps of the Brontës* to find that the fog has vanished and that we are passing over the Alps; they soar below us dizzily streaked and scarred with snow under stupefying radiance of evening sunshine. Feel sceptical yet fascinated and awe-stricken at Biblical couple and have started a poem in Irish about them: something is wrong however; I'll wait till they're no longer in sight.

Later still. Villa seems ravishing. No need for me to storm the Hôtel Hassler. Anyway Lou isn't there, I'm told by Signor Facchini, who introduced himself at Ciampino airport, and drove with me to Frascati. Facchini's position, though doubtless plain as a pikestaff to himself, is vague to me, but he seems to have some connection or other with the film and is a friendly creature. Speaks Italian only, so my part of conversation in car was remarkable for operatic vivacity, almost entire absence of grammar being atoned for by wealth of descriptive gesture and rich crops of Spanish words. He himself, short, stout and pale with a bald head and a babyish moustachioed smile, was very kind and asked eagerly for news of Orson, Rita, and progress of *Othello* rehearsals as we drove down long country roads marked by trees which had white aprons painted on their trunks, skirted the lights of Rome, and finally turned sharp hair-pin bend and shot up a steep hill towards a towering and dimly lighted gateway. Dogs barked as we passed a small lodge and then there was a long ascent through almost complete darkness: umbrella-pines and cypress trees, however, faintly visible against a handful of stars. Large doorway suddenly illumined, impression of glowing interior and of young man emerging on tip-toe who discussed luggage with the chauffeur, and led Facchini and me up flights of marble stairs to a big white dining-room, Roman style, with stone floor strewn with rugs, carved and painted ceiling, refectory table set for supper and all lighted by tall candles and a blazing olive-wood fire. Here over a vermouth Facchini gave me address of Hotel Excelsior as Orson's centre of activities and said the car is always at my disposal. After this, smiling and bowing like a benevolent gnome, he disappeared.

Strong sense of living in a fairy-tale was not lessened by beaming servants, two handsome country-women and the young man already observed, who brought me succulent and seemingly limitless meal beginning with olives wrapped in anchovies and working its way through fettucini, mushroom omelette, fish with mayonnaise, peas with ham, veal cutlets, salad, various cheeses, zabaglione, and all escorted by the wine of Frascati to a climax of freshly plucked fruit with the leaves on. Young man tip-toed in and out (do his boots squeak or is he afraid of being beaten?) and said 'Sissignore' or 'No signore' under his breath at intervals, finally appearing with coffee, array of liqueurs, and offers of hot bath, hot-water-bottle, and would I like coffee or chocolate for break-fast? He also unpacked (clothes, as I feared, crumpled as autumn leaves, but the two maids came smilingly forward and whipped them away to be pressed). All this I find not merely soothing but enchanting, and half expect to be lighted silently to bed (in the Cocteau manner) by tapers held in bodiless hands.

MARCH 31ST

Renato, still travelling on the tips of his toes, brought coffee and opened the shutters on radiance streaming down over a long apricot-coloured terrace and a wide garden with ponds, flowers, and fruit trees in a valley that rolls away to the hills of Rome and is filled with cypresses, pines, olives, and a sea of almond and cherry orchards; the tree-trunks all sprayed with pale blue and starred with blossom. A circle of mountains rises from woods of fig and chestnuts behind the house, all of them crested with brown and white villages cut out against the sky; men are at work in the vineyards, cocks crow, and the air smells of honey. Indescribably beautiful.

Wandered all the morning in paradise and wish I could share it with friends. Finished the poem about the American illustrations to Thomas à Kempis and the Bible and will probably send it somewhere. Their reception at Ciampino airport, by the way, marked once more by flashlight photo-graphs, and much more excitement shown by Roman public than by Parisian, one lady going so far as to shout 'Brava!'

Later. Rome this afternoon: magnificent as ever and with usual air of suspended languor, like a prima donna resting between two epoch-making arias. Spent most of the after-noon there in order to attend to Iago wig and clothes; in a

town one returns to the acceptance of the fact that one's
job is acting, but it is a jolt to the imagination.

Renewed acquaintance at the wig-shop with Vasco, one of
the world's great wig-and-beard boys; remember him very
well from two years ago in Hilton's Taormina film. The same
slim, pale, solemn-eyed, and natty little chap as always,
though his impeccable corrugated hair, previously raven-
hued, is now as though sprinkled with fine salt. Conversation
with him is easy as he speaks Spanish fluently and seldom
indeed pauses for breath. He reminded me that, like
Francesca, he hailed from Rimini (temptation, as he darted
about small dark shop with hair-nets and curling tongs, to
say 'Niminy-Piminy', though well-nigh irresistible, was
quelled). He asked feelingly after Mister 'Ilton Edwar', and
remarked that it was a pity that Carpaccio wig seemed
unlikely to help either my youth or *sex-appeal*, but added
that, as he hoped to be working with us on *Othello*, he
himself—Vasco!—would always be at hand to add, before
each take, various touches which would make me look like
Tyrone Power. Regarded my ageing, brandy-ball-eyed reflection in the glass (effect not aided by harsh grey light
filtering sideways through opaque glass window) with dislike,
and said Why not? without conviction.

Drove on to costumiers and spent tumultuous hour with
hordes of what seemed dramatic tenors surging about me
with tape-measures, pencils, papers, scissors and lengths of
cloth, all of these gentlemen in the last stages of ecstasy.
Emerged feeling, as so often after meeting with Italians,
flattered and battered, and having learned a lot more of the
language.

Back in this magical house, with the lamps lighted and
wood-fires burning in all the rooms and Renato tip-toeing
in from the terrace to ask would I like calamari or lamb or
both for dinner (chose, unhesitatingly, both), I feel more
than ever how I would appreciate a life not dependent on

fuss, intrigue, and organisation inseparable from the actor's world.

Have decided that if Orson does the Morocco film I will go home and wait there till he wants me. If he comes here and we continue with *Othello* at once, obviously I'll remain; shall be on salary all the time and cannot, in addition to this, live indefinitely at his expense in Luxurious Isolation.

APRIL 5TH

See the word 'isolation' used by me in last entry and can hardly believe my eyes, as parties in various houses in Rome (renewed pleasing acquaintance with Collie Knox at one of them) have vied in number with teas and luncheons with Joe Walshe, Irish Ambassador to the Holy See, and visits to the villa: Lee Kressel, Alan Curtis, Christine Norden, Lou Lindsay, John O'Flynn, Dermot Browner and a score of others in and out to meals, walks, and sunbaths.

These are interspersed with wild telephone calls from Hilton in Dublin: Orson has arrived and they talk all day of World Tour. H. severely practical and wants to know all sorts of things—mainly connected with orchestrations and electric current—I hadn't thought of.

So question of Isolation hardly arises, especially as Trauner has arrived to stay, still giving impression of gingerbread man, and laden with latest rumours from Paris and with new designs.

Later. News mysteriously circulated through staff by Renato (still on tip-toe) that Signor Welles is to be here to-morrow. Expect this will mean as much luxury as ever and still less Isolation.

APRIL 7TH

Orson didn't arrive, nor is there any news of where he is. Luke, our cook at home, who phoned me—ostensibly with message from H. but in fact to ask in awe-struck tones was I *really* speaking from Rome, and if so 'had I caught ere a glimpse of the Pope'—says that he (O.) has left Dublin. Nothing more seems to be known.

Later. Wire from O., who is in London, saying he's going to do *Black Rose* film in Morocco and would I like to wait in Rome, Paris, Dublin, or would I prefer to join him in Moorish desert, and we'll be shooting some time in May or June dearest love Orson. Seventh of April, you see.

APRIL 8TH

No news of Orson. Plane tickets arranged for to-morrow, 9th, Gina and Angelina, the two maids, fly round and round the house all day waving freshly washed linen: did this shirt belong to me? Or to il Padrone? Or to Trauner? Or perhaps to the German gentleman who spent Christmas here while working on a script of *Ulysses*? (Homer, not Joyce.) Finally everything packed by Renato, including about twelve editions de luxe of poetry and prose belonging to Orson which I had been reading and was obliged—with regret—to fish out again and leave on shelves.

Dined in Rome with John O'Flynn and afterwards wandered about in Pizza Navona. Met Trauner and some French friends in Caffé Greco and drove home.

Feel absurd at the thought of returning to Ireland without one inch of film shot, but think it the best thing to do.

DUBLIN. APRIL 9TH

Saturday. Left Rome at 9, changed at Milan at one (stone deaf from air-pressure, had to lip read porter's instructions, most confusing), at London at 5, was giving Rachel saucer of milk at seven-thirty, and talking to Hilton, Coralie, Eithne Dunne, and all the rest of them at side of Gaiety stage at 9. They were playing *Ill Met by Moonlight*, which goes to Belfast to-morrow to open on Monday 11th.

Made impulsive speech after the play and was so beautifully welcomed I felt very *émotionné*. This feeling was not dashed even by two ladies at stage door waiting for Hilton's autograph and saying in tones of deep disillusion as I passed them, 'Aw God, there's Meehawl back on us again; it's O.K., son, we got your name in our books last year, how's Italy?'

APRIL 10TH

They've gone North and I'm alone: I'm to follow them on Tuesday.

Was I ever in Paris or Rome? Is there a film called *Othello*? (Answer, in sequence, obviously, Yes I Was, and Not Yet.)

Garden all white and yellow with pear blossom and forsythia and daffodils. (Oh the Daffs, how I wish you could see the Daffs, Mr. Welles!)

BELFAST. APRIL 12TH

Impossible to fathom why I like this city but I do. Admittedly a cold, ugly sort of place, even in this radiant northern April, its setting of windy mountains and dark shipyards blotched with *fin-de-siècle* mansions and fussy streets full of plate-glass and cake shops and trams, but there's something about it all, its fantastic practicability, its bleak bowler-hatted refusal of the inevitable—what is it? To arrive here from Rome within the space of two days is a fabulous experience; from that languorous immemorial embrace one passes to Brooke's (Rupert, not Basil) 'rough male kiss of blankets'; Virgil and the Palatine Hill make way for the Bible and the bottle of Bushmills, and its air is that of a Business Man stepped straight out of Alice's Wonderland and marching side by side with the Jabberwock through yards of bunting and a gritty north-east wind to the rolling of drums.

Hilton, having lost weight, is now putting it on again and says brazenly why not? Adding that one can't be too fat for Falstaff or look too old for Lear. Fatal and agreeable philosophy. As for a film performance of Brabantio, he says, well, if that's to be the crowning-point of his career, who cares? As we seem immersed in subject of Shakespeare, I say what about revival of *Richard III*, as he is obviously still wicked enough for Gloucester. He replies that the trouble about plays with ghosts in them is it's so difficult keeping up disappearances. These corruscations take place in Donegall Square, round and round which we are walking in brisk shower totally unobserved by Hilton, and lead me to mention dark remarks frequently made by Orson to the effect that H.'s *real* place is directing movies. He says Oh really? and that this is possibly true, but enquires who is likely to give him a movie to direct? I say other people seem to direct them, and am told that is precisely what he means, and am then asked have I seen the average film lately? To this is added that Miss Lejeune is, on the whole, lenient, and that he has no wish to join the already seething army of mediocre directors of the mess of celluloid for which our profession is selling its (in most cases) non-existent birthright. He then notices it's raining, asks me do I enjoy being inundated with water, and complains that his voice, never his strongest point since pneumonia twenty years ago, has now completely vanished, adds my God! Taxi! in tones that shake the Gothic-Baroque-Romanesque-Victoriana of the City Hall, and we drive to remote suburb to see (me for the second time as I saw it a week or so ago with Trauner in Rome) die Dietrich in *Foreign Affair*.

Sound very bad and place full of children who skip, stamp, and screech without a single pause, but I hiss the inaudible jokes, rather late, into his ear. We both are suitably horrified by spectacle of once familiar streets now in unrecognisable state of destruction, and drive home humming the number 'Among the Ruins of Berlin', beautifully sung by die Dietrich, and nostalgically reminiscent of the old days before—(what's this his name was?)—Hitler.

APRIL 14TH

Arcadian day with H. and Coralie in a place called Craw-fordsburn where some clever people have turned an old mill into a hotel-restaurant and make one almost think that in the North, where Genius has died the death, Talent may be showing a welcome head, for the place has preserved its charm; there's not one instance of chromium plate and steel furniture, not one fireplace made to resemble miniature and regrettable majolica skyscraper: white walls and old dark furniture take their place. Lunch (for island standards good) followed by juvenile scamper in the glen, which is full of late blackthorn and early primroses.

Wild note from Orson (stamps are Moorish but there's no address), says I will love Morocco. Have no doubt of this as I loved it already in '32, but am beginning to wonder shall I have the opportunity of proving steadfast quality of this passion at any time in near future. Find it indeed impossible to believe there was ever any question of making a film in Morocco or anywhere else.

APRIL 15TH

Supper with Dr. Jim Ryan at his brother Arthur's (Monsignor Ryan) and long discussion with Arthur about Right and Wrong, most stimulating. Cannot fathom the moral mind, but find it full of endless fascinations. Have also yet to discover what qualities it possesses that make for handsomeness (admittedly of severe order) in the male, and for plainness in the female. All the thoroughly moral women I know, with two notable exceptions, not only plain, but have bad habit of humming tunes with loud, shrill, and persistent cheerfulness in cars. This surely to be discouraged?

APRIL 16TH

Rehearsed *Ill Met* all morning, *Drunkard* all afternoon.

APRIL 17TH

Easter Sunday; spent perfect summer day with Coralie, Hilton, and Paul in Antrim Glens. Irish Republic to-night at midnight. Dined at Harry McMullan's and argued pleasantly about it. The McMullans, though dissenting, most reasonable. Drank to it with H. on return to hotel. H. sympathetic but also analytic, and piously thanked God that England was free at last from 700 years of Irish domination. Found this a good twist, but felt too serious for badinage, and was suddenly fired with mad desire to drink to National Event with sympathetic compatriot. H. retired to bed, and I, regarding solitary bottle, was inspired, in desperation, to ring bell of lift, and on its appearance said to liftman who peered at me through the bars: 'Would you like to drink to the Republic?' Liftman's face, of vivid and trying shade of blue, brightened at the word Drink, but developed hitherto unnoticed network of veins at mention of Republic, and asked with great suspicion 'Which Republic?' and on being enlightened about this stated firmly that he was a Devout Unionist. (Probably has Orange Drum concealed somewhere.) Returned to room to drink alone, and to send telegrams to Maud Gonne MacBride and a few others.

APRIL 21ST

Drunkard doing hysterical business. Noel Atcheson to lunch.

DUBLIN. APRIL 30TH

A week out before playing Cork, so we are home. Summer weather. Commissioned by Seán MacBride, Minister for Foreign Affairs and chairman of new Cultural Committee, to write pamphlet on Irish Theatre. Decided to start in eighteenth century with Farquhar and all those boys usually billed as 'Old English Comedy', through Shaw and Wilde and Yeats national revival down to present day. Short but exhausting task: when and where am I to write it?

May Day Eve. Bonfires and crescent moon on the mountain at Howth.

CORK. MAY 2ND

Drove southwards yesterday bearing my Aunt Craven with us. Entirely delightful break on the way when we lunched at Kildare with Jack Dunne and his wife Una in setting of dogs, lawns, lilac trees, stables, beehives, and rooms smelling of potpourri, turf fires, and new books: an atmosphere I love because it's alien to me.

Cork as ever 'spicket and sparket, Mother', with memories. Impossible to imagine what life would have been like if one had never left it, as its peculiar intimacy can only be conceived as a hypothetical design from detailed point of view of the returning traveller. From any given point in the city you could see, if you had never been away, the entire pageant of your life: not merely the window of the room in which you were born, but also of that in which you had received your first experiences in education, ambition, dreaming, religion, shaving, drinking, poetry, seduction, despair, enmity, rebellion, failure, escape, death-wish, achievement, disillusion, decay, and a blank ultimate acceptance; these constant literal reminders of one's own cast-off skins must be stifling; it may be as well for me that life led me at so tender an age to a variety of places where one could not only cast one's skins but forget one ever had them.

Anyway, the soft distracting air and the river and the houses and the high leaf-covered walls with the gardens beyond them and the hills like tea-cosies emboidered with villas and trees and the steamers and the bubbling logical voices all welcome us; first night to-night a demonstration of wild exuberance, with comments from the gallery during post-play speeches full of a sort of caustic affection, one old man calling out insults to the films 'that take ye all away from us'.

Also discussed Ireland's relation with the arts into the small hours and came to doleful conclusion that, with her release into freedom and the delights of official nationhood, the great theme of her captivity is now cut off and she is faced, as far as her own principal art, which is literature, is concerned, with the problem of finding a new subject. What, in God's name, is she to do now that she is no longer the Princess in the Tower, superbly menaced by the Dragon Posing as St. George? Border question, though pressing, hardly possesses the stature to be used as a Villain, and art, like religion, like life, must have its Villain. So that now, the gaol gates behind her and the border problem appearing merely as a form of irritant on her left shoulder, she is presented a little late in the day at the Court of a post-war world, at this stage very bored, not merely with her, but with all the insignia of national entity she has been at such pains to acquire, so that she can think of nothing to show for the moment but the record of her past sufferings and struggles, now well known to everyone. This probably good for her soul, as in the end she will be compelled, like other nations, to look steadily at a world no longer veiled by the delirium of powder and smoke or by the excuse of prison bars, and find out what she really has to say about it all. Meanwhile I feel there's going to be a slump in Irish letters and drama: we can't go on about 1916 or even 1922 much longer.

MAY 3RD

Telegrams have arrived nearly every day from Orson: to-day he says: 'Airmailed letter to Hilton to-day impossible phone please try to get here May 16th cable address Fox Film Camp Militaire Ouarzazate letters c/o Don Cash Shelter Hotel Rue Horloge Casablanca all love Orson.'

Ouarzazate seems by map to be in middle of desert and

conjures up unpleasing image of self in shorts with oiled shoulders and pith helmet.

MAY 8TH

Finished last night in *Ill Met*, which has been enormous success: Eithne Dunne and Helena Hughes especially playing beautifully. All felt a little regretful and wondered when, if ever, we would play it again. Neesons and other friends carry us off to supper every night. To-day is Sunday and the sunshine a preparation for Morocco: we spent the whole day with the O'Learys of Macroom and drove in two cars over the mountains to Killarney. Indescribable if platitudinous paradise of lakes and fells drove my aunt Craven to paroxysms of delight, and Denis O'Leary and self to buy large bottle of whiskey for twilight journey back to Macroom: inevitable result of stories of ghosts, demons, and fairies ensued; Coralie completely lost her head and insisted on stopping car at every thorn tree and holy well to look for specimens of Underworld by moonlight.

Difficult to believe that the film of *Othello* is chief, if somewhat obscure, motif of my life at the moment.

MAY 14TH

Wire from Orson saying 20th will be early enough for me to arrive Casablanca. So played to-night for the last time (for how long?) with our own actors.

DUBLIN. MAY 17TH

Said good-bye to Hilton and the others yesterday and came home. Wretched interim alone in house with Arthur, who packs, and Queen of Siam, who is restless and reproachful. She will live partly with Winnie Menary during my absence in desert. (*Can* we be going to rehearse in desert? And is Orson intending to shoot film of *Othello* in setting of mosques and palm-trees?)

PARIS. MAY 18TH

Left Rachel (of Siam) in arms of Winnie (of Armagh); Arthur and Johnnie waved me farewell from Collinstown; photographers caught me (am convinced) at worst angles; Cecil and Lulu Lavery enlivened extremely bumpy journey. to Paris, where I lost sight of them. Lunched with *la famille Jéanne*, who proved themselves of the chosen race of friends by giving me a room to rest in as I'll be travelling all night, also by sending up tea and *mille feuilles*. Chestnut trees all in bloom, but queer, grey, luminous, melancholy day hangs over them.

Later. In Plane. Flying in series of bumps, jerks, and dives over Spanish mountains, and am informed by Walter Solloway, large and cheerful American business-man, who, since bus journey from Invalides to Orly, is my neighbour, that patch of lights blinking dizzily from apparently three hundred miles below us is Madrid. W.S. has amiably produced large bottle of whiskey, which between us we have almost finished. Sensation of acute unreality immediately assails me, and any thought of sleep, which one would have imagined was the purpose of whiskey to induce, is banished. Cold intense and we huddle under rugs. He glances at pen in my hand and diary on my knees and says, 'Writing to your wife?' and I say, 'No, to myself,' and he says, 'Gee!' with nuance of surprised admiration, and then looks at me with suspicion.

Plane has again dipped a few thousand feet, whatever the authorities say, and Walter (we are, after so many drinks, *Walter* and *Mike*) is waving the bottle at me. I shall write no more.

CASABLANCA. MAY 19TH

Approach to the town from the air in the dark morning superb; an armful of jewels flung over the black sky and sea.

Further inspection on landing revealed series of box-like, half-finished houses, promenades, arcades, dusty palms and a wild salty tang as of *frankincense, leopards* and *pepper* in the air.

No taxis at air-bus terminus. Walter S. had no hotel and had decided to accompany me to Don Cash Shelter (as I thought). Walked through arid new streets, now brightening with dawn, in wake of pock-marked Arab who pushed our bags on a cart. No one seemed to know anything of 'Don Cash', but 'Shelter' produced a gleam of light, and at last we arrived at hotel. Here Nightmare began. Mystery of 'Don Cash' soon cleared up: turned out not to be portion of hotel's title at all but American manager of *Black Rose* film (Tyrone Power cum O.W.) at present in the desert on location. No room had been booked for me, however, until three weeks ahead, said white-robed night porter in Turkish Delight edition of French, as he waved snake-charming fingers at a notice on the wall that read 'Complet'. As for Walter S., continued night porter, nobody ever dreamed of coming to Casablanca without booking a room at least four weeks in advance; the most that could possibly be done either for Walter S. or for Micheál Mac L. would be to let them have, in about an hour's time, a room in which to rest till 9 a.m., when the room would be occupied by wealthy French gentleman and wife arriving from Agadir. Sudden appearance was made on marble staircase at this point by a Mr. Frank Bevis, clad in striped pyjamas and flushed with sleep, who said he was production manager for *Black Rose* and he happened to know that Orson Welles didn't expect me for three weeks. Sympathy with my blank dismay at receiving this news was registered in bluff British Navy fashion, 'Very sorry of course, old man' being keynote of the conversation, with rider to the effect that he, F.B., was driven half dotty trying to fix rooms for actors who either arrived at the wrong time or didn't turn up at all. My riposte to this was that in future

I would unhesitatingly belong to the second group. This drove F.B. back to bed, still saying 'Sorry of course, old man.' I then repaired with Walter to landing furnished in Winter Garden fashion with basket-work and glass-topped table, easy chairs and illustrated guides to Morocco (pre-war), and discussed our plight. Myself, meanwhile, numbly ruminated on ignominious tricks of fate, and found I was haunted by refrain of rather sordid little song heard in child-hood beginning 'Why did I leave my little backroom in Blooms-bu-ry?' Finished remains of whiskey, its glamour now completely departed, also swallowed some black coffee brought us by Mohamet the Night Porter, and at about 8 retired to recently vacated room suggesting chiropodist's salon and echoing to loud Hammering (can Orson's workmen have failed to track him to Ouarzazate and be filling in time here?). Were not chucked out until noon (Mohamet now replaced by Abdullah, quite indistinguishable, apparently his twin-brother), when we sallied forth bathed and shaved to blinding sunshine and ice-cold wind respectively blazing on and blow-ing through white and yellow town surging with Arabs, French, Jews, and Spaniards. Walter gave me lunch and we parted regretfully, he to take train for Marrakesh and self to hunt for hotel.

Afternoon spent writing dismal letter to Hilton, on Winter Garden landing. Hotel of repellent aspect (the only one in the town with a free room) discovered at 6 p.m. in Rue Blaise Pascal. Mystery of my not being wanted as Iago for three weeks (at least) cleared up by telephone calls transferred from Shelter. First communication was from Rita, who is ill after an operation on her teeth in a clinic in Marrakesh. ('Quite ackonising, my dear, my face is really so like a football ge-schwolen.') Rita said wire from Orson to Ireland postponing dates must have crossed my departure. Second communica-tion was from Orson himself from desert ('Dearest Micheál I'm So Sorry but Miss Mud will provide you with large sums

of money, and why don't you visit Fez? Rabat? Marrakesh?
Morocco is such a Great country—now you *know* it's great').
Lee Kressel also had a lot to say and confided in a whisper
that, from point of view of his own taste, which as I knew
was inclined to favour Ritz bar at twilight, life on location
in Ouarzazate was a picturesque Hell.

Found myself being difficult and strenuous and saying I
was in the mood for Work, not sightseeing, but would be glad
of some money. 'Well, why not go to *Rome*,' says Orson,
'and try on your costume, you know I want you to look *good*
as Iago and you like Rome'; and his voice, diminishing in
weird mechanical fashion, was, after lengthy breakdown of
sound, replaced by voice of Lee repeating, 'They cut us off
but listen, honey, *Rome*, he wants you to go to *Rome*.' 'Why
Rome?' says I. 'Well,' says Lee, 'to try your *costume*, for I
know that is what Orson considers essential and it's worrying
him very much. You go to *Rome*.'

Opened my mouth once more and yelled that I had already
tried on my costume in Rome three times, also wig, and in
the midst of great eloquence discovered we were again cut
off. Jingled receiver like comic manservant in farce, also
shouted to exchange, but no good. Have spent rest of evening
in isolation and despair, but will now sally forth to visit town.

MAY 20TH

Twelve hours have finally revealed to me that while loneliness undoubtedly full of interest and profit for the soul
if experienced in beautiful wilderness, it is a barren affair
in garish modern town which, more than ever on close
inspection, resembles toy-town of yellow boxes, many of
them plastered with hoardings and regrettably revealing
worst excesses of Broadway in Franco-Arab edition.
Reminded as I paced about alone last night of Chesterton
saying what a grand place Broadway would be if one couldn't
read; and finally took refuge in Moorish cabaret where pretty

buxom houri waggled hips in *mouvement perpetuel* to the coruscating inanity of modern Arab music. This was provided by beaming male orchestra in European dress; audience, however, also exclusively male, clad in impressive robes and turbans.

Frank Bevis, Prods. Manager for *Black Rose*, rescued me to-day: lunch and dinner together in gales of laughter at each other's jokes.

A car has been arranged to bear me off to Marrakesh tomorrow to see die Rita.

MARRAKESH. MAY 21ST

Marrakesh of dazzling beauty as of Arabian Nights, all in deep reds and roses and purples, the streets full of bougainvilia and jacaranda trees in blossom under which droves of Arabs wander with linked fingers in robes of white, lilac, violet, and dark crimson. Was told by Rita, whom I visited at tea-time in her clinic, that I must dine in the Place de France, which she assures me is like the ballet of Scheherazade, and I certainly intend to obey her. She was looking very ill, *meine arme süsse Rita*, with face, as described by herself *so wie ein Füssball geschwollen*, her black hair in wild and I thought becoming disarray all over the pillows as she lay prostrate in a room so like a ship's cabin in its pale glistening chastity one almost expected it to roll. Very sad she was at first, too, as she devoured a purée of potatoes followed by creamed rice (surely a depressing diet to one already depressed, and inclined to be like English governess slightingly described by Blanche Ingram in *Jane Eyre*, as '*lachrymose and low-spirited*'), but cheered up at my imitation of Frank Bevis and told me, after a while, all the news.

Mogador. That is chief and, to me, staggering news item. We are to make *Othello* in Mogador, not Rome at all. Or Nice. Or Paris. Or Venice. Just Mogador. That's the latest.

Mogador: not the Parisian theatre noted for musical shows of the kind known as *light*, but a small town on the west coast of Morocco. No hotel, says Rita, lapping up her rice; der Orson will probably take a villa (the difficulty of that may be the sanitation) where you will all be one happy family. (This Family is disinfected throughout with Jeyes' Fluid). Mogador has a fortress built by the Portuguese (God forgive them) in sixteenth century. Quite perfect, says Rita, but she believes that there is little else. Just a few rocks, some hills—no, not mountains, quite little hills—a palm or two, and possibly an Arab quarter. (Quarter of What, pray, if there's nothing but rocks and a fortress?) There may possibly be, she continues, a funny little *inn* where we can eat kouskous *à l'arabe* and perhaps some fish, and even tea with mint. The sea of course will be *herrlich*, but being also *Atlantisch* it will be far too cold to bathe. Even in Summer. Also, she adds, still lapping her rice, the weather is windy and *foggy*. This too comes from the Atlantic, whose waves dash up over the Portuguese fortress all day and all night, and they cause this fog, which will give, she continues, now waving her spoon at me and looking suddenly deeply unattractive, this impression of mystery, of strangeness, this texture, this *Stimmung, was?*, so coveted by der Velles.

'*Ach ja,*' says Rita, handing me her platter (now licked clean and bestowed by my nerveless hands on black japan tray), 'it is not Monte Carlo you are going to. But the film, I am so sure, will be *wundervoll, fantastisch, fantastisch*'; and she lies back exhausted, as well she might.

Fell to pondering on Hilton's holiday planned to be spent with me in Rome or Venice or Nice or Paris or all four, and failed to picture him lost in fog among Quite Little Hills and an Arab or two, but realised this was not correct attitude for serious actor embarking on film career, however belated, and said nothing, but resolved to write self-sacrificing letter insisting on his holidaying alone and leaving self and der

Velles to face howling gales, kouskous, and yards of celluloid together.

MAY 22ND

Medina, which is the Arab part of the City as opposed to *Mellah*, which is the Jewish, surpassed all descriptions by Rita or anyone else; an orgy of Islam dyed in ferocious colour, scent and darkness, with sudden flaring lights that reveal multitudes of Arabs and Berbers who buy, sell, beg, dance, sing, juggle, charm snakes, read the Koran, tell tales, perform magical tricks by lantern light, and offer their services as guides, pimps, carriage-drivers, escorts, and purveyors of love.

Dined alone and was invited to drink coffee with pleasant French doctor who sat at the next table; we were afterwards driven by elderly Pandarus of Troy clad in embroidered trousers, a mackintosh, and a vast ragged turban to the *closerie d'amour*, where we were entertained for more than reasonable sums in a series of dazzlingly lighted marble rooms on long puce or sky-blue divans by bevy of unveiled houris smothered in *maquillage* and moles, and dressed, obviously, by Henri Matisse. They all in turn gave us honey cakes and tea with mint, which is revolting, stroked our cheeks, patted our thighs, pinched our biceps, smoked our cigarettes, and finally kissed us very coyly on the nose and cackled at each other in Arabic. This followed in each case by a lot of clinging and pouting and tut-tutting when we got up to go, and in one establishment by some spitting, at which I slapped all the bottoms within reach. This proved a triumphant success. They shrieked and slapped back, and one of them began to throw cushions about and tear off her clothes (in order, I suppose, to defend her virtue with more freedom), and Madame, who was very fat and dressed in what seemed to be a mauve tablecloth with a bead fringe, screeched with joy and threw a box of Turkish Delight at me, which we subsequently all ate together. French doctor was inspired by these activities to do a solo rumba, also triumphant success and soon joined in by the company; and Madame, fanning herself with the lid of the sweet box and jingling her bead fringes, said she had never seen such merry French gentlemen as ourselves before, the French being for the most part, she vowed, her mouth full of Turkish delight, dull, solemn, and cheese-paring and inclined to forget her own existence. This delicate hint at her faith in her own past charms as in our present generosity did not go unrewarded; Madame got a nice tip, and to express her gratitude flung herself on the floor at our feet with howls of gratitude, then found herself unable to rise, and that was the last we saw of Madame.

Berber dancing boys visited in turn: these, dancing in long white night-shirts with bracelets on their ankles, proved as quiet and docile as if they had been brought up at St. Margaret's Hall (which they probably had, or at Schleu equivalent). After the dancing was over, a gentle and very pretty affair concerned chiefly with a soft stamping of bare feet on the floor, and with a fluttering of tiny metallic castanets to the accompaniment of a stringed instrument played by their tutor, a sort of Mussulman Santa Claus, they squatted in the corner to whisper together and drink mint tea, never taking their eyes off us, and Santa Claus, after a brief chat with them, explained in French that they admired our ties and would like them as a souvenir. (Of What, I should like to know? Anyway they didn't get them.)

Everyone friendly, and delight with us expressed by all with the exception of Sir Pandarus of Troy who, sitting morosely on his driver's box, tut-tutting sibilantly whenever we remounted the carriage, said he couldn't understood why we stayed for such a short time at each port of call, adding that we seemed very difficult gentlemen to please and suggesting a visit to other haunts of pleasure where we would

undoubtedly find what—surely?—we were seeking. No
demands, however complicated, would be found impossible
of fulfilment. These offers (in spite of half-formed 'Oh do
let's!' which sprang to my eager lips) were severely turned
down by doctor and we drove home (Pandarus in condition
of bewildered despair), and talked Islamic civilisation (discussion highly speculative as our interest far greater than our
knowledge) till small hours.

To-day is fantastically hot and spent (stripped to skin in
shaded room) partly in writing pamphlet on Irish Theatre
(have got through eighteenth century, also Wilde and Shaw
and arrived at Yeats) and partly at clinic (fully clad) with
Rita, who, true to Orson's promise, gave me lire for journey
to Rome. This discussed at all angles. I still think it crazy but
agreeable plan to go from Morocco to Rome and back again
in order to try on one tunic already tried on, but am now
in mellow condition and ready for anything. Die Rita herself
will be flying there on 26th and have decided to fly with her.
Plane via Paris: surely a long way round, but in addition to
being mellow am also getting as used to these whirling
journeys as Les Invalides station must be getting used to
the spectacle of self arriving at all hours of day and night
en route for somewhere else.

MAY 23RD

I wandered about in the Souks after dinner and listened
to two young girls who stood hand in hand by the roadway,
singing for coppers. They were both blind. Their songs, like
the *flamenco* songs in Spain and the traditional songs one
still hears in Connemara, were set in a mode unconnected
with modern European singing, and held me listening there
for more than an hour. It seemed as though one heard a kind
of whispering of the inmost secrets of two lives addressed to
no audience in particular, but to the universe at large; as
though the singers were trying to make the air understand

the sorrows and ardours, at first simply of two individual
girls, and, later on, of a whole people, a whole race. I wished
I were a musician, or at least that I could have taken down
some of the airs, because they were at once sad and joyful
and indescribably stirring. I would like to have known too
some of the words they were singing, for when I asked a
Moor who spoke a little French what was the subject of the
songs he said, after listening for a while: 'They are making
up the words and the tunes as they go along. Now the
younger one is saying that she has never seen her father or
her brothers, and cannot imagine what it would be like to
watch the sun coming up in the morning, or the crescent
moon on the first night of Ramadan, the feast of the Prophet;
and now the older one is saying she wishes to meet a young
man as blind as she is herself, for then, though her sister
has told her she has no beauty, she could deceive him into
thinking her the fairest of all women,' and I was reminded
of Synge's *Well of the Saints*.

Yet when he had gone away, and I gave them some more
money and begged them to sing again, they tittered and grew
shy, and at last began to sing some vacuous air that must be
popular in the cabarets, for several people passing by joined
in, and a guide, seeing my interest, whispered that they were
not *femmes de plaisir* but that if I wished it something might
be arranged, and the spell was broken.

CASABLANCA. MAY 26TH

Returned by train and have had recurrence of old miseries
of dizziness and lassitude. Sent for doctor and he cured me.
Frank B. delightful and kept me amused all the time, also
helped me when I got better with difficulties of journey.
These very tedious indeed, and involved hours at office of
Air France and similar institutions, which increased dizziness. Drove about with Frank and to dispel these symptoms

took long walks with him by the sea every evening, these followed by dining at various places. Casablanca, in spite of regrettable resemblance to Toy-Town and general air of Much Ado about Nothing, is full of good restaurants, La Reine Pédauque I think the best, Frank, however, preferring Le Petit Poucet because, as he says, Petty Pussy is such a *soppy* name, adding that only the French would get away with it, oh yes old boy, I mean, when you come to think of it it *is* the end, I mean *isn't* it?

It's going to be Pédauque to-night, however. Die Rita arrives and is to meet us there: we then fly to Rome via Spain and Les Invalides, leaving poor old Frank behind, and I am still wondering what all this cavorting through the air has to do with the art of the films.

PARIS. MAY 27TH

It was amusing to watch the sun go down over Africa and rise over Europe, though the second of these spectacles was watched through eyes swollen with lack of sleep. Six babies on the plane, and they were all laid to rest by their mothers with the aid of steward and hostess in little hammocks slung under the luggage racks: a pleasing arrangement, but the sky was pale before they stopped yelling and we were paler still. Nothing available but Cointreau and warmish water, and coffee this morning made with tinned milk, and on the plane's alighting at Orly in sharp, early French sunshine (so different from Moorish) die Rita, busily combing her black hair and powdering her large handsome nose beige, glanced out of the window to observe the earth slanting dizzily towards us, and what should she see but a *Hare*.

'Ach schau Mal, ein grosser *Hase* I think you call a *Hare*,' says she, 'and he is looking at us quite cheerfully.'

She couldn't understand until I explained the ominous meaning of this: a hare crossing one's path at dawn and looking at one (however cheerfully) is a Witch in disguise and bound to bring confusion and ill luck. I looked in terror and saw the loathsome thing loping away over the fields. Rita laughed at these superstitious fears, but has earned for herself forever the name of a heroine of popular Irish fiction of my youth known as Kitty the Hare, and it was not long before the Hare began to demonstrate her power. On arrival at the Lancaster at the hour of 6.30 there were no rooms for us, in spite of Rita's (K. the H.'s) having engaged them in advance. Paris was full to the last bathroom, the last billiard-table. Crab-like servants were crawling about over the vestibule with buckets and mops; the concierge was adamant; and we had nine hours of waiting before us, as the plane for Rome leaves at three. Coffee was brought after much winsome pleading from us and we were given two long sofas in the salon where we fitfully slumbered with coats and rugs till nine, when we heard a voice saying 'My! this certainly seems to be occupied,' when we threaded our way through throngs of beautifully dressed Americans back to the vestibule dragging our coats and rugs after us.

Kitty the Hare, however, miraculously restored by her three hours' rest, vanished after announcing that she was going to bathe, have her hair fixed, shop, and make several telephone calls. Sat in vestibule feeling flat, dazed and shabby when M. Wolf, always sympathetic, appeared and offered me his own room. This turned out to be large, pale, quiet and elegant. Slept till one and dreamed of the Queen of Siam. Then phoned Hilton, who said, 'But where are you *now?*' and asked how many scenes we had shot. Told him the news as far as I could and he says he'll come to Mogador if that is where I'll be and that the new car is behaving beautifully.

Lunch with K. the H. (new and striking hair-do, geranium nails, lips and gloves, and general air of gleaming poise) and with dear gingerbread Trauner (very depressed).

Am writing this in the vestibule, still swarming with super-elegant Americans, who make me feel more than ever travel-seared and crumpled.

Later. Writing in plane. Spell of the Hare pursues us: her victim Kitty especially, for she forgot to declare some lire in her bag and was marched off to small boudoir at Orly to be searched by relentless-looking lady with a forage cap at a jaunty angle over a Buzz of elderly brown curls, magenta lips, and a bust like a shelf. I as her companion and suspected confederate met with same fate at the hands of swarthy dwarf and vast blond *père de famille*, both in uniform and both from Brittany; these on finding me guiltless became all smiles and cracked a few hearty Breton jokes about my passport and our mutual Celtic heritage. Rejoined Rita (also pronounced guiltless but now complete nervous wreck), who tottered on my arm across windswept airfield in the manner of Mme X after her trial and fell crashing to her face on iron step-ladder as she mounted plane, bruising her hand and chin. Gave me stricken glance as we strapped ourselves to our seats and murmured 'der Hase, der Hase!'

We have once more passed over Lyons, Grenoble, Alps, Blue Coast, and Appenines, and are now above Rome, which is sloping sideways towards us, a diminutive model of itself with St. Peter's, Castel San Angelo, the Vittorio Emmanuele wedding-cake, and all the rest of it, rising up like gilded toys by a gilded winding stream.

Later still. Everything at the Villa Bottai as it was: Renato (still on tiptoe), Gina and Angelina all wreathed in smiles, welcomed us with succulent dinner. Garden more melo-dramatically lovely than ever, burnished sunset having changed to green bronze night accented by stars, cypress, umbrella pines, and distant hills veiled in silver, but fruit blossom, not unnaturally, disappeared, and rather poorly replaced by deafening chorus of crickets. Took coffee and Strega lounging on the terrace where Kitty the

Hare said we were all catching pneumonia ('der Hase, der Hase!').

Say 'all' because Bob (Roderigo) Coote is staying here, also Michael (Cassio) Laurence, both in condition already bordering on lunacy. They have been here for several days doing nothing, and have decided during their enforced idleness (stimulated no doubt by the subtle frustration of fresh air, many apéritifs, and much comparing of notes), that never have they heard of such a film, or of such a strange way of doing things, and for their part they think it is a lot of unprintable expressions, old boy, no honestly I mean, laugh as you may, but in Hollywood or Ealing one signs one's contract and makes one's picture: one doesn't get sent out to a (no doubt pretty) villa to sit on one's fanny with no one to talk to except one another and a horde of gibbering foreigners, and nothing to do but drink cocktails and eat olives and hear rumours about some outlandish place called Mogador. Mogador, good God! Just rumours, oh yes, but no news, no real news, and as for the costumes, well they'd tried *them* on till they were dizzy, and what was the use of costumes if there was no news and no film and no work and no nothing? It is different for me: I can make myself understood to the gibbering foreigners and seem indeed to be quite at home among them; also I'm a stage, not a film actor, and probably haven't half a dozen contracts I could be and should be fulfilling elsewhere. (This perfectly true.) Also I have, according to my own admittance, already abandoned my own season in Ireland, and would very likely be holidaying among gibbering foreigners in *any* case at this time of the year, but really, no *really*, it was beyond a joke. And where *was* Orson anyhow? In the desert, was he? That was funny news. Very funny indeed. And when was the work to begin? And how much longer were they expected to sit in this villa waiting to be told what to do and where to go next; with their agents, by this time perfectly frantic, wiring them almost hourly to Stand Firm and Go Home (could one possibly do both?) and teach somebody a little sense.

Felt on the whole in sympathy with them as their mood reflected my own on arrival in Casablanca a few days (is it possible?) ago, and appealed to Rita-Kitty to explain what she knew of the situation to them (she, though a foreigner, could not be described as gibbering, as her command of English, in spite of an occasional 'mit', is astonishing). So Kitty, with frequent promptings in cascades of Italian from Giorgio Pappi (who had met us in Ciampino and was now catching pneumonia with us as he walked unhappily up and down on the terrace looking agitated and bored at the same time, a combination of expressions requiring careful practice), did explain things, and they said that was all very fine and large but When was *Othello* going to be Shot? This produced short silence which enabled one to hear again the chorus of crickets, and Kitty said at last, He would Return probably sooner than any of us expected, as der Velles, when he did move, moved like lightning. At this some incredulous Pshaws drowned the crickets again, and we all went bristlingly into the house with, by this time, firm conviction that no film was ever going to be made at all.

In spite of this depressing background to our professional lives at moment I was glad to see Bob Coote again, and even gladder to see Michael, who is one of our own Gate Theatre actors and has played with us a lot at home. We talked together about Dublin in intervals between the *Othello* storms (out of the corners of our mouths in Irish so as not to appear to be breaking too openly with the burning matter under discussion), and this seemed to soothe Michael, though the momentary identification of ourselves with hordes of gibbering foreigners had a perfectly frightful effect on poor Bob ('my God! are you two starting to do it *too*?'), so we turned back to English.

Were joined later on by Betsy Blair, the new Desdemona, who has the same gentle beauty as her picture in *Snake Pit* and infinitely more to say about life than she had on the screen. Just arrived with immense enthusiasm (how long will this last?) from Hollywood, is staying in Rome, and had driven to Frascati accompanied by long thin American journalist called Slim who takes incessant photographs of everybody at all moments as if it were a nervous habit (which by this time it probably is). Also has astounding method of conversation resembling cross-talk monologue of intimate and jocose nature studded with names of film stars. From it emerged humorous story of attempted interview with Churchill, which sounded like custard-pie comedy and in which Slim seems to have had (or given) last word (or pie). A happy good-natured fellow with the sort of militantly Irish face only seen on Americans and which is, I believe, accounted for by almost undiluted Scottish ancestry; he invited us all to dine with him in Rome to-morrow and disappeared with Betsy B. in diminutive car followed by loud series of explosions.

ROME. MAY 29TH

Afternoon yesterday in Rome occupied by *turismo*, with Armando driving and self as highly imaginative guide (even if historical exactness dubious). Experienced usual pleasure in showing off beauties of the city to Michael and Bob, who cheered up immensely and forgot for an hour or so that they were Screen Players. I tried hard not to feel I was entirely responsible for design and execution of Colosseum, Forum, Campidoglio, and all the rest of it. (Does everyone initiating friends in their first experience of known and beloved masterpieces experience this unwarranted sensation?)

See-Rome-in-a-Day episode was followed by refreshing bath in Lou Lindsay's rooms at Excelsior, and this by dinner with Slim and Betsy at the Tre Scalini on the Piazza Navona,

which was a huge success: Slim bargained vivaciously with
cab drivers, and apparently feels about Italian customs and
language much as I did about the Forum. We all wandered
through the amber-coloured moonlit streets after dinner full
of wine and wild strawberries and singing superbly at the top
of our voices.

Kitty the Hare has returned to her flat on the Via Anto-
nelli, but to-night came to dine with Betsy and told some
wonderful stories about Rome during the war; also reported
rather nervously but with dedicated expression, No News
from Orson.

Betsy charming and of genuine intelligence; argues beautifully about acting, women, communism, America, friendship,
and religion without losing her head when she loses a point
(a rare thing in a woman), or even becoming winsomely
inarticulate (even rarer in a pretty woman). Only thing that
worries me is: will Orson find her right for Desdemona?
'Modern' a tiresome adjective for a personality, but that is
what she is, with an undisguised frankness in her eyes and
free loose-limbed gestures and walk. Would cast her unhesitatingly for Jo in *Little Women* or equally for any girl who
walks straight and alone into life, but cannot feel the Renaissance, the Latin world of the fifteenth century, or hear her,
in answer to Emilia's 'Alack, who has done this deed?', reply:
'Nobody. I myself. Commend me to my kind Lord.' Must
keep these thoughts inside my own head.

MAY 31ST

Neatly but simply clad in a swim slip and walking up and
down in order to observe beauties of garden from all angles,
I drink my coffee every morning on the upper terrace, and
yesterday crooked my back while lifting cup from low wooden
stool. Unable to walk straight ever since, and am undergoing
daily treatment which includes injections and massage from
Orson's Dr. Hirschfeld (cousin of dear old Magnus of Berlin,

Code 175 and all that), who says I have a *Hexenschuss*. This, as everyone knows, means a Witches' Shock, and Kitty and I are convinced it is the continued Work of the Hare espied by us in Paris airfield. Injections disagreeable, and massage acrobatically agonising (so different from Moïse in Paris), and after them I hobble slowly to Rosati's or Doney's in the Via Veneto for an ice. At one of Doney's tables on the pavement to-day was confronted by strange gentleman, large, plump, elegant, and impressive in soft beige gaberdine suit, silk shirt and tie, with a heavy good-humoured face like someone in a Gogol story and what I took to be a strong Russian accent. He said 'You are Iago, I think, isn't it? May I give myself pleasure to offer you an drink? I, also, am called Mike.'

It was then revealed that he was Dr. Mihail Waschinsky, the Polish film director about whom continual discussions were held in Paris, and who is going to assist Orson in film (if this ever happens: am now strongly influenced by M. and B. school of pessimism: by M. and B. I mean, of course, Michael and Bob; powerful and curative drug, very lowering to the spirits, is suggested by joint usage of their initials; this impression not entirely misleading).

Waschinsky a charmer of the first rank, and his conversation, at once barbed and indulgent, passes from German to English and back again, both tongues echoing to the music of his own Polish and encrusted at moments with French and Italian; like me he is unblushingly at his ease in at least five languages and incorrect in nearly all of them. Like me, too, while feeling a little bewildered by the history of *Othello* to date, he has not the slightest intention of allowing it to blot out Life with all its Ecstasies, as Walter Pater might have said but didn't, so we had several drinks together and compared so many notes about Italy before the war, Berlin before Hitler, Stage before Cinema, and Orson before *Othello*, to say nothing of *Othello* before Orson, that I forgot all about my *Hexenschuss* and roared aloud with the sudden pain when I got up to go, causing all the eyes in the (now twilit) Via Veneto to glance uneasily in my direction as I hobbled to the car and drove back to Frascati.

JUNE IST

News. We fly to Morocco day after to-morrow. Via Paris. M. and B. so revived by this that they remarked what a lovely house this was, and what a beautiful landscape, and Rome! what a glorious city: really, it seemed quite a pity to leave it all behind.

JUNE 2ND

Writing solidly for two days on pamphlet about Theatre in Ireland. This carried on in cool white room overlooking garden and filled with Orson's painting things with photograph of O. in matador's clothes killing his bull in the arena at Seville. (Is there no activity he has not at one time or another pursued?)

Renato tiptoes about in the courtyard below and swears softly at Gina and Angelina, and M. and B. sunbathe. All is peace, and Theatre in Ireland makes rapid progress. Have read almost nothing since I came here but O'Casey's *Innis-Fail, Fare thee Well*, which fills me with admiration and deep, deep dislike. It made me wish more than ever that Ireland showed signs of a new mood in letters, as the nail-biting, tooth-baring school, still fashionable among writers whether they remain in Dublin or take refuge in Devonshire, becomes wearing to the nerves in the end, however dazzling in execution; there is much to be said for the creation of a new era of generosity.

JUNE 3RD

Really this is June 4th, as the midnight bell sounded long ago but its music was drowned by sounds of revelry issuing

from gaudy night arranged by M. and B. and taking form
of wild supper party. Betsy among the guests, also Slim
(camera dangling around his neck), Erwin Shaw, Doris Dowling of Hollywood and Rome, a handsome creature who I
hear is to play Bianca with us, and a seething horde of other
guests whose identity remains for the most part a mystery.
Kitty the Hare, who is not, I'm sorry to say, coming to
Morocco, very busy hostessing, and Renato flying round on
tiptoe with cauldrons of ravioli, lobsters, chickens, pâtés
and bottles of wine. Local band has now been summoned
from village to play mandolines and harmoniums and perform spirited tarantellas; Gina and Angelina proud but
anxious that the delicacies they have prepared are giving
satisfaction. M. and B. very *flushed*, though poor B. complains of several ailments of ominous if indefinite nature—
'Feeling pretty cheap, old boy, heart a bit rocky—probably
this ruddy strain I've been through'—but has struggled
bravely to the feast and is now contributing to its gaiety.
Have come upstairs at last to pack as we leave at 6 a.m. for
Morocco (via Paris) and can already visualise with painful
accuracy long journey in plane, the eyes grilled with in-
somnia. I'm sad to leave this house, which I feel will be
visited by me no more, and wish Hilton could have seen it.
Ponder nostalgically on its grace and beauty, on the first
night I arrived at the door with Facchini, on the white walls
and carved ceilings and olive-wood fires, and the birds singing
in the garden and the hills of Rome rising out of the cypress
trees and Renato tiptoing over the marble floors with coffee
in the morning and opening the shutters on to the sun.

These thoughts turn from honey to saccharine as the
strains of *Turna a Surriento* float up from below a little off
the note, and so *to bed—to bed—to bed*.

PARIS. JUNE 4TH

Panic, whether caused through my written quotation of the

traditionally unlucky Macbeth on the subject of going to bed, or through the relentless pursuit of us by the Hare, reigns. Les Invalides reached safely. Waschinsky, in sparkling reminiscent mood, told some fantastic stories of Berlin and sketched lightning prophetic impressions of our immediate future in Morocco where we would all live in Kasbahs and have black slaves to wait on us. Through this M. and B. slept soundly, also Betsy (mouth wide open, even this did not detract from her charms). Rested at the Lancaster. M. Wolf, friendly as ever, placed rooms at our disposal; dined with Lou Lindsay, who looks overwrought, and drove back to Les Invalides preparing for long night flight to Casablanca: Betsy, Waschinsky, and Italian technicians sailed through barrier to the plane, their passports in perfect order; M. and B. and self stopped at small unpleasing *bureau de contrôle* by small unpleasing *contrôleur*, who said, Where were our Moorish visas? In our passports said (very firmly) M. and B. and self. Oh no. Not at all. Not a sign of visas in our passports. Would we step this way and see for ourselves? Plane due to leave in eight minutes; these dragged themselves out interminably through thickets of discussion led rather feebly by me (no good at this sort of pleading or threatening at all), and ended in blank refusal to let us through. We alternately sat on our luggage and leapt madly to our feet at sight of any new official of either sex and pleaded with them in varying stages of sardonic resignation (Michael), congealed fatalism (me), and burning, towering, stuttering, palsy-shaken fury (Bob). 'Tell that frog-faced fool je suis outraged, je suis absolument disgusted—where's an interpreter? Je—oh well take it or leave it, we've damn well *got* to passer, nous avons rendezvous. Film! Monsiou Orson Welles—Here, stop! Retourner ici, vous! Listen!—je can't imagine what the hell they mean, stopping us like this, hi! Monsiou! Écoutez! *Vous*, let us passer, voulez vous? Come on, Monsiou, let us through—look at him, bloody unprintable expression fool,

shaking his silly unprintable expression head—three minutes
to go before she leaves; my God, old boy, if I could parler
français I'd parler it all right I can tell you, hi! Monsiou!'

None of the Monsious any good at all, and we ended up
in the bar and are now back in Paris. And thanks to the overwrought Lou we have rooms in the Reine Elizabeth in the
Avenue Pierre 1er de Serbie. Here I suppose we remain till
Moorish visas in order: while Betsy and the others fly merrily
over Spain, and are just beginning to observe, I suppose,
that we are not in the plane.

JUNE 6TH

Still in Paris; wires sent to Orson (God help him), who
has arrived in Mogador, to inform him of mishap. Also series
of complicated telephone calls to Dublin result in Hilton on
the phone this morning speaking from Beauvais: he is driving
the new car to Paris on his way south; he will park it in Nice
or Marseilles and fly to Mogador in a few weeks' time. His
holiday mood shaken to foundations on hearing of our mis-
adventure, but says it's typical of me (think this unfair), also
that it's probably lucky on the whole as we can have a day
or two together in Paris. No sign of Moorish visas yet, so
probably day or two will stretch out indefinitely.

Dined with Lou and afterwards visited the Glimpses of
the Moon off the Rue du Colisée, where a few friendly looking
ladies, their dinner jackets straining over their unconsidered
(though ponderous) busts, danced steadfastly with some
other ladies, rather lachrymose, and dressed for the most
part in sad pastel shades. All this in a dubious mauve twilight
to admirably nostalgic and muffled (but male) dance band,
though I deprecated absence of classic flutes. (Surely there
is a fortune to win by some enterprising lady who would
introduce these to similar establishment in appropriate setting, with chlamys and chiton *obligatoires*?) Lou said it was
all kind of hard for a guy to understand, but it just fascinated

him; this I remember thinking conceited of him at the time but cannot now imagine why I thought it.

Arrival of Hilton, bursting with health, in resolute holiday spirits, and suggesting attitude of 'why go to Morocco at all?', though this not openly expressed. Lunch and dine happily together, and he tells me he thinks of driving Paul to join Alan, who is in Monte Carlo. He will then park the car (which is brand new and complete Obsession with H., who is in agony if a speck of dust touches its gloss) at Marseilles, and fly thence to Casablanca to join me at Mogador. All this sounds very rich and idle to me. Paul to arrive to-night, his first visit; H. and I both experience familiar proxy-ish thrill of showing off all its beauties to unfamiliar eyes, but can think of nothing more original to begin with than dinner somewhere or other, a glimpse of Josephine Baker at Folies-Bergères, and a night club.

Later. Two of these novelties achieved; Paris a triumphant success with P., whose eyes pop out of his head (as well they might) at succulent dish of snails at the Méditerrané and drive across dazzling nocturnal city followed by spectacle of Josephine B. appearing in a series of roles that portray the Quest of Love down the ages, from tropical Eve (accompanied by ash-blond Adam, several doves, and misty Jungle of Eden at dawn under gigantic waterfall) through bevy of startling incarnations that include Greek princesses, Eastern impératrices, and Queens of France. After this she dodges about a good deal (after the manner of Mr. Dunne) in Time, and skips on and off as a Southern Belle, as a Grande Mondaine (in lovely number called 'Minuit'), as the Empress Josephine in sumptuous beige-and-white number which introduces le Petit Caporal, and as Mary Queen of Scots (several scenes). This diversion reaches its height in dark purple cathedral where she is publicly executed (in trailing black velvet), after which the lovely headless thing, now robed in dazzling diamanté, sings Gounod's *Ave Maria* to crashing strains from the organ, and scores of stained-glass saints descend luminously from their windows to celebrate triumph of Mike over Matter, and execute stately saraband in violet-ray. All this *émouvant* in the extreme: we find ourselves far too tired for night club, so drive back across the river, put poor tired (but pleased) Paul to bed, and drink cocoa at the Dôme to calm our nerves.

JUNE 8TH

Peaceful day with Hilton ended in dining together at Bouteille d'Or and departing in new car through dancing, streaming rain to Les Invalides. Great reunion between M. and B. and H. at now embarrassingly familiar bar, where barman looked at me faintly smiling and said *'Toujours là, Monsieur?'* with jocular upward inflection. Said goodbye till Mogador to H., with ominous feelings now so well known as to be instantly quelled, and travelled in bus to Orly.

Unbelievably, passports *still* not in correct order, but helpful lady, replacing dyspeptic male colleague of four nights ago, most kind and saw us through; God bless you, Ma'am, whoever you may be, and the Curse of Cromwell on the other old bowsie, though but for him I suppose I would have missed not only H. but Josephine B. as well.

We are now in the plane and flying dimly to the south. Usual feeling of unreality descends as I regard the steward scurrying silently to and fro between shadowy sleeping passengers huddled under rugs, babies in hammocks slung from luggage racks, and points of reading lamps pricking the gloom, ponder on the fantastic fact of my own and other people's existence, and reflect that in a few days' time I shall be, I suppose, a Film Actor, whatever in God's name that may be.

PART III

June 9th to July 31st, 1949

CASABLANCA. JUNE 9TH, 1949

LIGHTNING flashed continuously through the night and illumined our plane, bouncing up and down like a rubber ball: this might have looked amusing to spectators seated on top of the Pyrenees or of the Giralda at Seville but felt grimly unfunny to ourselves, strapped to our seats inside. Casablanca made usual appearance at dawn (routine growing repetitive) —I effected excitable meeting with Italian technicians on the now reminiscent and atmospheric landing of the Hotel Shelter. Italian technicians were headed by Brizzi, famous cameraman, a tall Florentine with Dante profile, grave goat's eyes, silver hair, and olive green gaberdine suit. Was deeply impressed. He was surrounded by his flock, all noisy, expressive, and agreeable; and Vasco, emerging immaculate and with loud screams from a bathroom, cried 'Ah! Signor Michele, Signor Iago, bravo, bravo, bravo!' V. then went on to say that they had all been warned in Rome not to drink Moorish water or eat Moorish fruit, salad, or fish, and would probably all be dead of typhus before a month had gone by, ending up with an heroic cry: 'Ma cosa vuole? Siamo in Africa!'

Lunched, after morning's rest, with Frank Bevis, and discussed what have already become Old Times. Frank very roguish, and said with dead-pan face he wished he was coming to Mogador with me, old boy, who knew, he might liven things up a bit, and from all he'd heard of Mogador it needed it.

Michael, Bob, and I now preparing to leave in car.

Later. Mogador achieved. All three of us thrilled to the marrow by the unabashed beauty and wildness of the country and its people, Bob revealing hitherto unknown side of his nature and beaming with delight: this transforms his features

87

and personality into a radiantly pleased schoolboy. Michael also at his best, and grew lyrical about the Mussulman schools of painting whose source, even as far west as Morocco, you can trace, or imagine you can trace, in every twist and turn of the landscape.

Mogador reached at twilight by a long winding descent that seemed as if one were driving straight into the sea, and there it was at last in a conflagration of flame and copper and gold and bronze over the rocky coast, a couple of square squat towers with pinnacles at their corners by the water's edge, a long stretch of brown battlemented walls, some groves of palm-trees, a little white town shining like a moth's wing in the embers of a fire. Then you drive along the shore past rows of bathing-huts, when (noticing gradually that everything is white or blue—white walls, blue shutters and doors, no other colours seem visible except in the clothes of the people) you pass through the high square gateways of the city walls past a corner of the market streets. Little shops filled with fruit and bread and vegetables, horse-carriages, merchants, Jews in black kaftans, veiled and blanketed women, French and Arab policemen, sweetmeat sellers, restaurants, the edge of a small ornamental park, a mosque or two, and at last the Place du Chayla. This, also white and blue, is surrounded by French and Jewish shops and has at its farthest corner two hotels, the Beau Rivage where we eat, the Paris where we sleep, and opposite this is the chief Mosque of the town. The Muezzin had just called the faithful to prayer; a queer glowing atmosphere pervaded it all; the Arabs and Jews lounged at the street corners and conversed affably together; we are eyed with approval rather than curiosity: I like it already. Was shown up to a room which looks on to the Mosque and has a faintly studentish air (appropriate for one embarking on a new technique), large, stone-floored, shuttered and ramshackle, a *cabinet de toilette* with a trickle of water in the tap, an enamel jug and a tin bidet, a roomy

wardrobe, handles that fall off when you open things, a
chaise-longue, and a sallow light over a vast bed that
squeaks in a skittish elderly fashion when you touch it.
But I like it.

Lee joined me as I unpacked, looking, in spite of his sufferings at Ouarzazate, plump, and, as he was just in the middle
of dinner, full of garlic and scandal, strikingly dressed in a
yellow sweater and black silk Moorish trousers embroidered
in white. After five minutes of sensational news (only half
grasped by me as I flung shirts and socks into a tallboy
whose drawers either stuck or collapsed as I pulled and
pushed them out and in) he escorted me to large stone dining-
room on first floor of Beau Rivage next door where, from far
end of long table bristling with steaming dishes and bottles
of wine, Orson rose thunderously from hordes of tumultuous
diners and swept towards me waving his napkin like a flag
and crying, 'Welcome, welcome, dearest Micheál!' then, fold-
ing me in bear-like embrace, stopped dead suddenly to say
'Hey! what have you been doing? You've put on about six
pounds. God dammit, I engaged you to play Iago and here
you come Waddling In To Do It!'

Loyal cries of 'he hasn't, he hasn't' from Betsy and the
others failed to reassure me, as I remembered the risottos
and fettucini consumed at Villa Bottai as well as numerous
fell delicacies of highly fattening nature enjoyed so heedlessly
with Hilton in Paris. Orson was right, and I dined on eggs,
fish, and raw tomatoes in chastened mood. Dinner, however,
on orgiastic conversational level in five languages, and the
rest of the evening passed by Orson and me visiting (in
English and by moonlight) peerless fifteenth-century Portuguese fortress and citadel, with long ramparts over the sea
and ancient harbour walls. He has discovered a complete
Island of Cyprus with towers, bastions, bells, dungeons,
battlements, and green bronze cannons, pointing out, not to
the Mediterranean (and what member of the public would

know or care about that?) but the Atlantic, frothing and surging over the black rocky coast above which the town lies scattered out like an early Picasso in sharp greenish-white cubes.

Pacing up and down under the moon, I learned of his endless difficulties about money, Italian wardrobe, and cost of labour: everything as I see it is against him before he starts, but his courage, like everything else about him, imagination, egotism, generosity, ruthlessness, forbearance, impatience, sensitivity, grossness and vision, is magnificently out of proportion. His position at the moment is grotesque in its lack of stability and even likelihood, but he will win through and all at the end will fall into his hands, the bright-winged old gorilla.

JUNE 10TH

Rehearsal from nine this morning: scene of Iago tempting Cassio to drink. All is far more detailed and down to brass tacks than in Paris: Orson even more Pre-Raphaelite than Hilton in unbelievably inventive detail. Dexterity (not my strongest point) in great demand for business of pouring wine into two goblets from goatskin held by elderly Arab and cheating him over payment while saying, 'Here is a brace of gallants that would fain have a measure to the health of black Othello.' Complications of this outrivalled in afternoon's rehearsal with Bob Coote (who says he didn't sleep a wink, old boy, owing to infernal shrieking of Arabs below his window).

Startling news that entire male wardrobe from Rome held up indefinitely (women's stuff all safely here) has caused inspection of large assortment of costumes (reeking of camphor and far more Veronese than Carpaccio, but capable of re-adjustment) and some fine armour all spread out in office rented in the Medina. This presided over by pleasant woman from Seville, who flew at me on being told by Lee that I had lived in her native town when young and spoke Spanish: she then spent every minute not occupied in trying on tunics and helmets singing Flamencos and Cante Jondo, and such favourites as *Rosario la Cava* and *Camino de Quintillo*, with much expert snapping of fingers. Chose several magnificent pieces of armour for Orson, also impressive black cloak stretching from here to Cork; also workmanlike but unattractive jerkin in yellow leather for me (to be altered by local tailor), tights, shoes, and some extremely painful armour and greaves. Thought I would look far more fetching in several other things and wistfully tried them on, but was called to order by O., who kept on snatching smart embroidered and brocaded numbers (distinctly slimming effect) from my back, and saying that if I wished to look like a slightly decayed Romeo I had better re-read my part, and would I kindly look at *him* for a second (if I could spare so much time from intervals of attempting to pass myself off as a romantic juvenile and brushing up my Spanish) and see if I didn't think that *this* tunic, if neck and sleeves could be fixed, would be rather impressive (if worn with white burnous) for Epileptic Scenes? (Undoubtedly Hilton, his first director, has influenced him off stage as well as on, and not always to his advantage.)

Clothes now seem settled, my own anyway, for I'm only to have one suit (if you please) and ring changes with two cloaks and hats and relentless bits of armour, though a lot of work will have to be done with them all and my two journeys to Rome, while giving me exquisite pleasure, are now proved a complete waste of Orson's time and money.

JUNE 12TH

Finally it is made clear that while my clothes for Iago *may be* in a fit condition to wear in a few days' time, no such hopes are entertained by local tailor about Othello's, Roderigo's, or Cassio's. Orson in despair as sequences for the arrival at Cyprus with which he wanted to start shooting all include, inevitably, these people.

But this is where the winged gorilla is entitled to respect as well as to that jocular interest he can so easily inspire in the ignorant and impressionable public, always more attracted by the glittering bauble in the crown than by the gold of the crown itself. He has decided to open fire with the camera on the attempt on Cassio's life and on the subsequent murder of Roderigo by Iago, and as these incidents usually take place, as the script suggests, in a street, and as this would necessitate clothes for Cassio and Roderigo (no less than their arrival at quayside), he has emerged from a sleepless night with the idea of making the murder happen in a *steam-bath*, with M. and B., God help them, stripped and draped and turbaned in towels. This, as well as dealing with the clothes question until it can be settled, effective and sinister twist of the bloody business of Act Five Scene One with which he is opening.

Roderigo, draped in towels, discovered lying on small straw divan in a rest room after the bath and playing with ears of lapdog (not yet discovered) as he says to Iago (fully clothed and peering playfully round doorway) 'Every day thou doffest me with some device, Iago.' Action then proceeds through comedy scene of Iago's instructions about the murder of Cassio to series of shots in crooked stone passages and wash-rooms hung with dripping towels and full of vague shapes of bathers and of negro masseurs carrying jars of oil and vats of boiling water through clouds of vapour. Bob (in *négligé*) and me (in leather tunic) plotting and peering through ominous gratings and barred windows at Cassio being massaged while I hiss 'It makes us or it mars us, think of that'; and we come right down to Roderigo, having made his abortive attempt on Cassio and been himself imprisoned under slatted floor, crying 'O damned Iago! O inhuman dog!' During this Iago stabs him through the slats with his sword in the manner of fish-catching in tropical waters, the vapour growing denser as he does it (mercifully for audience, and luckily for myself as my aim none too good; God, let me say it again, help poor Bob!).

All this seems to me effective and ingenious and will certainly save much bacon, as we can now proceed to sequence for which one of the square towers on the fortress is being prepared as steam-bath. This carried on by hordes of Arab workmen supervised by dear gingerbread Trauner and his assistant Cap from Paris, who affects short pointed golden beard and large beret and looks like a Van Gogh. We have rehearsed this to-day and are to continue to-morrow at dawn (or thereabouts) and when we are not rehearsing we spend hours on end in the hands of Vasco and Santoli (S. is make-up man), who thin out our wigs under the eagle eye of Orson and experiment minutely with beards and eyebrows; and other hours with the local tailor, who snips and slashes and is rapidly heading for a nervous breakdown.

JUNE 14TH

Work continued without a break for two days, but diversion created this evening by visit to Civil Governor and his wife, M. and Mme. Ducroz, both of them charming. They bore us off, after drinking cocktails in their house and admiring the banana trees in their patio, to dine with the Caid in his town house. Orson, overcome with surfeit of work, worry, and new ideas, didn't come, nor would he allow Waschinsky to stir from his side, or Trauner or Brizzi or Cap, so party was made up by self, M. and B., and Betsy Blair. Ducroz speaks no English, and M. and B. no French, and Betsy, though making incredible strides, is at early stages, so it was a busy evening for me and Dr. Jean Ritter (of Strasbourg), who speaks not only a little English as well as French and German but a good deal of Arabic. So liaison was established between ourselves and Caid, who looks exactly like Lady

Gregory in a white beard, a fact which makes his lack of
any tongue but that of the Prophet confusing, as at absent-
minded moments one kept expecting him to make some
allusion, however slight, to the Abbey Theatre or the Swans
at Coole. A dear old man with impressive entourage of
secretaries and male relations, all of them, like himself, clad
in honey-yellow, dove grey, or snow-white robes and turbans.
They escorted us through a series of arches, courtyards, and
gateways to superb house like an old-fashioned house in
Seville, with a patio all in marble studded with citron and
peacock tiles and full of fountains, sunken gardens, cypresses,
and orange trees, with rooms opening out of this and
furnished with carpets, divans, honey-combed ceilings, incense braziers, hanging lamps, and mountains of cushions.

Usual super-succulent dinner of sixteen to twenty courses
eaten from vast central dish and preceded by washing in
rose-water offered in brass bowls by gigantic Nubians. One
then drapes oneself in a finely embroidered towel and proceeds to abandon all hopes of retaining one's figure by devouring *pastilla* made with milk, honey, almonds, butter, sugar,
and saffron, and plunges ahead to lamb with fresh figs, and
chicken with rice, and quail with honey-cakes, and mutton
with green peas, and then more chickens and more lamb
and a variety of unknown little birds, and kouskous and
melons, all manipulated with three fingers of the right
hand. Observed Betsy, after a couple of involuntary moves,
putting her left behind her back with rapt expression of self-
control. The feast is washed down by mint tea, though wine
was offered by the Caid (looking more like Lady Gregory
than ever, if one could imagine Lady G. in such an abandonment of inarticulate gaiety). The wine was refused (I thought
unnecessarily) by us all, and then the male relations, after a
long discourse by the Caid, played to us on an ancient musical
machine resembling a water clock and functioning rather
precariously by means of big metal discs, old Viennese

waltzes and polkas and quadrilles. Caid beamed with rapture and clapped his hands and showed us some faded photographs hanging on the walls of Edward the Seventh and the Kaiser Wilhelm and Alfonso of Spain. Then we were given coffee and cigarettes, and incense was held by the Nubians between our feet until we and our clothes and our nostrils were saturated in sweetness, and the water clock played *The Whistler and his Dog* and *Bluebells of Scotland*, and then we drove home through the shuttered town smelling faintly of pepper and musk under a sky glittering with stars.

JUNE 16TH

Rehearsals still in progress: tailor, by this time, wearing soured expression and afflicted by what seems St. Vitus's Dance, still at work on my costume. Result of this continuous energy is strikingly simple and Relentlessly Unbecoming Effect, but Orson pleased and says daily, '*Now* it's beginning to look like Carpaccio: what I cannot tolerate is that Forest of Arden look. And I don't care how much you desire it, dearest Micheál, because you're not going to get it.'

Telegrams arriving daily from Hilton; he hopes to arrive round about the 21st. Had Cassandra-like premonition last night that he had met with some frightful fate: this apparently unfounded as wire again arrived this morning, but cannot rid myself of uneasiness. Premonition was during dinner, not sleep.

JUNE 18TH

Ramadan, the Feast of the Prophet, has begun. The Arabs neither eat, drink, smoke, nor do anything else all day long and atone for it after sundown by making night hideous with singing, dancing, blowing rams' horns, beating drums, and general revelry. These activities carried on mainly in Place du Chayla below our windows and I have changed to small

room of lugubrious aspect at back of house. Rehearsals
continue.

JUNE 19TH

Shooting began at 7.30 this morning. Made my début as
a voice off (hope this does not turn out to be a prophecy of
my film future) saying 'It makes us or it mars us, think of
that'. Bob, draped in towels, did a lot of stuff with a dagger
as he wound his way in and out of the labyrinthine ways of
the Vapour Bath. This followed by several close-ups, as my
tall laced boots, of purest Carpaccio inspiration, not yet
finished. Owing to story told by Waschinsky of Pola Negri's
first efforts in English on arrival in Holywood, the close-up,
with all its joys and terrors, now known to us all as 'One Big
Head of Pola'.

Orson the soul of patience, and I have an uneasy feeling
that, like a tactful dentist with a drill, he is starting me off
with a deceptively light and gentle treatment. Made about
seven takes, each one from three to fifteen times over.

Find what I have long suspected: (a) that one's first job
is to forget every single lesson one ever learned on the stage:
all projection of the personality, build-up of a speech, and
sustaining for more than a few seconds of an emotion are not
only unnecessary but superfluous, and (b) that the ability
to express oneself just *below* the rate of normal behaviour is
a primal necessity, especially where Big Heads of Pola are
concerned. One single sudden move of eyebrows, mouth or
nostrils and all is registered as a grotesque exaggeration. One
can feel this as one does it without the humiliation of seeing
the result on the screen, which Orson wouldn't allow in any
case even if there were a screen to see it on: none of us are to
be allowed to witness the showing of the rushes, his theory
being that to do so makes one self-conscious. (It would probably make me sick as well, so I raise no protest.)

Such taboos on the favourite activities of the mummer, the

dressing up of his personality and the projection of this to the furthest reaches of the cheaper seats, points to what seems an almost conscious trades-union instinct on the part of the camera, whose business it is to perform both these functions. At the same time one discovers that, far from finding one has nothing to do, one is confronted with a complete and bewildering set of new and rigorously negative tasks, the first of which is the stripping from the bones of all the tricks learned in the theatre as if they were rags until nothing is left to one but the naked and shivering ego.

JUNE 20TH

Stripping process continues in all senses of the word. Still at work in Turkish Bath. The long hours between the shots spent on the ramparts in dazzling sunshine, boisterously blown on by salt sea breezes. We loll about on stone parapets or, when we can get them, in deck chairs, M. and B. and self alternatively reading, smoking, and talking about acting, while Orson and Waschinsky, deep in the gloom of the Turkish Bath interior, harangue the Arab staff in Italian and English. Pandemonium reigns. Interior, in contrast to the sunshine of the ramparts, is a very beautiful inferno of violently projected mauve lighting, black crisscrossed shadow of barred gratings and latticed windows, scurrying naked forms and coiling vapours.

JUNE 21ST

Dreamed that I was choking to death in a desert sandstorm and being blinded by handfuls of dust, and woke to find that the part about being blinded was true. Could neither open eyes nor shut them, and spent an hour or two trying to do both without success and in scorching pain. Groped my way to Bob's room, which is opposite mine, and said 'I'm blind.' Bob all kindness and bounded out of bed, switching on light (only visible to me as distant and excessively unpleasant red glare) and saying 'Don't worry, old boy, you've got Kleig eye.' Not understanding this, I cried despairingly 'Kleig eye? My God, what are they going to do to us next?' (Haven't lived this down yet: Bob, thinking it awfully *moving*, which of course it *was*, told old monster Welles, who thought it *funny*, which it isn't At All.) Bob then poured some burning liquid into my sightless eyes and led me back to bed. Have spent all day in black spectacles, and Picistrelli, the sound mechanic, whose head, shoulders, and legs are pronounced exactly like mine from the back (both of us deeply flattered), has doubled some long-distance shots for me.

Am writing this in black spectacles and mood to match, as Jean Ritter has come round to see me and says I shouldn't work for two or three days.

JUNE 22ND

Telegram from Hilton announcing his arrival by bus tonight. Took off black spectacles for nocturnal walk with Orson and discussed Italy and her people, deciding that former was a large and sumptuous Aviary and the latter its feathered inmates, pecking, fluttering, scratching, hopping, cackling, making love, and rhapsodically singing. Our only point of disagreement was that I am partial to Birds and Orson not at all, and he cited humorous drawing in the New Yorker which depicted the Birds with flapping wings and yapping beaks lecturing hell out of a cowering St. Francis, and said that was how he always felt in Italy. Attempt to picture Orson as St. Francis under any circumstances at all met with swift and abject failure. Went together to the Rousillon, a bar in the patio of a house in a narrow backstreet, where we drank cognac with Bob who was leaning over the counter looking very smart in a blue jacket with brass buttons: the sudden glare caused me to pop on black spectacles again. Cognac and further discussion of St. Francis, Aimee McPherson, the art of Al Jolson, and other topics carried us on till two, at which time Hilton's bus was expected to arrive in side-street off the Place du Chayla. Witnessed arrival of bus, which belched forth enormous crowds of French, Jews, and Arabs, carrying, among other things, bunches of live chickens, God help them. But no Hilton. Wandered by the sea leaping in mountainous waves under calm moon-flooded sky, Orson alternately quoting *King Lear* in magnificent thunderous voice and giving famous imitation of Alabama hostess, and finally went home to bed. Bob came to my room for final drink, when the door flew open and there was Hilton with bandaged head, arms, and hands, but otherwise looking boisterously well. He and Paul had had a smash on the road at Brignolles, near Nice, and Paul was in a clinic with a fractured shoulder. Car (the new one) in frightful condition in garage in Nice, and endless legal complications (it was the other man's fault and favourable results almost a certainty) were already in motion. Recollected, even while emotions of horror at H.'s recital were in full swing, Cassandra-like forebodings experienced by me on the 15th and recorded in this diary on the 16th, and was faintly disappointed to find that the accident happened on the 14th. Am loath, however, to be cheated of any manifestations of telepathy, and can only conclude that the message came through a little late.

Bandaged or not, it's good to have Hilton here. Yet he has brought with him a mood of which he seems himself to be unconscious: it fills up this room where I am writing and the sky above the flat roofs when I look out of the window at the darkness, a breath, a sigh, a sort of *pastoral regret*. Does this come from Europe, from Irish mountains and English fields and French woods and hills where you can drink water and pluck apples or strawberries, and milk a cow or a goat (if you know how), without fear of typhus or scorpions or all the poisonous coiling spells of the desert countries? And why should the beating of the Arab drums and the laughing wail of Arab voices and the scent of the Arab night seem, for the first time, unbearably alien and remote?

JUNE 25TH

More arrivals: Doris Dowling to play Bianca and Julien Derode to manage Affairs (badly, says Orson, in need of firm handling). Julien D. is a handsome Parisian who reminds me he came to a party at our house in Dublin years ago and who has the national eyes (like Yvonne Jammet and Anatole France), small, friendly, and of an indescribable shrewdness and tolerance, expressing the two qualities that combine the strength and weakness of the European Matriarch; he also possesses a good knowledge of English and a head like a dark plush pincushion.

Doris, decorative as a flamingo, has started work already. Did a street scene to-day in which a camel, stealing up nimbly behind her, thrust its nozzle into her neck during a Big Head of Pola, against vivid background of Cypriot life, and she unexpectedly burst into tears. Hilton on being told of this expressed no emotion, but produced academic query about the likelihood of camels on the Island of Cyprus, which seemed to me not only beside the point but lacking in sympathy.

JUNE 29TH

Have decided that one's first film has all the less attractive features of the principle of reincarnation. One is born again in pain and gloom, and, accompanied by half-forgotten images of an adult past, one discovers oneself ignominiously as a baby. One says, 'What, Born Again? My God! Again! In a setting of napkins and petting and slappings, crawling art-lessly on the floor and endeavouring to walk and to speak, to express oneself and yet to obey the rules, to expand within the limits of a cot, a minute cramped cot, and one of a frequent and hideous dampness.' The work is more difficult than I had ever dreamed (and I had dreamed a good deal), and never again will I have anything but the deepest respect for any actor who can move or speak at all, however ignobly, before a camera. Have taken however what seems the only possible course: blind, unquestioning obedience to and dependence on the will of the director. This quite easy to do before the day's work begins by the abandoning of my face at six each morning to Santoli and Vasco, who paint, beard, and bewig me as I sit inert in a chair, not even glancing into a mirror, a towel tied under my chin to keep me, I suppose, from dribbling on my doublet. This over, I totter on to the set (will soon have to be led, probably carried) and wait, generally for several hours, to be told what to do. Result of this is a form of complete and paralytic inanity: for the past two days I have had to be instructed how to raise my arm, turn my head, or place my feet, and have little doubt that if this continues I will soon be led away like Oswald in *Ghosts* babbling 'The sun, Orson, give me the sun.' Orson says all this perfectly in order and that I am doing marvellously and worrying without cause. Can only think that if he really means this, his own brain, as a result of dealing with me, must be softening too. ('Rather nice, Mother, like cherry-coloured velvet.' Oh, horror, horror, horror!)

Am too exhausted to appeal to Hilton about it all: at any rate, when I did venture on the subject, all he said was: 'You seem like all the others to me: no one can judge a performance by snippets.'

Snippets! Yet it's true. Hardly a shot has lasted more than fifty seconds; the meticulous inferno of tripping over the rails, arriving on the wooden stool, hitting the wooden blocks with one's toes, turning to go, turning back again, twisting the dagger, and saying the line, has no sooner begun than it is all over, and one does it again. Sometimes we make a shot four times, sometimes forty, with intervals between each shot for Santoli to mop up our sweat and Vasco to comb out the dank strands of our wigs, and Orson to say, '*That* was the one, I *think*: mechanically it was perfect, but you were becoming a little bit *mechanical*, you'd lost the freshness of the second shot which you spoiled by falling over the stool: now let's see if you can get back the *freshness* and keep on your feet. Wait a minute, let me adjust that hat. Gee! you look so cute, and you're getting so beautifully skinny! Now here we go—and Remember—*Everyone loves the fellow who is smiling, he brightens the day and lightens the way for you* . . . good, hold it! Ready? *Vai*, Picistrelli! Number 127. Take Five. Action.'

JULY 7TH

Fantastic day on the beach at the western side of the town, where we play the scene where Othello (concealed) miraculously misses hearing Iago saying to Cassio 'Now if this suit lay in Bianca's power how quickly should you speed' but hears distinctly Cassio's reply, 'Alas poor rogue, I think i' faith she loves me', and all the misleading and Desdemona-damning talk that follows, when Bianca joins them from a solitary hike (in long distance) among the rocks. This scene, made so far in three takes, carried on in blazing sunlight in the fangs of smart N.W. gale with the waves leaping mountain high at our feet over stony strand utilised by Arab population as fishing ground and public toilet. So several scouts employed in chasing them away from both these pastimes. Precisely the same uses for this wild and lovely spot are found by multitudes of seagulls, who were at once pressed into service by Orson, boxes of fish being sent for to tempt them to become actors. Obvious results: between the takes the air was thick with white fluttering wings: every time we were ready to shoot they had mysteriously vanished. Morning passed in congealed condition (instead of customary boiling process) and with Orson in dungarees (as takes of the listening Othello are to be made at a later date) jumping up and down on the wall and waving clenched fists in the air as he yelled 'Take 13, oh lucky thirteen, come on, Fish, God-dammit! Action! Hey, cut! *Cut!* Can't you hear me, Grease-balls? Look at the silly pronks, all flying away out of the shot! Hey! Come back, you great big overfed Jezebels—hey! Here they come again! Action! Fish! Quick, tell those Arab cretins, someone, quick! Action! Hey! *Fish*, Goddammit!'

So passed the day till glacial twilight drove us to the Club (mainly Jewish, very friendly, rather Refined) to drink Pernod and thaw ourselves out before dinner. Doris, Michael, and I, still dressed in our mummer's clothes and shuddering violently with the cold, listened with dazed ears to Hilton and the inexhaustible Orson discussing bird-life, Existen-tialism, corn on the cob, Sam Goldwyn, Californian cham-pagne, censorship, Arab sanitation, athlete's foot, the life to come and the Lunts, and gaze dumbly at Waschinsky execu-ing admirable Mazurka, accompanied by his own delighted basso profundo singing, to dumbfounded members of the Club.

JULY 8TH

Work unceasing. Bob and I perched on dizzy heights of scaffolding with Arab crowds milling below us for 'He takes her by the palm' scene. Bob has height complex and suffered agonies as he clutched at me with one hand and with the other tried to prevent large Picture Hat (époque Julia Neil-son) from blowing away in the hurricane.

JULY 10TH

Work. Jealousy scene begun.

JULY 12TH

Bulk of jealousy scene achieved, opening with long track shot and Orson and self pacing battlements together. Hilton helped us with the book. Got it, miraculously, in four goes.

Infinitely easier than the short shots which pick out the middle of an emotion. This scene followed by more complicated ones of Cassio drunk sequence: Michael extremely good. Turkish bath episode now a thing of the dimmest past.

Find I am slowly emerging from psychic paralysis caused by retarded embarkment on new technique, as no comparison conceivable between old silent film methods with those of present time: two lines of chalk, in those days, being lightly drawn on studio floor to mark where one was and where one was not in view of the camera, and the rest left largely to oneself and one's stage training. Average result, the over-projected genius of Sarah Bernhardt tearing a handkerchief to bits, and the smoother but still uncontrolled ecstasies of Theda Bara. How Messrs. Hayakawa, Lloyd, and Gilbert, the Misses Frederick, Nazimova, Gish, and Pickford were so good remains to me a mystery, to say nothing of Jannings and Chaplin. Anyway, I'm emerging, and find that the blood is beginning to circulate again through my torpid veins.

Life, however, is strenuous, and no time to write here. There have been in the intervals of shooting two more Arabian Nights' Entertainments with the Ducroz's at the houses of two new Caids (Hilton so nimble at tearing the best bits of the lamb from the bone with three fingers of right hand, and so loud in his praise of this method of eating, that I fear he may insist on adopting it for good and will have to be discouraged from accepting all future invitations to luncheon-parties). Also the arrival in Mogador from Paris of Jean Davis, who is not only distributor of films for France but a fine figure of a man as well, with an Assyrian profile and a flow of English, and may play Montano (alas for old shamrock-smothered Pal of Paris Night-Clubs on St. Patrick's Eve). Ramadan pursues its wild way and prevents any of us from getting a night's sleep, and now comes the news that Fay Compton has been engaged for Emilia and will shortly be in Morocco.

JULY 14TH

Betsy sent on mysterious holiday to Paris by Orson, who has bloodshot eyes again. We all miss her badly, and the dining-room Symposia, now that Doris has finished Bianca and returned to Rome, are completely Stag and frequently Rude. I was desperately sorry to see Betsy go away and to hear from O. after her departure that he was worrying about her being too modern. Felt as guilty as if I'd spoken my own thoughts to him, and find completely selfish satisfaction in reflecting that I didn't. Orson himself has not yet informed her of his feeling, for in this matter, as in all others, he is an eerie mixture of atomic bomb and keepsake album; but it seems he is already looking about for yet another Desdemona.

JULY 15TH

Our numbers increase: a script girl has arrived at last. Her name is Gouzy and she comes from Berne via Casablanca, her present home. Gouzy is short, plump, cherry-cheeked, diamond-eyed, and of an untiring energy and gaiety; she speaks five languages including Arabic (six, if you include her own lusty Schweizerduitsch), and agrees with everyone heartily in all of them. She drives herself, and everybody else who wants a lift, all over Mogador in a bumping, thumping little car, has a fine appetite, smokes like a pottery, wears a lot of bracelets, scarves, watches, gloves, berets, veils, cotton frocks, and, when the fit takes her, a pair of ample pearl-grey slacks, and about her there flaps an assortment of scripts, sandwiches, pencils, bags of sweets, handkerchiefs, aspirins, attaché cases, and good-will. Add to these props a small campstool on which she perches on perilous ledges in sun or storm, a bottle of beer or coca-cola between her feet, a smile and a burble of information ready on her lips (frequently anointed with cold cream produced from a handbag to prevent chapping) for everyone. Gouzy is what the English call a Poppet.

Another lady, not sharing the success of Gouzy in my eyes, is one Riquette, a *soi-disant* lap-dog of repellent aspect, borne in the arms of extremely pretty mistress (French), and adored by everyone except me. Riquette plays the part (shamelessly inserted by Orson) of Roderigo's pet, and has not merely monopolised the attention of everyone and made my life unbearable (I play innumerable scenes with her) but is referred to by Orson as Angel, Honey-Child, Sugar, and Chicken-Pie, and is also, quite obviously, going to steal the film.

JULY 16TH

Spent all day on ferocious rendering of that portion of the jealousy scene in which Othello says 'Villain, be sure thou prove my love a whore.' Orson, beautifully dressed up and painted a dark chocolate-brown by Santoli and Vasco, paced to and fro for hours thinking it all out on the edge of the farthest watch tower, among a thicket of cannons and anxious shivering technicians, black rocks and leaping waves below, and a tempest howling overhead. Finally, with warnings frantically hissed and shrieked at us by everyone, we assume stout leather belts to which ropes are attached and, held fast by Marc, Pierrot, and other members of the French crew (the Arabs being considered too emotional for the job), hang at right angles from the battlements in order to play the scene, camera at dizzy levels conveying sense of terror and (not wholly unfounded) feeling of physical danger (thank God for not endowing me with more than rudimentary height complex). This occupied the morning hours. During lunch the wind freshened and we passed the time from two to six-thirty clinging to large cannon on still windier Promontory doing the 'I lay with Cassio lately' speeches culminating with 'And sighed and kissed and then cried "Curse fate which gave thee to the Moor!" ' These lines, which I have always visualised played quietly into Othello's ear in atmosphere of sultry stillness with flies hovering in the breathless air (probably because Hilton produced it that way and always begged me to imagine the flies), these lines, I say, were shouted by me across some twenty feet of battle-mented area at Orson sitting joylessly on the edge of the wall, his burnous flapping up every now and then to extinguish him completely as the Gale rose higher and higher in manner worthy of *Lear, Wuthering Heights*, or what you will. As neither of us could hear the other speak and as we were both continually engaged in pulling portions of our clothes out of our mouths whither the wild winds had tossed them, intimate and rather spicy information proffered by Iago was difficult. Finally gave it up and came home in despair and frustration. He's going to try it another way when the wind drops a little, but when will that be?

JULY 17TH

Nicholas Bruce arrived the other day to play Lodovico (his advent coinciding with such a rush of work that I forgot to write it down), and seems to be exactly what was wanted, being tall, elegant, and soldierly, as well as agreeable and of a pretty wit. Wears his clothes as only Englishmen can—and very few even of them can do it either—but has extra-ordinary exotic eyelids and back to his head. His mother, somebody told me, is Russian; can this account for it? Most of the Russians I know look merely tired and over-experi-enced, but N.B. has a genuinely strange and un-put-on expression of imperiousness, languor, almost of voluptuous contemplation that doesn't go with the rest of him.

He and all the rest of us were in for it to-day as some further shots of the drunken Cassio sequence turned into real Orgy, for Waschinsky let loose a few barrels of red wine among hordes of Jewish extras—the Arabs stuck to coca-cola, drinking it in classical manner out of prop goblets and cups with much gurgling and rolling of eyes, and as they always look intoxicated in any case all was well. But the Jews had the time of their lives and screeched and spluttered like wild fowl; their excitement was not decreased by the sight and smell of smoke torches lit and waved about by the staff in order to produce atmosphere of infernal Dionysiac revelry. Complicated business for me of pouring wine into proferred goblets, slapping various breasts, backs, and backsides with short stick (continually getting lost and rescued invariably by Gouzy), was met with good-natured but full-blooded retaliations, and after a couple of hours' work (wine still circulating and no means of stopping it) the whole sequence assumed form of free fight, accompanied by fervid (if incorrectly rendered) singing of *And let me the cannikin clink, clink, clink*.

Hilton, nothing loath to help in this sort of scene, rushed up and down on one side of the harbour armed with stout stick and yelling directions in English, with some scattered but vivacious ejaculations in French, with Waschinsky on the other side screaming in any language that came into his head. Orson stood on a rickety pile of boxes and stools behind the camera yelling in American and Italian; Lee tore backwards and forwards waving a script; Riquette, insufferable as ever, yapped her head off and got under everyone's feet (emerging from it all unscathed); and Brizzi, looking like Dante having decided to search no more for Beatrice, muttered '*La contraluce, mama mia, la contraluce!*' Vasco sat very neat and despairing on a suitcase declaring that all his wigs would be ruined and he would never get back to Rome again, and Gouzy stood clad in white shorts on the top of her car waving a *belegtes Butterbrod* as she screeched Arabic versions of everybody's commands. Panic indescribable as Bob (carrying the unspeakable Riquette alias Chicken-pie), Michael, and I dashed about among the crowd bawling what we could of Shakespeare's lines and being slapped, pushed, and winked at by now totally inebriated Israelite soldiers, also by Arabs, who enjoyed it so much that one hardly minded emerging, when it was all over, black and blue, and feeling too exhausted to do anything but wish one had a bathroom in the hotel and was not forced to dally wretchedly with an enamel bidet. Was led however by Simon, the Jewish dresser, to Arab bath at the far end of the town, where usual strenuous process was endured of being hurled about on a wet stone floor, having buckets of water poured all over one, and being scrubbed down by bunches of rushes.

JULY 19TH

All the morning gobbled up by spirit of desultory Mischief which exhausted us without achieving any worthier result, but on arrival at luncheon table a surprise awaited us. For there she sat. I mean Fay Compton, and unless you peered into her face so closely that it would have dazzled your eyes, the face was completely unchanged. And anyway the tiny things that time has done to nostrils and eyelids fly away the moment she speaks, which is at once, and with the same gay unhesitating music; and we were told about the journey from London, and the hotel at Safi, and the way the Moors treated their horses, dirty dogs, and the noises her cat made when she bade her farewell, and what Ivor had said at the Ivy, and how she'd only just learned that We know Who was not being brought from London to play Desdemona, Thank God! no, really, the poor darling would have closed down the picture before it opened if we saw what she meant, and where *were* Mac and Mana anyhow, and what had happened to their children? She had a fellow feeling about children because of her own Tiny Son (thirty-seven years old and at the moment directing new movie), and imagine my remembering *Moon, Moon, serenely shining*, *Don't Go In too Soo-oon*, and she sang it for me more beautifully than ever. We spent the afternoon in the office going through some scenes, and she tried on the Emilia dress, which was all wrong at the waist and My God! what a bust, and what a weight; all that lovely blue velvet and all those dam' gold braids, imagine wearing that in the heat, which was simply nothing but Tropical; something flimsy to slip on and off was what she would have preferred, but one must remember it was Emilia—so all those tucks and smockings and slashings were Carpaccio, were they? Anyhow, Orson was a lamb and she'd wear anything for him, and why had she never met Hilton and me before?

What I found about her most unexpectedly were the two small Angels, one at each side of her head about a foot and a half above her shoulders. They are very small angels indeed and rather stiff like the angels in a French primitive, but they are there all right, rolling their pale blue eyes up to heaven and puffing out their cheeks, one of them blowing a little golden trumpet and the other fiddling away like mad. There may possibly be a devil or two under her right foot as well but the skirts of her psyche are long and trailing so one can't be certain; the angels, however, are indubitable and follow her everywhere.

Later. Mystery of Nicholas B.'s eyelids more than fully explained, as it is revealed that the Russian mother so casually referred to is Tamara Karsavina. Feel indescribably awed about this piece of news and follow him with my eyes since I was told it, half expecting him to produce a gold bow and arrow from his hip pocket and float into the air to wound a bird with flaming plumage, busy among enchanted midnight apples. No such activity however yet visible, as he, like all the rest of us, is madly packing his shirts in order to leave for Safi. Why this all of a sudden? Fay C. the only one of us with nothing to pack as she is already installed in Safi, so she sits with Orson and Hilton (already prepared for the journey) over a gin fizz at club, her two angels undoubtedly entertaining them in their own celestial way, while Simon and Baby Brother Armand (aged six), who has been giving excellent imitation of dressing me for a week or so, give extremely poor imitation of packing.

Had better see what they're up to.

Safi. After midnight. Spirit of desultory mischief, observed by me in this morning's work, seems to have grown wings and talons like a griffin's during the day, and on arrival in spacious and flesh-potty hotel, took complete possession of nearly every member of the troupe. Pandemonium has reigned for two hours largely on subject of Rooms: contentions, (*a*) bathroom or no bathroom, and (*b*) to share or not to share. Hilton and I, who generally work together on these occasions, found ourselves neutral as we both have beautiful rooms with baths, and H. actually acted as dove of peace with striking (if ephemeral) results; but Griffin of Strife found plenty of material for Me to do a little Shouting too, chiefly about the call for to-morrow, which was for seven; and it was nearly two when we got here. This question has now been settled, and I have usual reaction of shame. Would be glad to know if anyone else in the world is constituted in such a way as to make defeat or triumph equally unendurable: sense of impotence and failure resulting from the former more than balanced by deep consciousness of guilt, meanness, and indescribable *vulgarity* from the latter. Poor Julien Derode came in for most of the all-round abuse (none of it being his fault at all) and in the end most of the problems were settled by Orson, who began by sweeping through the field of battle (which was the bar) offering everyone his room (and bath), saying he would sleep, if necessary, on the kitchen table, and ended by roaring so much louder than anyone else that they all crept away to their rooms (with or without baths) in a cowed condition, but fortified by promises from charming and apologetic management (eyes starting out of their heads with terror), that all would be well to-morrow.

Having won my point about early call, the least I can do is to go to sleep. Apart, however, from any interior complex of guilt, this room disturbs me. Really it's no more than an ordinary good room, with deep-curtained windows opening on to small balcony beyond which is a garden full of palms and rose trees; rugs by the bed, gleaming bathroom, writing desk, telephone, chaise longue, peach-coloured reading-lamp, wardrobe which opens and shuts without a single handle falling out. Yet merely to contemplate these things, transformed by contrast with Mogador into images of Sybaritic luxury, is enough to keep me awake for hours.

JULY 21ST

Life now in a new rut: work at the Château (built above the sea) in atmosphere of ruined stones, burning sand, horse-flies, tepid coca-cola, and streaming sweat, from seven-thirty every morning; a nerve-clattering drive up the hill for lunch, return to Château, and work till twilight. Then we dine, and then we sit in the bar and drink gin-fizz. Somerset Maugham-ish atmosphere of semi-tropical friction and frayed nerves produced almost nightly, though this not referred to. Fay began first day admirably by saying to us all:

'Now, boys, I can see you're all in a Bad Way. Well, I mean, I don't wonder at it. Who wouldn't be? A lot of men, all working together for weeks on end, all tired and strained, all getting highlier and highlier strung, if you see what I mean.'

As a result of this description I immediately saw us all as members of chic but highly neurotic lumber camp, but, as habitual with me of late, I kept thoughts to myself and merely frowned at Hilton, who was knocking his pipe up and down on the table, and who immediately said, 'Now look here, Micheál, just you stop *governessing* me; damn it, I'm forty-six and this is My Pipe, and if I want to knock it about I'm bloody well going to,' and Fay said, 'There! That's exactly what I mean, you see. You've all been too much *together*, and when I think of what it must have been like, well, I think you've been marvellous, and I think you're all *going* to be marvellous in the picture, too, and all you need is a Fresh Point of View. A *Woman's* point of view. Well, here I am, and I bet you anything you like I'll cheer you all up. Now *don't* start getting nervy, because, my Lambs, There's No Need. Don't, just because you've different temperaments and outlooks, let silly little things get you *Down*: We *all* know that Dear Orson has been having a hell of a time, and we *all* know how wonderfully he's been working—and so have you *all* of course,' she added hastily. 'So remember: Just look on the Best Side of Things, and don't go getting into a Slough.'

So much for our fairy godmother on the first day, and she didn't say she'd be a Little Mother to us because she was Fay, but bedad if she'd been anyone else she would have. So we all rallied and smiled, and clapped each other on the back like mad for at least an hour; but on the second morning she herself appeared in the lounge at seven-forty-five in her blue velvet, wearing a deeply *withdrawn* expression under her crown of plaits, and saying in hollow tones: 'It's getting me down, it's getting me down. Any news? God, I've got the jitters. I've got them. I've got them.'

Now: what is wrong with us all?

'And as for Morocco,' continued she, waving away a proffered cigarette with every sympton of nausea, 'what a country! What a country! Beautiful? Well, of course you *might* find beauty in Clapham Junction, but you'd want to have something oh! so dangerously wrong inside you to see it, wouldn't you? Oh, and the way they treat their horses! And their hens! And that Château—Château! it's a public lavatory, my dear, that's what it is. Oh, and there's something so arid and cruel and dried up about it all. Hilton, you look as if you hadn't slept a wink. Well, who could? Well of course, darlings, I shall be carried out. That's how *I* shall end up. Simply carried out. Bob, what's wrong with your *eyes*? You look feverish to me. Have you been drinking the water? Oh, but, my dear, you mustn't ever clean your *teeth* with it. Very well, you'll soon see. Oh yes, that's how it will all end up. We'll just be Carried Out. All the lot of us.'

Since then she has cheered up herself and us by incredible imitations of monkeys, parrots, cats, dogs, and her brother Compton Mackenzie, and by being so good as Emilia that all, for a moment or two, is transformed.

JULY 23RD

Hideous hour spent this morning in deciding that the Sun, as well as transforming landscapes, houses, streets, and human beings into radiance, can invest these objects under certain circumstances with an aspect of strange squalor in the same way in which it can turn milk sour. To wander among the curdled gamboge and cheesy off-white of these Safi streets, among the smells of incense and wine and stagnant drains and fermenting fish and fruit, the shops with their wares sprawled out on dirty mats, the printed cottons, the tin cans and pots, the deciduous dates and oranges, the curry-coloured pottery daubed with spots of gorgonzola green, the spider-web brassware, the baskets of spice, the sallow, pock-marked boys and women carrying kettles and glasses of mint tea from door to door, the mangy camels and donkeys nosing the garbage, the trickling of latrines, the bunches of gaudy shoes and beads and candles and dried herbs and entrails and sweetbreads hanging from worm-eaten rafters, the cab-drivers and newspaper-sellers yelling, the cars hooting, the trams slowly screaming, the stone-masons hammering, the new concrete houses flaunting up under the turgid cobalt sky; all of it is cheapened, jaundiced, made harsh and common by the sun. This is sacrilege, but in Safi it is, disgustingly, true; I suppose this is how Fay has seen Morocco all the time.

There is nothing to do when on a morning of freedom you feel like this—(would love to call it *Spleen de Safi*, but think it more probably liver)—except to stay in the hotel or sit in its garden. Nothing could be easier, and both are pleasant enough: the hotel spacious and shadowy and cool as a fish, and the garden full of flowers, but a demon pushes me, wherever the Arabs have built a street or two, to roam and peer and bargain and shudder and admire. I can't resist them. Neither they, however, nor the world they have made, nor the dragon of a sun that gilds and festers and enraptures and corrupts their world, are intended for the stomach when it is delicate: what I would really like at the moment is not their sun-spawned, seething magnificence at all, or the urbane and expert French escape from it, but a cleft in the grey rocks at home and a stream coming down from the mountains with cresses and green rushes growing in it, and the curlews crying, and the clouds smelling of rain.

Later. Afternoon spent on scene of 'How comes it, Michael, you are thus forgot?' and Cassio answering, 'I pray you pardon me: I cannot speak.' Wished these had been my lines as I would have said them beautifully with minimum effort of imagination. As it was, I briskly intoned endless speech beginning, 'I had rather have this tongue cut from my mouth' and including such remarks as 'But men are men— the best sometimes forget', which I delivered with great rapidity feeling I was about to die, death to be preceded by vomiting. Orson delighted and said I'd never been so good. So much for the Importance of Being Healthy.

Our efforts—Jean Davis, as Montano, continually whispering, 'Mais tu ne peux pas vomir ici, non, tu ne peux pas— plus tard, mon petit, plus tard! Courage!'—our efforts, I say,

were backed by gangs of local soldiery of indescribably
repellent aspect, a seething army of Hobgoblins who ruined
three to thirty shots by scratching their backsides, blowing
their noses, and hitching up their unspeakable tights during
otherwise impressive action. Great effort of imagination required from me in order to bestow enigmatic glance suggestive of mingled desire and loathing on Desdemona (out of
shot) on line from Othello 'All's well now, sweeting, come
away to bed', as of course Desdemona is still not merely
absent but also, so far, non-existent.

Have come back to my room still feeling death is in store
for me. Hilton worried and has gone out to buy a thermometer. God help him, what's the use of a thermometer when
one is obviously destined for the tomb?

Later still. Aha, I thought so, I have 37·6 degrees of fever.
Hilton has dosed me with anti-grippine: I have no pain, dear
Orson, now.

JULY 24TH

Fever gone, but day spent in feverish manner doing
handkerchief scene with Fay ('Handkerchief—what handkerchief?'). This carried out on immensely tall flight of steps
augmented by swaying rostrums, all very tricky indeed. Fay,
in spite of many false starts when she not unnaturally dis-
played tendency to glance down to see where she was going
and prevent herself from falling headlong into sandy abyss,
played superbly; she has mastered the art of being directed
without losing herself in the act; our most difficult lesson.
Especially with directors like Orson and Hilton, both of
whom incline to the Melting-Pot school, the price they pay
for seeing the image of their heart's desire so clearly.

JULY 25TH

All life is changed.

Two axes have fallen. The first one: Hilton is down with

what the doctor first called 'une forte bronchite' and now describes as 'une légère congestion'. Am worried to death, fearing pneumonia, and hover about with the thermometer he bought for me. The second one: Orson, pale as his shirt (only it was a black one), announced yesterday that money crisis had again arisen and we would have to knock off work until things were settled. Complete scattering of our forces: Orson himself has already disappeared, feeling and looking ill, to Casablanca; Fay, Michael, Nicholas, and Bob are to go to England, Italian technicians to Rome, Jean to Paris, and so on. Julien, who is in charge, has been rushing about with a moon-white face, dark pincushion hair on end, and hands full of tickets, suggested to Hilton and me that we might go to St. Paul de Vence near Nice, where, he says, there is a famous Inn, standing among orange and mimosa trees, with original Picassos and Braques on the walls (inside) and doves a-flutter about the walls (outside), hence its name, which is Colombe d'Or. Heaven on earth, Julien assured us, and the favourite haven and refuge of all the great poets and artists—Gide, Picasso, Prévert, etc. (Immediately conceived insane dislike of Colombe d'Or: reason for this undiscovered.) Julien was sure that this *Othello* delay, regarded so tragically by Orson, would only be a question of a week or two and pointed out that if we flew all the way home to Ireland we'd probably have to fly back again almost at once. (Fly away Peter, Fly away Paul, surely something to do with a lady-bird?) Tickets for St. Paul de Vence, in fact, already arranged for and rooms at the Golden Dove booked, when H. develops this illness. He is attended by Dr. Frédéric van Varseveld, who has grave *accusing* eyes in a long, grave, well-drawn face, and an ominous manner, but is, I am sure, a fine doctor.

Later. Everyone has gone: the hotel seems vast, pearl-grey, and full of echoes and reflections as if it were a cavern under the sea. Fay, even more than Orson, heads the procession of ghosts, her image in gold and blue—a sea strand at evening —flits up and down the silent corridors, but there's nobody there: Hilton and I, alone together again, embark on a new period. His room, even to eyes as accustomed to hallucinations (if that's what they are) as mine, is saddened by frequent spectacle of hooded Figures, who sit in the corners watching him under their eyelids as their hands wind and wind: I wonder is it flax or wool? He dozes, and seems unaware of their presence; I ring for Abdul and order tea in a lowered, sick-room voice, and now fall to pondering on this *Othello* film of ours and on what will happen next.

JULY 26TH

Dr. F. van V. calls every day and gives penicillin. Practically admitted to-day it was pneumonia. Temperature has fluttered between 39 and 40.

JULY 28TH

Miraculous recovery of Hilton; we have both decided Frédéric van V. is the world's greatest doctor. Life now takes on a sort of Parched but not Unpleasant Monotony: I read Simone de Beauvoir with deep interest but little profit on H.'s balcony and sunbathe at the same time; have passed the boiled mulberry stage and am arriving at usual dubious piecrust which gives me appearance of fever-stricken half-breed. Have searched every *papeterie* in the town for English book for H. but nothing to be found but ancient *Reader's Digest*, *Trilby*, and *So You're Going to the Mediterranean?*, which we're not. H. however insists on it, reads it avidly, invites me to read bits of *Trilby* aloud, and demands cigars. I agree to *Trilby* but am austere about cigars. Painful scene ensues; Frédéric van V. lets me down completely by taking lenient view and says he is fond of them himself, and that in a few

days' time we must dine with him and his wife. Nurse,
meanwhile, attends every day and gives H. *piqûres*, also tells
ghoulish stories of her operations and of how Freddy van V.
twice saved her life. She, however, hasn't a single organ left
in her body as far as one can judge. The thermometer is
popped into the patient's mouth as she ruminates. 'La voilà!
. . . oh oui, il ne me reste rien—mais rien du tout, vous
savez, mais je suis heureuse! Heureuse! Ah! Comme il est bon,
ce cher docteur van Var! Ah. . . . Mais c'est un génie, vous
savez . . . Il ne m'a rien laissé, du tout du tout du tout!
Et je me sens si libre, si bien, si maîtresse de moi-même!
Et puis sa femme! Quelle gentillesse, quelle intelligence, et
surtout quel charme! Ah! tenez. . . . oui! toujours normal,
Mr. 'Ilton, grace à votre constitution et à ce cher van Var!
Et maintenant votre petite piqûre,' and she advances holding
long, unpleasant-looking needle as Joan of Arc probably held
her sword.

Othello, ushered by Orson and the rest, seems to have
faded out of life.

JULY 29TH

Hilton up again, a chastened version of his old self. Smoked
his first cigar with blissful expression, and we dined with
Freddie van V. and his wife and her mother. Great success,
and H.'s French progressed astonishingly. Returned with
Freddie after dinner to private cinema at hotel and witnessed
Wild West picture in glorious Technicolour ghosted into
French. My first picture since I became a screen player—was
it true?—and found myself regarding it with totally new and
not altogether delighted eyes. Counted eleven different shots
to portray heroine of the Lady-that's-known-as-Lou school
moving away from boy-friend, whose trust she is expecting
to betray, to join group of dangerous toughs at adjoining
bar-counter, and decided that she had failed to do it in one

long take, poor thing. Eleven goes, however, certainly landed
her there, and she then said audibly 'C'est qu'il ne veut pas
le faire. Bref, il refuse. Sortons!' This delivered in close-up,
and her lips said as plainly as lips could speak 'Says he don't
want no funny business—so break it up, kids! Let's get outa
here!'

Shortly followed her advice and said regretful farewell to
Freddie, who is all the nurse says he is. We are now going
to pack as we go to Casablanca to-morrow. Maybe, if we hear
no news there, we'll go to Picasso and Prévert and the Doves
in St. Paul.

CASABLANCA. JULY 30TH

Travelled here in bus and journey can always be recalled
to my mind, should the necessity arise, by reading Gorki's
Lower Depths or some little thing out of Henry Miller, also
by holding burning feathers under nostrils, drinking hot
coca-cola, and playing effects record of Arab music and Farm-
yard Effects. Discovered on arrival that I had lost twenty
thousand francs; whether they had been charmed out of my
wallet or flown away of their own free will remains a mystery.
H. bore journey and money crisis well, and in the bus gave
some illustrations of how to breathe without smelling the
air, so technically complicated I decided to pursue my own
instinctive methods and risk typhoid. The Moors, like all the
Arab peoples, must have real charm or after a journey like
that one would have turned on them for ever.

Wallowed in baths for an hour on arrival then dined at
Reine Pédauque: a note from Julien D. informed us that
Orson had been ill but had now recovered and had left
Morocco, that all was going well and that we should be start-
ing work in Venice next week. Decided to fly there in easy
stages.

JULY 31ST

No way of getting to Italy by air except via Paris, and no boat for ten days. Am inclined to blush at mere thought of Les Invalides, but after all it's about six weeks since my last appearance there, and anyway what is one to do?

PART IV

August 2nd to September 25th, 1949

HABITUAL feeling of never having left Paris at all descends. Dined last night at Tour d'Argent in great elegance and marrow-piercing gale as place so crowded that Claude had to put us on the balcony, where we ate a duck in company of hordes of Argentine millionaires, gold teeth all chattering in the breeze. Curious illusion of the French that they have a warm climate only equalled by English illusion that they like fresh air and that Continentals don't; reverse of this is painfully obvious. What the English really like is *talking* about fresh air and pretending they want the windows open when foreigners are present. Can think of several other national illusions, such as Italian one that they are musical, and Irish one that they are chaste, but one could go on for ever. Anyway, we have both caught sore throats.

Dinner to-night *à l'alsacienne*. We went there because it was on the Place St. André des Arts, which conjures up such sentimental musings about Taffy and the Laird; this identification of the place with du Maurier's St. Anatole des Arts my own discovery many years ago, and if I am disproved will upset me badly.

Storm, which had been brewing in the heavens as well as under the waiters' boiled shirts, broke when all was over, and we had coffee under an awning somewhere and watched the water descending like a million hawks on the leaves and the red glare of lights, and dancing up again from the pavements: both of us confirmed in theory that whereas rain obscures and distorts other cities or makes them merely wet, it reveals Paris in all her wonder. Passed enchanted evening witnessing performance of magnificent symphony—*L'Orage sur les Dalles*—so far unwritten, and wished we were both musicians: so easy if one could write music fast enough, one would simply put down the notes.

AUGUST 3RD

Julien D. rang this morning and made appointment for us to meet at the Dôme. Great excitement, as he brought with him prospective Desdemona. And there is little doubt that Orson's eyes will soon cease to be bloodshot. French-Canadian; experience: French tours and two French films; bi-lingual, a lingering echo of Canada in her English here and there, but voice warm, flexible and soft; her face a Bellini with large grey eyes that bestow lingering and slightly *reproachful* glances, perfect nose and mouth, chin a little too broadly modelled, age just twenty, figure good; a gentle dignity is her authentic hallmark; name Suzanne Cloutier. Manner rather *fin de siècle*, the childish, vague intensity of Mélissande; but Hilton and I agree that this is the merest article of clothing and as easily discarded as the mackintosh she incongruously wore (rain has ceased), and feel sure that somewhere in her There is Steel. Interesting; I smell Ham, Character, Individuality, and above all Indestructible Will, and prophesy that Orson will have trouble with her (as she no doubt with him), but that somehow a Desdemona will emerge. Her eyes seem never to have looked on planes or trains; even the shape of her ears expresses a lack of familiarity with radio or the roar of traffic or of saxophones: I mean that she is by all appearances a genuine Renaissance type, and this, even if she listened to the radio all day long and read nothing but *Paris-Match* and Georges Simenon, would remain aesthetically the truth. But what a time we're all going to have with that chin!

She's going to Rome for the test and to have her hair, which is a dark smoky brown, alchemised into gold.

VENICE. AUGUST 4TH

Our colds, begun in Tour d'Argent, steadily worse and both have sore throats. Journey to Venice in plane: from Milan, where we changed, we sat on the floor, as plane very full and Italian hostess too soft-hearted to leave us behind. Dazzling approach over a wilderness of ivory and emerald flats, swamps and islands in lapis-lazuli water; then bigger islands with pink churches and castles, and then St. Mark's and the Campanile and the whole gilded hen-coop of the Piazza and the Schiavone and the Rialto and the Giudecca and all the rest of it. Then we flew away and landed at distant Customs House, and finally made usual approach by series of motor launches crowded with Americans and British. Deep emotions as our boat turned the corner and the water changed from mere sunset brine to the authentic turgid rolling jade and gold of Venice under the coral and amber of the old sorceress unseen by us since '39; almost forgot our sore throats and felt that probably they were caused by emotional lumps. All this, however, shattered on arrival at wooden jetty of Hôtel Europa (whither Julien D. had directed us and where Orson was supposed to be found) by sight of Nicholas Bruce, looking very flushed, and Bob Coote, bright scarlet and Dancing up and down with Fury. Both of them had had a few martinis and were reacting, as people do, in their own fashion: Nicholas, being one who enjoys being pleased, fades a little when things happen to be not pleasing; Bob, like Hilton, enjoys being indignant, and takes possession of the situation like an obstreperous general occupying a town.

'So there I was, old boy, perfectly happy in Marseilles—not a bean of course but perfectly happy, I mean absolutely *happy*, you get me, oh yes, having a wonderful time—when up turns this ruddy wire and orders us here. This foul hole. Well, we arrive, like ruddy fools, to find instructions to go straight on to Rome. I ask you! Rome! Facing all that mob again in the Europa, lot of gibbering incompetents, my God! I'll let them have some Italiano, I can tell you —no I mean, honestly, old boy, what do *you* both think about it all? The situation? Poor old Nick here, not a bean I mean, either of us; not a very dignified position I mean, is it? And when are we shooting, if one may ask? I merely wish to know: When? If ever? And What? Absolute farce. Complete farce. My hat, when I think of all that work in Morocco— poor old Micheál working away like a slave. Well anyway, here we are on the old Grand Canal—hi! Porter! where is that moron? How many pieces—one, two, three—I'm sure I had a—four, five, no there it is! Have to pop that in the pop-shop if this sort of thing is to continue, simply *pop* it, old boy, I mean, that's what it will come to—come on, Nick; hi, Porter! *Portiere!* Ruddy languages. Get you down in the end. Berlitz School, that's what this picture is—Hugo's Grammar. Hi, you! Bagaglio, see? Oh well if you both think you're staying here you'll probably find you're *not*, boys. Probably find you're not at *all*. Oh no, you'll find yourselves in Stockholm before you know where you are! . . . Orson? Don't ask *me* about Orson. No, Dad's not here. Dad's far away. Dad's the shattering limit if you ask me—there's our boat—come on, Nick. Well goodbye, Hilton, goodbye, dear old Micheál—God knows if we'll meet again, give everyone a kick in the pants for me, old boy, will you, no, seriously, I'm very, very—hey! mind that suitcase, you fool—seriously, very fed up. Very fed up indeed. Well, good-bye!'

They were gone, and the last rays of the Setting Sun dipped in the canal.

So we found out Orson wasn't in Venice at all; he was in Torcello, an island far, far away, and he didn't answer the phone, so of course he must have been out for a nice walk. Now really. So Hilton gave a superb though unintentional imitation of Bob, and we got two rooms with marble floors and mosquito nets and dark green shutters, and bathed, and sent laundry, and here we are. So we dined in the hotel garden over the canal, and heard people singing, and drank some Soave bianco and ate scampi and peaches, and knew we were in Venice again because we watched the moon rise over Santa Maria delle Salute and went for coffee to Florian in the Piazza San Marco, and wandered home through streets of mosaic and majolica. And what with one thing and another, as Hilton, slowly recovering from his Bob Coote mood, observed, there is no blotting it out that Orson, be he as changeable as the wind, as elusive as the Pimpernel, as unpredictable as fate, as maddening as a mosquito, as movable as a Christian festival, has a knack of finding the perfect place in which to be these things.

AUGUST 5TH

Throats still sore, and no sign of Orson. Venice, however, would atone for the world's ills. After long weeks of letting it lie have fished out ancient article of Theatre in Ireland and contemplate it as if it were the Rosetta stone. Must finish it here or drown it in the Canal. Meanwhile we have no money, nor is there anyone in sight who might give us some.

Hotel, however, all that could be desired, and Hall Porter sympathetic and gets everything we want chalked up for us.

AUGUST 7TH

Writing every morning. The Mostra Bellini (Giovanni) this afternoon. Admire his enormous range, also his use of that thin hard line Leonardo hated so much, but cannot believe he is in the first circle of the elected ones. Am quite willing to believe this is my blindness and not any fault of Bellini. Anyway, find him incomparably nearer to God than Veronese, Paolo the Pest of Venice, who should have had a house in Park Lane in the reign of Edward VIIth. What a satanically cynical and skilful Vulgarian, or is it again something wrong with me?

AUGUST 8TH

Met Dearest Orson wandering like a thunder-cloud in indigo overalls among the streets behind the Frezzaria. All three of us deeply moved, and he swept us off to lunch at Harry's Bar. Lunch highly succulent. The best paella I have eaten outside Seville and superb and unknown (to us) white wine; must get the name. All chalked up. O. said wasn't it terrible having no money, and we agreed, but it doesn't really make much difference, we'll doubtless have some soon. O. also said why didn't we go and live with him in Torcello? Quiet, fresh, and beautiful with orchards and green fields all round and a perfect country hotel under same management as Harry's Bar, also motor launch to carry one to and fro. Couldn't understand that we enjoyed Venice so much we didn't want to leave it. But in the best form I've seen him since early days at Mogador, and says he hopes we'll be starting work in a day or two. Then invited us to see Suzanne Cloutier's test for Desdemona, to be shown somewhere at dead of night.

AUGUST 9TH

Waschinsky rang from the Lido and we went to lunch with him and his great friend—'I svear you, Mike, she is en vonderful voman and she like very much meetink you both'—Contessa de Fraso. A nice, good-tempered woman with a white face and a friendly tongue and Italy, as you might say, tucked away comfortably under her arm as it can only be under English or American arms (hers is American). Loathe the Lido and all it stands for, if you can call it standing, more than ever, but heaven to see Waschinsky again so smart and sleek and all in snowy white. Lunch an orgy of melon and smoked ham and scampi in a sort of Cecil Beaton setting and joined afterwards by several members of what I have heard described as International White

Trash Society, all so kind and so absorbed in and bored
with each other, and so eager to be amused, one almost burst
into keening. Really they're very nice people, even if many
of them have got minds like furnished lodgings (rather smart
ones) and even if all of them do remind you irresistibly of
Guests in the Second Act, and you'd have to cut them down
a little on tour or use local extras to save the salaries. Then
we all sunbathed and talked about selling villas and getting
divorces. Had never seen any of the villas and didn't know
any of the co-respondents, and quite suddenly found myself
dreaming, not unpleasantly, that I was dancing the Walls
of Limerick with De Valera and Barbara Hutton—what
would they say to that I wonder?—and woke with icy wind
blowing on me to find strange Englishwoman in a white
bathing suit staring at me with mild distaste and saying how
extraordinary seeing me here and how *funny* men always
looked when they were asleep. (Why does she know so much
about it? Especially if she merely finds it funny?)

Indignantly pulled towels round me and found I was caked
with sand. All the others, said unknown Englishwoman, had
gone away to play Canasta. (Hilton and Waschinsky playing
Canasta? Might have known there was something fishy about
this from the start.) So we had dead-pan and dazzling conversation, and I found she was really very kind and her name
was *Wendy*, and didn't I remember all the fun we'd had at
Oban? Didn't, as I have never set foot there, but distinctly
heard myself saying wasn't it heaven, as I uneasily threw
handfuls of sand at the sea (didn't reach it). Well, Wendy's
two children—I *hadn't* met them had I, no, as a matter of
fact nobody *had*—Wendy's two children in Norfolk were
simply worrying her to death and she thought of taking
them to Florida because she thought people would be more
or less *kind* and there'd be room for the children to *expand*.
Why should one expand in Florida and not in Norfolk?
Didn't ask this question but assumed expression of intelligent

sympathy and stared across eye-searing expanse of bathing
huts, dazzling sands speckled with bronzed and shrimp-
coloured bathers, butcher-blue sea, and fringe of Turco-
Genoese Exhibition castles designed by Disney in a lesser
moment, while Wendy went on to say that the trouble about
staying with Americans was that they were so *kind* and gave
one so much to *drink* and one never got away. (Then how
again could one expand?) And then Wendy's children drank
too, and would simply grow up fit for cocktail parties and
nothing else, and of course Florida *was* Deep South, and
before Wendy knew where she was they'd all be dressing
in white suits and luminous ties and talking Deepest South;
and had I heard about the Coddington-Powys divorce? and
wasn't it absolutely ghastly about Rosemary and Pug? All
Pug's fault really, of course, and poor Bunny had been perfectly frantic about the whole thing and had cabled several
times from Bermuda to say it was all a complete and utter
fiction about Mary running off with Daphne's governess, and
the invention of that filthy little Yugoslav who simply stayed
at everybody's houses and Stole the Silver as she had done,
so Wendy had been told, from my hut on Lake Placid: was
it true she had tried to set Fire to it too? No? Well anyway
she was always being thrown out, did I remember her name?
No, *she* didn't either, but anyway it didn't matter, it was that
mess with the green eyelashes that was always giving herself
piqûres in the leg at lunch-time, and she wasn't even allowed
to *land* at Capri. So she'd gone off to Penang or somewhere
frightful with that sinister Bolivian chauffeur who'd left poor
old Frieda Withers-Cholmondeley absolutely stark naked in
a cellar in Antibes, hadn't I heard? And what news, if any,
of my awfully amusing friend Sidebottom? Was it true he
had married that circus dwarf who said she was a Hapsburg,
the one Wendy had met at my darling little house at Cap
Ferrat? (Never had one, any more than I had ever met a
single member of Wendy's *dramatis personae*. Uneasiness

ORSON WELLES AND MICHEÁL MacLIAMMÓIR
'Work. Jealousy scene begun'
Mogador (July 10th, 1949)

'In the fangs of a smart N.W. gale'
Mogador (July 7th, 1949)

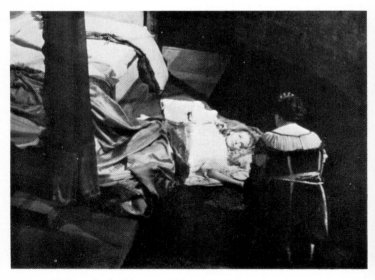

'Schnucks looking ravishing in shell-pink nightdress'
Viterbo (October 23rd, 1949)

'Orgy of work all over Venice'
(August 29th, 1949)

'Worked away with me at the corner of the balcony'
Venice (August 28th, 1949)

'Freezing . . . in Ca' d'Oro'
Venice (November 3rd, 1949)

'The November sun . . . streams over Doge's Palace'
HILTON AS BRABANTIO
Venice (November 7th, 1949)

'Work all day; a good day'
SELF, SCHNUCKS, ORSON, TROIANNI, FANTO

Schnucks being made up by Vasco; Troianni taking measurements
Mogador (February 1st, 1950)

'Work has been in progress . . . for last two days'
SELF, SCHNUCKS, BELLE OF STOCKHOLM, HILTON, ORSON
Mogador (February 5th, 1950)

'Work today was scrappy'
Safi (February 13th, 1950)

now turned quietly into panic.) Threw some more handfuls of sand at the sea, and Wendy said I'd changed a good deal since Jamaica, and was I getting on any better with Hermione, and did my wife approve? Answered, I thought rather brilliantly, that there were certain things I just couldn't *talk* about, and Wendy, looking pensive, said she'd often thought of all those things I'd said to her on the river that night, it seemed such ages ago (no wonder) and she wished she'd listened more sympathetically. And but for Bogey, who'd turned out the utter cad I'd warned her he was, she would have done so. Long and pregnant pause. However, she knew it was too late now, she whispered at last. Aoh! Aoh God! what a fool she'd been. Then she began calling me *Henry*, and saying I really *had* changed in the subtlest way, she wasn't sure, was it altogether an improvement, and then asked me with stony manner, suggestive of heroically repressed emotion, had she hurt me *frightfully* at Thames Ditton? Now seriously alarmed at this Noel Coward flavour to pre-Elizabethan comedy situation, I was just deciding to throw myself at her feet and explain all or else to jump into the sea and drown (could one at the Lido?) when Dorothy de Fraso, oh blessed blessed sight! accompanied by Hilton and Waschinsky, appeared, and said 'Micheál!' At this Wendy gave me a really petrifying stare, put on a gigantic pair of black sun glasses and tottered into a hut, the door of which she banged so loudly that everyone jumped. Dorothy de F. said, 'Who on earth was that?' but I remained dumb; didn't begin to recover until I found myself drinking tea with Hilton on the Piazza San Marco, and don't really feel well yet.

AUGUST 23RD

Have been in Venice nearly three weeks and not a stroke of work on *Othello*. Both Hilton and I have achieved a rhythm of life which makes us feel we have never been anywhere else. Have finished *Theatre in Ireland* pamphlet and sent it off;

rest of time making notes for new plays and not working on them, making some comic drawings (why? am not very good at them), also visiting the Accademia and all the exhibitions.

We have met a lot of people and gone to many parties, and have not so far experienced the feeling of suffocation I have occasionally known in Venice through absence of green trees or grassy places on the one hand, and on the other, through a surfeit of ambiguous idlers of many nations and all sorts of sexes willowing their way through the shadow of endless marble colonnades in shorts and net shirts. How irresistibly Italy attracts them, the aimless agreeable things, as they murmur their sibilant criticisms of Tintoretto, whose name on the lips of so many of them sounds like the fluttering of a gas fire, or discuss the price of carrots—for many of them carry string bags on their arms as they wend their way like determined Agags towards the market for a morning's shopping—and it all boils down to the fact that everything is *fabulous*, my dear, *fabulously* good, or *fabulously* expensive or *fabulously* frightful—Tintoretto or the carrots or the Lifar matinée or the Film festival or the arrival of the American battleships in the lagoon or whatever new diversion turns up; simply *fabulous*, my dear.

Work starts the day after to-morrow. Arrival of Bob and Nicholas last night, also Fay in glorious form, her angels fiddling and trumpeting away like mad as she beholds Venice for the first time and reacts to its beauty. We drink gin fizzes and float up and down in gondolas. All this will stop when the shooting begins. Waschinsky has already abandoned the Lido and the snow-white suit and has taken a room at the Cavaletto where Hilton and I used to stay before the war. Orson whirls backwards and forwards in his motor launch between Venice and Torcello. Brizzi and the Boys have re-appeared, also an entirely new wardrobe staff.

Saw at midnight of some day or other last week Suzanne Cloutier's test, which is fine, and Orson, heartily backed by all of us, has approved. So she, I believe, has also arrived, though nobody can be discovered so far who has caught a glimpse of her. Presume, however, she will finally be run, if not to earth, at least to marble pavement, and that very soon.

AUGUST 24TH

Hilton started Brabantio this morning perched up on balcony of Desdemona's House on the Grand Canal in grey wig and beard, also night cap and long embroidered night-and dressing-gowns, shouting his head off at Bob Coote and myself, once more rigged out as Roderigo and Iago and now seated in gondola (managed with great skill by delighted gondolier, looking, as is the habit of Italians, perfectly at home in his Cinquecento finery) as we hurl epithets up at Othello's father-in-law.

Suzanne has been discovered and looks all that could be desired in confection of shot-silk puffed sleeves, pearls, and pale gold hair; she and Fay sat in another gondola, which wobbled uneasily but regained its balance as Fay did scenes from Panto with superb gestures and wistful tripping walk of Principal Girl saying 'And ahll the schemes—and Cinderellah's dreams—nevah, it seems—come trew!'

Blazing weather and hard-working morning enlivened by sudden spectacle of Lady Diana Duff Cooper appearing in yet another gondola with an enormous cyclamen and white mushroom hat almost eclipsing her face and singing out, 'Orson! All hard at work on *Othello*! And there's Desdemona's Dad on the balcony! What fun!' This, especially as she looked so cool and summery and we were dripping and dropping into the canal, was, of course, unqualified success with us all, and Fay is busy on faultless imitation.

AUGUST 26TH

Work continues: we are covering an enormous lot of ground and are followed everywhere by hordes of extras all

wearing their clothes beautifully and acting with such abandon that they have to be toned down by Waschinsky.

AUGUST 27TH

Location now moved from Grand Canal to Doge's Palace;
its magnificence blotched by our yards of cable, standard
lamps, boxes, and baskets overflowing with senators' robes,
wigs, hats, shoes, tights, doublets, and jewelled chains: the
extras fight like wild cats as to who shall wear the grandest.
Wardrobe mistresses in despair; all of them chatter and
scream like magpies; Orson is right: Italy is an aviary. But
what a gorgeous aviary, and what gorgeous birds, flapping
and trilling and shaking their wings in their setting of marble
and gold and mosaic under the dazzling violet-coloured sky.
We pace up and down through bars of light and shadow
under the colonnades of the great balcony among the bronze
busts of doges, senators, architects, musicians and poets, and
look down, when we are not in action, across the Piazzetta
over the Schiavone and eastward to Salute on one side, and
on the other we watch the Piazza San Marco. Crowds of
people stroll about or sit in the shade outside the cafés, the
jangle of string orchestras play Scarlatti, Irving Berlin, Franz
Lehar, Puccini (we'll have to do a lot of dubbing at some
future date, I can see *that* coming), the pigeons trot about
or flap affectedly into the air when the gun goes off or anyone
says 'Bo!' to them, the newspaper boys thread their way
through the ranks of yellow chairs collecting cigarette
butts.

And why do people talk about the smell of Venice? To
me it's the best smell in the world except carnations, strawberries, or a turf fire—that whiff of cold brackish water lapping on hot marble and mingling with the smells of all Italy,
lemons and fish and brilliantine and black roasting coffee
and market flowers and shuttered rooms; and I'd work all day
in this country and never mind it at all, if at the end of the

work I can sit with Hilton and Orson over an ice or a glass
of wine, and watch the gilded boys striking the hour and the
sun rise and set over the lagoon, the golden domes, the
crinkled roofs, the crumbling houses, the bridges, the gondolas floating like long black leaves, the women selling fruit
in the back streets, the city smiling drowsily in the sunset,
the stars appearing one by one in the water.

We've finished the scene of rousing the alarm at Brabantio's
house, and the preceding scenes (which we made later) of
'I'll poison his delight', which I say about Othello, not
Brabantio, and which is played outside the church in which
Othello and Desdemona are being married; and to-morrow
we do a long speech: in the play it comes in Act One, Scene
One, God knows in the film where it will be—

> Oh! Sir, content you;
> I follow him to serve my turn upon him;

down to

> I will wear my heart upon my sleeve,
> For daws to peck at: I am not what I am.

This to be played at the San Marco corner of the great
balcony; the effect of Setting Sun is essential for Orson's
happiness, so the morning will be spent elsewhere.

AUGUST 28TH

Morning passed successfully with scrappy shots between
Bob and me rushing madly up and down sumptuous interior
staircase in Doge's Palace with crowd of senators on our way
to listen in to Midnight Council. We were joined by Joseph
Cotten, who's here on a holiday and walked on as a senator,
thus satisfying Orson's superstitious beliefs about Joseph C.
figuring somehow or other in every picture he makes and
ensuring its good luck. Charming and friendly and accompanied by Joan Fontaine, who appeared as a page-boy.

This evening a nightmare; Orson as cranky as a dromedary,

and the sun setting much too quickly. Bob Coote, whose face wore that patient, over-boiled expression that comes from frantic internal combustion, worked away with me at the corner of the balcony on speech about following Othello 'To serve my turn upon him'. This was shot after three halves of a rehearsal which never reached end of speech, so naturally imagined (was it, on second thoughts is it ever, natural to imagine things in movie work? Anyway, I'll never do it again) that a cut would come after 'In following him I follow but myself', which was as far as rehearsal had ever taken us. Orson in such panic before we shot at all that entire cast and staff, Hilton included, became infected with his mood, lost their heads and yelled at Bob and me, particularly me. Panic spread. I started off; Orson, eyes visibly suffusing with blood, darted rapid glances between sinking sun and my face, expression changing from supplication (for sun) to blank yet pregnant loathing (for me). So I fluffed in the first take and did it again. Got through so nicely with second take that I stopped dead on 'follow but myself' and said, beaming with pleasure, 'There! was *that* better?', to receive storm of unleashed abuse: I should have finished right down to 'I am not what I am'.

Mortified, but obviously nothing to do but take it again, and by this time the sun had sunk too low. (Didn't seem too low to me, but confess I am no judge of heights or depths.) So more pandemonium broke forth and Orson bade us all good night and marched away with Trauner. Called my dresser to my side with as much *hauteur* as I could, pulled trousers and coat over Iago clothes, and walked back to the hotel seething. Dined in garden with Fay and Hilton, joined later by Bob, and finally by Orson looking like a dropsical black Panther. Brooding silence followed as he sat down with us and began to devour several lobsters. Then began to abuse Bob. Then me. Then storm broke out. Then we cried and made it up, but only after he'd told me that any other director would have Thrown me into the Canal. (This feasible, but directors not noted for logic, good behaviour, or sense of justice, especially when engaged in racing with sunsets.) Then we both said it was *our* fault. His fault, no my fault, no *his* fault. Nearly rowed again about this but not quite. Now I have to go through it all again to-morrow. Oh, St. Anthony, St. Christopher, St. Michael, and St. Genensius, pray for me.

AUGUST 29TH

Wild orgy of work all over Venice resulted to-night in almost leaving things too late again for setting sun, but I got the long speech, after careful rehearsal, in two takes. Orson jumped up and down and kissed, first me, and then everybody else, on both cheeks and gave complete version (Major Key with Actions) of

> Everyone loves the fellow who is smiling.

Momentary and slightly priggish sense of triumph dimmed on the way home by Sergio, the dresser, saying he didn't think me nearly as good in the speech as I was yesterday. Informed him coldly that I was not interested in his views on the art of acting, and would he prepare a bath at once and send for a barber. Sergio said I took too many baths to be healthy, adding that it was Monday and the barbers were all shut, and repeating his conviction that I wasn't up to much as an actor to-day. Had to remind myself that at seventeen one can't be expected to know anything about acting or valeting, but that one *could* learn to do what one was told and to shut up. Said so aloud. Sergio after correcting several mistakes in my Italian said meekly '*Sissignore*' and began very shrilly to whistle *Parlami d'amore, Mariù*. Told him to shut up again. Sergio said *Sissignore* and proceeded to take his revenge by filling bath with boiling water. Blistered my foot, put on dressing-gown again, and commanded him to add cold. Began to write diary, and Sergio, now humming *Vissi d'arte, vissi d'amore* in piercing tenor voice, emptied bath completely and presented me with ice-cold one. This bath game still in progress, and am now convinced he is right about the 'I am not what I am' scene and that it will, in all probability, be finally cut out of the picture.

AUGUST 30TH

Have been observing, accompanied by Hilton, the character and pursuits of Suzanne-Desdemona both on and off location, and we have come to the conclusion that she is a Peculiar Girl. Always ready on the set an hour before she is needed, and emerging from the hands of Santoli, Vasco, and her dresser as freshly washed, combed, painted, begowned, bewigged and bejewelled as if she had arrived from an exquisite toy shop and one had to peel off layer after layer of tissue paper in order to see her at all, she then dumps herself untidily in a chair and stares wistfully into space, or wanders up and down trailing her silks in the dust, till Orson or Fay or someone says, 'Hold your dress up, it's getting filthy!' or 'For God's sake don't put on your train till you're called, it'll be ruined.'

To us she shows so many facets of her nature: guileless, artful, amusing, remorseless, kittenish, intelligent, and plain phoney in turn, that we are in darkness as to the truth about her. We have decided she is an Iron-clad Mass of Egocentricity (Orson: in the main endorsed by us all); Obstinate (Fay: ditto); One Scharming but Difficult Girl (Gouzy: ditto); a Fascinating little Baggage but I wonder (Bob: ditto); sweet but Sticky (Nicholas: ditto); en Vicked Girl, so en Baby Lucrezia Borgia, I *svear* you! (Waschinsky: ditto); Attractive but something Funny About Her (Michael: ditto); Talented but Good but a Mental Ju-Jitsuist (Hilton: ditto).

For me she has one salient feature: she is Indestructible. She will discuss herself tirelessly for hours at mealtimes in

French or English in a faintly *gilded*, clipped drawl (like sunshine on snow) without pausing for breath. She will, with or without the attention of an audience, interrupt, declaim, misquote, advise, question, beg for advice, recount, flatter, boast, invent, be amusing and embarrassing but never stagnant: even when she is silent you know that, like a cat, an immense activity is in progress.

And, Orson having called her Schnucks in a moment of desperation, it looks as though the name was going to stick to her: Schnucks the Indestructible, the admirable, maddening, solemn-eyed, bilingual Schnucks, a terror among the Desdemonas of the world, a daughter of the demi-gods. And Orson is planning to save the strangling scene till the very last for, as he says, the public will undoubtedly want to see her all through the picture as Brabantio's daughter, and who knows, honey, he continues, rolling his ominously patient eyes over her small and exquisite throat, what may happen by the time the murder is due?

SEPTEMBER IST

We have been working for two days in Torcello, using Orson's rooms (of a sybaritic rusticity) to dress in and to rest when there is time.

Torcello, apart from the astonishing beauty of the church and its Byzantium forest of mosaic, where Hilton, dressed alternatively as Brabantio and as Hilton Edwards, wanders fervently up and down gazing, Torcello is of endless charm. A strange pleasure, too, in beholding again things that grow —long deep grass and thickets of flowers and trees laden with fruit. We set off every morning at seven-thirty and arrive while the air is still cool, and all of us enjoy it. Work, however, of the severest order; most of it in the cloisters of the church, and many scenes, as they are artificially lighted, are carried on far into the night. Last night we were on the passages following the 'What committed? Impudent strumpet' scene between Othello and Desdemona when Desdemona is joined by Emilia and later by Iago: an enormously long take running from Emilia's

> Alas! what does this gentleman conceive?
> How do you, madam? how do you, my good lady?

down to Iago's

> Go in and weep not; all things shall be well

and all things in one unbroken shot and not so well either, though we worked till 2.30 a.m. and didn't get home till nearly 4.

SEPTEMBER 2ND

Orson not happy about our long take last night, so we did it again to-night, and all things, he says, were well.

The dresser, Sergio, dilated with rapture at *motoscafo* journeyings, bowls of spaghetti under the orange trees, and late nights, brings us all cups of coffee whether we want them or not (we generally do), and spills most of the coffee in the saucers, trilling out arias from Puccini with such unbridled passion I haven't the heart to stop him. All of us, in spite of overplus of work, in high spirits, and Fay as brightly burning and whirling as a Catherine wheel.

Schnucks has developed mood of enormous demureness and calls Fay 'Miss Compton' with lowered lids.

'Quite right too, my dear,' says Miss Compton. 'There's a great deal too much of this "Fay darling" business among the younger members of the profession. My God, I caught the call-boy calling me "Fay" in London the other day.' She also refers to us as 'Mr. Orson, Mr. Hilton, Mr. Bob' and so on. Have yet to discover the precise effect she intends to convey by this, but it's so Schnucks I am inclined to like it except when she applies it to myself. There's something nauseatingly alliterative and Peter Pannish about 'Mr.

Micheál', so every time she does it I sing *Animal Crackers in my Soup* at her and now the 'Mr.' is disappearing, but 'Micheál' is pronounced with much diffidence and a repeat performance of lowered eyelids. (Does she want to be cast as Prunella, Hannele, or Wendy? Or all three?)

Later. Trauner has told me of a wonderful dream he had in which all the pigeons of the Piazza San Marco, having lost their power of flight, strutted *heavily* up and down the marble pavement while the tourists, miraculously transformed, fluttered madly into the air, billing and cooing, and the Venetians scattered handfuls of maize for them. The Freudian angle on this glorious conception leaves me cold; but what a subject for Chagall!

SEPTEMBER 4TH

4.15 *a.m.* Venice, the pigeons, the Palazzo Ducale and all the rest of it have vanished into the air, for we've been ordered to Rome, and Hilton and I sit in the spotless neon-strip-lit dreariness of a vast station buffet at Bologna waiting for a train. Series of maddening accidents have trod upon each others' heels, so fast they came, and now Nightmare is in full gallop. Led by Walter of Parma (famous for violets and cheese), a short, pleasant and hitherto little-encountered young man with fair hair and a misleadingly tranquil manner, who is the present Manager of the Troupe and obviously Giorgio Papi's left-hand man, all of us arrived as called at the station in Venice at eleven to catch *wagon-lit* to Rome. Sudden discovery was made by somebody that no luggage was on the train. No suitcases, no wardrobe, no wigs, no props, just nothing at all. Slight panic among our ranks unhesitatingly topped by Walter of Parma, who elected to go suddenly raving mad by way of protest, screaming, cursing, weeping, foaming at the mouth, clutching at porters as they scurried past us wheeling their trucks, and doing admirable performance of last act of *Cavalleria Rusticana*. (Why? Though in charge of

ourselves and our luggage until train moved out, Walter
wasn't himself travelling to Rome, and his own belongings not
in question. Surely, therefore, we were the ones cast for the
tragedy?) Hilton, in one of his diabolically inspired boy-scout
moments, decided that someone ought to stay behind and
see to it all. He further decreed, waving his walking stick
about and puffing cigar smoke faster than the engine, that
he and I were the ones to do it and that we could, if necessary,
take a later train. This involved a lot of vigorous rushing up
and down the platform on the part of himself, Bob, Nicholas,
Gouzy (eating sandwiches), Suzanne-Schnucks (waving sin-
ister-looking black-faced rag-doll called Louis), and myself
(giving Superb Performance of rushing but in reality not
covering much ground). Fay, looking like the Madonna, gazed
enigmatically out of her *wagon-lit* window, and gave excellent
advice, unheeded by all. Finally whistles blew, everyone but
H. and self shot into their compartments and were borne
away, and as they vanished Bob's face appeared at the opening of the luggage van saying 'I say, you two, it's all on the
train, hard luck!'

So then we were left Alone with Walter, who proceeded
to totally unrehearsed performance of the last hours on earth
of Mr. Hyde, ex Dr. Jekyll. (Again: Why? Could have done it
quite as well myself, and Hilton a great deal better.) So we
bore him off to a café to soothe him with ices. After consuming three, followed by three glasses of water, the wholesome
Jeykll look returned to his small, blond, classically propor-
tioned features, and he smiled sadly and said '*Minchia di
Dio che truppa!*' which seemed to me unfair. He then took
himself back to the station to learn the time of the next train
to Rome, and returning to our side informed us that there was
a direct, if somewhat slow, train at 2.15 a.m. Hours drooped
by with diversions of salami sandwiches, red wine, coffee,
and anecdotes of Walter's past life, sketchily translated by
me for Hilton's benefit in increasingly sombre tones. Trudged

back to station at 1.45 and walked up and down with now exhausted but gently smiling Walter (Jekyll) between two trains among clouds of evil-smelling smoke. Climbed into empty train labelled Rome, said, hypocritically, *arrivederci* to Walter, and were about to settle into our corners when Mr. Hyde suddenly reappeared at the window, face again contorted with fury. We were, he yelled, in the Wrong Train: it was the one *opposite, Madonna mia!* Too weary to protest, we dragged ourselves and our overcoats out and were propelled by Walter Beelzebub Hyde into opposite train, which was packed tightly with people, mostly women with babies. Practised haughty first-class glances on them all without much effect as they were first class too, though this hard to believe, so wedged ourselves in somewhere and said *arrivederci* again. Usual terpsichorean orgy of nocturnal Italian travel set in: everyone shouting, singing, laughing, weeping, consuming oranges, sausage, cheese, and bottles of wine. Train just moving out when Walter once again appeared in full spate as Hyde, and more totally abandoned to rage and passion than on either of his previous demonstrations (these seemed, in fact, mere rehearsals in comparison with this leaping, caterwauling, epileptic reading of the part). The train we were in, said Walter, was not going to Rome at all, but to Bari. And what was more, he screamed, flying after us as we shunted away down the platform, his hands and legs waving in all directions, if we wanted to get to Rome at all we would have to change at Bologna, *mama mia*, Bologna!

So here we are.

Red Bologna. Decided, when we emerged from train, now a shambles of orange-peel and spilt wine and rocking with arias from *Tosca* and *Fanciulla del West*, that we would stay here for the night, but not a room to be had anywhere. So have taken refuge in this draughty mausoleum (obviously designed for Fascist receptions in the bad old days), and here we remain until six-thirty, when a diesel, destined to arrive in the Eternal City at noon, is due.

ROME. SEPTEMBER 5TH

We are staying at the Ambasciatori opposite the Europa at the corner of the Via Veneto. Rome horribly noisy after the deep, plashing stillness of Venice: motor-bikes, cars, buses, and taxis all hooting away like mad. Hotel very pleasant: striped, strawberry-coloured bedrooms with balconies at the back of the house. We bathed after unspeakable nightmare of diesel journey (bolt-upright slippery seats, eyes like hot bull's-eyes staring at parched landscape crawling by under bright unwinking sunshine), and after bathing were presented by Waschinsky with pots of flowers: mine an enormous dark cactus, most peculiar, with lovely scarlet blossoms. Waschinsky also lunched with us on terrace restaurant of the hotel decorated in terra-cotta canvas to resemble large tent and embroidered with zodiacal designs; three-piece orchestra played by a brother and two pretty sisters, operating on squeeze-box, fiddle, and double bass, worked their way through strange but agreeable assortment of tunes, chosen mainly from Debussy, Brahms, and Cole Porter.

Utter exhaustion has now descended on us both. Hilton, having retired with book by Ouspensky in his room which opens out of mine—bathroom between—is now gently slumbering. Work at Scalera Studios begins to-morrow.

SEPTEMBER 7TH

Nostalgia for Venice gradually recedes as the siren Roman spell, in spite of the hooting and screaming of the traffic, steals inexorably over us both. In the warm and luscious apricot light of September, the peach and plum and gold and amber of her body lying lavishly over the dusty hills under the high dark blue of the sky, accented by parasol-pines and broken marble and cold stone fountains, the faint ambiguous ageless smile, the unfathomable sensuality, I keep muttering aloud, 'What a country! My God, what a city!' and every corner I turn causes me to catch my breath as though I saw it for the first time instead of knowing it since '22: it is inexhaustibly wonderful.

Can still find nothing remotely connected with the Invisible Life in St. Peter's or indeed anywhere but in the most unlikely places on the Palatine or in remote and little known churches: St. Peter's is a great salon (*not* 'saloon' as old pal, the Rev. John O'Flynn, thought I'd said: *salon*), for the contemplation of the achievements of man, not all of them admirable, but then not all man's achievements are.

These apparently leisured impressions (or confirmations of impressions, for many of them are old) are received in the morning: Orson has a new scheme of work and we don't go down to the studios till 2 p.m. So we wander about in labyrinths of unleashed splendour and unleashed vulgarity (the entire gamut is there between Trajan's Arch and the Vittorio Emmanuele Presentation Cake: Orson says it's *all* vulgar and begs me to consider the Colosseum before it grew elderly) and then we return to the Ambasciatori to eat lunch on the canvas-covered terrace and listen to the family trio playing *Clair de Lune* or *Kiss me, Kate* or *South Pacific*. And this hour's relaxing after the morning's exertions in September sunshine has created already a keynote to this Roman interlude that I know will set the tune of it all for me, if, at some future date, I want to remember it. I will too: it is a wonderful interlude.

The work is tough. Good to have dressing-rooms again, and each one is provided with a sofa and cushions, but is also at the moment haunted by microscopic Ants which swarm over everything, also by a vast motherly dresser called Mathilde who allows the fact that she looks like a handsome man absurdly dressed as a woman to permit her to burst into the room whether one is stark naked or not and help one with one's socks or tights or whatever it is. No protestations, no turnings of the back can stop her; she bounces in, loudly whistling bits of *Mario Cavaradossi*, and assuring one that she has a husband and six sons and regards one as so much furniture to which she is obliged to attend. She also assures me that the ants come in from the garden (which she seems to think annuls their unattractiveness) and reminds me that we are all Children of God. Find this Franciscan school of thought admirable but uncomfortable, and Fay and I are combining to buy bottles of germicide and cause havoc in the ant-world.

Fay lent me her spectacles to-day as my eyes got tired and I wanted to read. Horrified to say that the spectacles are a great comfort, and think I'll see an oculist and get some of my own. Am reading for the third time Aldous Huxley's *Art of Seeing* and am deeply impressed, but am too dense to follow his instructions, though I find his philosophic deductions clear. I can get no one to teach me the exercises, and take sardonic pleasure in the fact that the very phrases condemning artificial aids to perfect sight are much more easily enjoyed with the aid of Fay's glasses.

Working in a studio for the first time since, I think, 1915, when I made *Coming thro' the Rye* with Alma Taylor and Stewart Rome, and find it all very different from my childish memories, which seems reasonable, as thirty-four years of improvements have gone by since. One large set of the Hall in the Castle designed by Trauner, in which we play a mass of loosely related scenes round and about the handkerchief episode; we're also going to use it for Iago's murder of Emilia and for his being brought back into Othello's presence to say 'Demand me nothing, what you know you know'.

So we start off at two-thirty every day and work until eight, when we dine together on balcony of excellent studio restaurant overlooking the garden, which is full of roses, oleanders, palm-trees and fountains; and we choose our food from an apparently unlimited menu and drink wine, and I compare it with British and Irish canteens where poached eggs and sausages are so frequently Off To-day and one ends up with tea and a Chelsea bun in an atmosphere of steaming dishcloths and frayed nerves and wishes one had never been born, and then I wonder what it is about our islands that makes everything so difficult. Well then, after coffee and a Strega we go back and work, and when we're not engaged on a scene we wander among the trees in the garden within reach of our call, and the work goes on generally till one or two in the morning, and then baskets of sandwiches and bottles of Chianti arrive, and then we drive home.

SEPTEMBER 10TH

John O'Flynn to lunch and came with us to watch work, with Orson's permission, at studio. Couldn't believe his eyes at seeing us rehearse small scene of three lines eighteen times and achieving it only after seven takes, and said quite rightly that life in Vatican City seemed simple in comparison.

SEPTEMBER 11TH

Tough going with Schnucks; her chin and Orson's bearing strong resemblance to sea and wind in Hamlet when both contend which is the mightier. Thought her as steely as she appeared all day until I found her crying in her room after-wards (ants now chased away), and we had a long brother and sister session. I like her and believe in her in spite of all the nonsense. She has, as well as beauty and talent, an endless supply of courage and determination, and her remarkable powers of endurance would be far less called upon if she could only emerge from the sort of leaden wrappings under which she hides when being directed. You see her staring at Orson when he's explaining things to her with large, dewy, unseeing eyes and small, shell-shaped, unhearing ears, absorbing nothing, registering nothing, incapable of receiving his aid. Why? roars Orson, his patience breaking at last. Why? ask I, busily petting and patting her as she weeps. Why? queries Hilton, struggling with her inflections in private and finding her composed of maddeningly equal quantities of fire and dough. Why? demands Fay, gazing mournfully into the dewy eyes with her own penetrating and analytic (though azure) gaze, as she waggles a finger at Schnucks and says 'It isn't as though you were a fool, dear. You could do it perfectly well if you'd let yourself, if you'd just listen and concentrate and do what you're told. So why?'

Well, says Schnucks, it's like this: sometimes she feels like a poor little snail inside its shell, and they begin cooking the snail and it just *can't* come out of the shell for it knows it would get burned if it did, so after a moment's panic-stricken reflection it decides to stay where it is, and then the oven grows hotter as the snail feared it would and the snail curls up inside and gets cooked and then of course there's nothing to be done with the snail but to eat it. Which is precisely, say Schnucks' tearful eyes, what is happening to her Right Now; and then of course one has to hug and pat her all over again. I take pains, however, between the kisses and slaps, to point out, rather tartly, the absurdity of the parable, saying that Direction is not comparable to Cooking any more than she, Schnucks, is comparable to a poor little snail; what she *is*, I assure her, is a great big beautiful peroxide blonde with a chin like Pallas Athene who is learning how to Act for the Movies, and I add wistfully that it's much easier to do that at twenty than at forty-nine. So then she cheers up and is in great form for the evening's ordeals, and Orson, emerging wild-eyed into the moonlit garden after a long session of saying 'Oh thou weed!' to her, murmurs: 'The incredible thing about that Iron Butterfly is: that she is going to be So Good in the part. Oh yes she is, she's going to be So Great. Bring me a bottle of Cognac. I'm through with everything.'

SEPTEMBER 14TH

Wild night spent by Hilton and Orson teaching me a dagger fight. O. says, 'Oh you're so *clever*, you're so *artful*, you're so bad in long shots and so good in close-ups I have to keep on giving you Big Heads of Pola; no actor has ever had so many since Jack Barrymore. God, you're so artful! And it's all because you *move* so badly.'

I say indignantly that this, if true at all, is only so when I am faced with the camera and the ridiculous limitations it demands: on the stage, I say, I move very well indeed. Oh no, says O., I do nothing of the kind because he's watched me, and I just give an excellent *performance* of moving well: in reality I don't do it at all.

Feel not only indignant at this but detect definite symptoms of paralysis setting in, and doubt if I shall ever move again.

SEPTEMBER 15TH

Fay's death scene. I thought her superb. The latest night yet: we weren't home till nearly five, and on the Toby Belch principle of it being too late to go to bed, Orson, Fay, and I had drinks together in the downstairs bar of the Europa across the street, which is where Fay is living. Bar-room had a soothing, early morning *ambiente* and large leather chairs, and we talked about Christianity, Ethel Barrymore, English institutions such as muffins, week-ends, punts, Worcester sauce, cricket, and the Christmas Pantomime. Then we glided into abstractions such as the habit of generalisation, about which Fay and Orson were severe. Yet, though in most cases it is an absurdity, generalisation at least serves thought as the rafter serves the bat: as a dependable starting-place for flight. (This of course leaves a good deal to be said about the essential inferiority of the bat as a flyer.) Anyway, generalisation led to its own unavoidable conclusion, the little matter of death. So we talked for a long time about that, and Fay, she assured us, had been dead once for quite a long while after an operation, and it was extremely pleasant. In fact, said Fay, sipping her gin-fizz and looking about sixteen, it was so nice that she's quite looking forward to it as a permanency, much as she enjoys life in bits. All this surely very cheering, and am thinking of it quite a lot as I tiptoe about the room so as not to wake Hilton who has been asleep for hours in the next room, and watch the dawn opening in the blue air over Rome like a vast rose-coloured shell and listen to the birds singing.

Later. Orson's little daughter Christopher has appeared: an enchantress of the very first order. Not beautiful, which surprises me because her mother Virginia is lovely, and she resembles her closely, except that she is dark instead of fair. And Orson himself, though admittedly no Hermes, is not without a certain lunatic radiance; maybe Christopher will turn into a beauty, or at least a siren, because she already has merely to glance your way (which she frequently does if you're near enough, whoever you are) and you melt. We lunched at a country restaurant in a garden overlooking the Appian Way and she sang *Some Enchanted Evening* and did some shattering imitations of various celebrities beginning with Ethel Merman, making hay with several Barrymores and a few famous political figures, and finishing with her own Daddy. When that was over she came to the studio to watch us work and produced admirable impressions of Fay and Schnucks. Tremble to imagine what she will do with me. She's on her way from some Italian villa to the Heart of Africa, Virginia's latest fancy, and will have there, I'm sure, plenty of new material.

SEPTEMBER 16TH

Scene of reception to Lodovico devised by Orson as

sumptuous spectacle in pavilion of silks and tapestries:
Nicholas looking magnificent. Have worked on this sequence
for two days; it leads through a jungle of cuts, counter-
shots, and general complications to (a) a climax of 'Goats
and monkeys' and (b) to Othello's striking Desdemona across
the face. This planned by Orson with hierarchic backgrounds
of banquet tables and crowds of distinguished guests, Othello
out of camera but long shot of Desdemona slowly approach-
ing camera for the lines:

> DES. Trust me, I am glad on't.
> OTH. (*out of camera*). Indeed!
> DES. My Lord?
> OTH. (*still out of camera*). I am glad to see you mad.
> DES. Why, sweet Othello!
> OTH. (*still out*). Devil!

Des. by this time is in Big Head of Pola; black hand of
Othello suddenly strikes her across the face. Cut.

Poor old Schnucks did it countless times, moving beautifully (unlike me, hmph!) towards the camera, but once Big
Head of Pola obtained could not prevent herself flinching
before black hand of Othello appeared, thus ruining the shot.
Her lovely face went slowly numb under this treatment and
its constant repetitions, her make-up repaired and repaired
again by Vasco. Hours wore by, we all wilted. Unfortunate
joke on somebody's part that it must be time for lunch was
sternly unheeded. Schnucks did it again. Flinched. Again.
Flinched. And again and again. And at last Orson, his face
(unmade-up) now pale green and hanging in festoons, his
hand in its Renaissance sleeve blacker than ever, said
'O.K., Schnucks, you can't do it. So here's what's going to
happen. You just do it once more and I'm not going to
strike you, see, we're going to cut on your line on your last
"Why, sweet Othello!" and we'll take the blow in the face in
another shot and we'll make that to-morrow when you feel
fresh. So here we go, last time; we cut at "Why, sweet

Othello!" and Remember: *Everyone loves the Fellow who is smiling . . .*'

So off we went again, and Schnucks, reassured and radiant, sailed into her close-up, no sign of a flinch, and got the best puck in the face you ever saw and 'Cut!' says Orson, and it was all over. 'Perfect. Thank you, Schnucks.'

Followed a short silence while Schnucks wiped the salt and smarting tears away, and then deprived us of our breaths by saying very sweetly, 'Of course I'm very grateful, Mr. Orson, it was the only way to make me do it, but of course I *did* know all the time you were going to hit me: I guess I'm psychic.'

Orson is right and so am I and so are we all; she is everything we accuse her of being, but above all else she is Indestructible.

SEPTEMBER 17TH

Lunch with our Minister to Rome, Michael MacWhite, and with his Danish wife. They bore me off to Monte Cavo where we ate on a broad terrace under plane trees. Both of them nice to me, and Michael produced a miracle—is he unconscious medium or saint?—by fishing a noggin of Irish whiskey out of his pocket and we drank it together as an apéritif. Immediately manifestations of miracle: the entire classic countryside half sleeping under the sun was transformed at the winking of an eyelid, as the old familiar bouquet mounted to the nostrils, into a windswept landscape: the cypresses and chestnuts and olives turned to straggling colonies of hazels and thorns, the junipers to blossoming furze and heather, the mountains pulled veils of clouds about their heads, and the peasants' houses changed into thatched cottages; a wilderness of stones with pools of water sprang up before the eyes where before there had been plantations of almond and cherry, and far away there were desolate reaches of bogland sweeping up to the breast of the hills, and soon the air grew melancholy with the floating breath of turf-smoke blowing through miles of sun and rain. And not until a waiter appeared with a piled up dish of *tagliatelli* and we were immersed in its savour did the landscape readjust itself, and Ireland steal away from us over the edge of the horizon, and Italy step back on her throne. Mme MacWhite said, 'Ah! the sun is coming out again; I am afraid after all it's going to be dreadfully warm,' because of course, being Danish, and not having been touched by the bedevilment of the whiskey, all she had noticed was a passing cloud.

SEPTEMBER 18TH

Fay's birthday, and she is going back to England, having finished up last night at the Studios Scalera in a blaze of glory. We all gave her inadequate presents and were sad at her departure: a blankness follows her exits in life as on the stage, and looking back at the various phases of this picture's history up till now, she, in the gallery of its personalities, is one of the very brightest portraits. Perhaps she stays in my mind more as an enamel than as a portrait, for the first thought of her is visual and she seems made out of turquoise and gold; and then, such a cool and glowing little space of sky behind that comely head with its crown of plaits, and the two angels—why have I never mentioned them to her? —one fiddling away and the other blowing a long slim trumpet, and such a festive billowing of draperies and wind-blown clouds. Of course there are demons under her feet, but they're very small and amusing demons and she has them beautifully under control. Besides, they add a little body and darkness to a scheme otherwise so aerial, and where would St. Anthony be without the temptation I should like to know?

Well, she's gone to play in a new show in London, and we linger in Rome—Hilton and I being half contented in this gilded weather, and half fearful at the thought of life slipping by and the picture not finished yet, and Nicholas and Bob (for Michael has gone away too) at the restless stage, and Schnucks trumpeting up and down and bemoaning the fact that Desdemona, much as she loves her, has impelled her to turn down countless offers in Paris, and Orson looming about and in and out, and saying he wants us to do *Julius Caesar* in the spring with me as Brutus and Hilton directing.

Why, says H., should Orson think that he could direct a movie? It is, answers O., quite patent to anyone with the embryo of observation and the minimum of movie experience that he would be a perfect movie director. In fact if he, H., possessed either of these faculties himself, he would know it already without waiting to be told. H., pleased but full of doubts and suspicions, says it is precisely *because* he has no experience that he doesn't know for certain, and that a good deal of learning would have to be achieved before he could be convinced, and O. says Well, he had better start directing bits of *Othello*. This H. is more than willing to do, but news then comes through that money once more is fast disappearing, and that until some more turns up there will be another Break. So we all go out to dine and spend the breathlessly warm evening, which is of the colour and smell of a prize convolvulus with bright gold spots which turn out to be street lamps over the Tiber, wandering about in Trastevere.

I'd like Hilton to direct *Caesar*—who wouldn't?—but all these plans have an air of vagueness which disturbs me. Find I am growing indeed middle-aged and am beginning to put things into compartments as the Nordic races do their emotions: a place for seriousness, a place for passion, a place for humour and so on. This is what singles them out for their sense of order and decency, and for their ultimate winning either of success or of destruction, but always, I think, of attention and respect. Certainly it is what distinguishes them from the Latins and the Slavs and from racially indeterminate peoples like ourselves, in whom all these qualities are liquid and overflowing, and who may at any moment laugh in the midst of love-making, or play cards in a corner of a parade ground, and who never win a battle or build a complete system of our own, however we may contribute to the greatness of others, but who on the other hand are never so close to destruction as, say, Germany has come. The English were the triumphant heroes of the Hitler war, and see how lengthily and laboriously they are building up again, and the French and the Italians in their various ways skipped and staggered and skedaddled through and seem at any rate to be flowing with milk and honey in spite of a growing and not too hidden undergrowth of wretchedness; and that's how we in Ireland would do it if we were in the world at all, everything flowing and liquid and brimming over the edges; but England and Germany do it in slow portions, bit by bit, and either win through or perish and rebuild in agony.

Well, I could go on with that forever and so of course could anyone else, but what I meant was that I'm getting to the slow portion and the bit-by-bit stage myself about certain things in my life and in Hilton's, and I like to be executive and to know: are we going to do a new film with Orson? Or when are we going to finish this one? Or when are we going back to our own business, which is the theatre in Ireland? Or what the hell will I do with myself meanwhile, or Hilton with himself? If I had a ha'porth of guts I'd sit down and write a play, because playing Iago in bits isn't enough to fill up my mind, but all I can do is to sit in Rome and write a diary and let life push me about.

I might write a comedy about the making of *Othello*: God knows the characters are here; from Rita to Vasco and from Orson to Schnucks there are plenty of them, but heavens! what a lot of sets it would want. And I can't see it, somehow, played in the Elizabethan manner.

SEPTEMBER 19TH

Entire day spent by H. and self in Forum. Guide-book and all. Loved it. There's something wholesome, unpretentious and grand about going round with a guide-book and another man and learning about things. Talked a lot about Caesar and the possibilities of the new picture. But caught myself also thinking of all sorts of English novels of the 'nineties or of the age of Edward VII, where so many lost relations find each other's descendants after years of fruitless searching: 'That little boy has such a look in his dark eyes of our beloved Mabel, do you not think so, dearest? And that brow—surely there is a strain of the Willoughbys there? Oh, Aubrey, do let us ask him.' And sure enough the child's mother turns out to have been a beautiful *contadina*, and the father that handsome scapegoat Gerald, Mabel's second son, who had left home in order to become a painter and had died in poverty on the Piazza di Spagna; so the little fellow is taken back to Wimbledon, where his perfect manners and quaint struggles with the English tongue endear him to everyone, and all ends happily with tea under the dear old cedar on the lawn and his meeting with Cynthia over the tennis net.

Later. Incredibly lovely walk with H. through a warm and stormy night in the Borghese gardens, where we discovered an enormous and apparently forgotten courtyard of low marble balustrades and half-ruined statues among a forest of pines and cypresses, swaying and tossing against a swollen umber sky. Everything was dark brown—sky, earth, trees, and low swollen sallow clouds—and the broken statues glimmered in dull yellowish ivory.

SEPTEMBER 20TH

Lou Lindsay has turned up again and was sitting at lunch with Hilton on the pink canvas terrace when Nicholas Bruce and I returned to eat after a long walk through the gardens and across the Piazza del Popolo, where we complained bitterly about this new hitch in *Othello* and said no, really, it was past a joke. So it was, but we both felt it was worse for Orson than for any of us and then felt it was priggish, quixotic and sanctimonious of us to feel it. Probably, also, *phoney*, as we were much sorrier in our hearts for ourselves, and *our* trouble was, we declared, being so much in the dark and never knowing how long the breaks were going to be so we couldn't do anything else. I decided, watching the Piazza from the gardens as we swooped towards it down the zigzag road lined with acacias and statues, that one might be distressed in many places possessing less attractions than Rome, and Nicholas agreed; but added that he and I and Hilton and Schnucks would doubtless go on doing *Othello* for ever. Had disturbing vision of the picture as a whole with the four of us appearing reasonably young or in prime of life as the case might be, and developing in many of the shots a sudden and unaccountable maturity, and in my own case, if things continued much longer, the definite stamp of a ripe old Age. Thank God, said I, that the line 'I have looked upon the world for four times seven years' has been cut out of the script by thoughtful Orson, for by the time I got to it it would doubtless get the wrong sort of laugh.

What has been really good about this latest stage of things has been that so much of the picture is now achieved that the idea of not going through to the end is surely out of the question, and still more wonderful has been the setting in which all has been achieved. Because, knowing that these days mark once more the conclusion of an interlude, I seem to hear an entire opus played back to me on a record, at the making of which I was present ages ago.

The Moorish section is all there in my mind without any aid of this diary to remind me of it: it is *audible* in brilliant angular forms cut as it were out of blinding sunshine and

shadow, with the sea foaming below the yellow battlements
of Portugal's heyday in Africa as its leit-motif and chief
inspirer; the Venetian section is a grave andante in rose and
blue with long delicate passages of tranquillity and a series
of trills and shakes at the most unexpected moments, and in
the most astonishing variety of tones. And this Roman
section: ah, who can define it? In some ways, in spite of the
sweating nights in the studios, the swollen-eyed dawns witnessed on the way back to the Via Veneto, with Schnucks
chanting her grievances at the back of the car and Fay staring
through the windows with haggard eyes across the empty,
brightening streets, yes, in some ways, in fact in most ways,
it has been the best of all so far. For, apart from the colour
and form of the original musical structure, the prima donna
—what was it I used to think about her resting between two
epoch-making arias?—the great Diva herself, throwing her
arms about us and putting her lips close to our ears, has
added her voice to the harmony and transformed the thing
into a work of magic. So to Rome, so far, I give my chief
thanks: if we never made another shot of *Othello*, I have lived
and worked with her for a little, not merely visited her, and I
have heard her voice, and seem already to know its passion
and rich languor all in retrospect, as though the conductor
of this particular movement of the Chorale had laid down his
baton and she were bowing low and low among the flowers
and we, players and audience alike, had burst into rapturous
applause.

SEPTEMBER 21ST

Plans to leave for Dublin to-morrow until *Othello's* finance
shall be readjusted—somewhat shaken by tottering of English pound; heartrending spectacle of tourist hordes all heading
for home and in the meantime being offered lifts in the cars
of those who have dollars, francs, or even lire, meets the gaze
on all sides, and God knows if there'll be a seat on any plane

The idea of travelling by land and water never seems to occur to us. Curious: I must ask Hilton why. Probably, however, trains and boats will be as crowded as planes.

Orson and Hilton discussing plans for next film and madly signing Gentlemen's Agreements together. Can make head or tail of nothing whatsoever except that I wish we could finish *Othello*.

PARIS. SEPTEMBER 25TH

Exotic and highly excitable dinner given by Jean Davis and his wife, who is as charming as you could wish Jean's wife to be: a Russian restaurant in the Rue Bréa; décor, for some reason I cannot fathom, reminded me of the illuminated inside of a whale. One sits encased in gold and vermilion boxes consuming imperial delicacies and being entertained by gypsies, so it was the general *Stimmung* that provided the exotic qualities of our evening, combined with the glowing and somehow *Assyrian* features of host and hostess. Maurice Bessi was there too, and Orson, and one or two others, and Orson and I got somehow on to the subject of what was European and what wasn't, and this provided the excitement. He said something about a manner of living, I forget what, and I said we didn't feel that way and he said 'Who's we?' and I said 'Europeans,' and he said 'You don't consider yourself *European* do you, you benighted Harp?' and I said 'What else am I?' and then discovered that neither British nor Irish people were counted by Orson as belonging to Europe at all. So then Hilton came pouncing in like a Large Enthusiastic Retriever and said Of Course we were European, and Orson said Oh No Not at All, and we all began shouting. God knows why, because that sort of definition seems more or less beside any point of importance and is surely a question of the convenience of terms, Orson choosing to use the word European as we use Continental, but Orson said No, it was *deeper* than that, and that our islands (tea-drinking and other habits briefly referred to) were further removed from Europe in spirit, even, than America was. And then I discovered that Scandinavia, Spain, and Russia were also in question as far as their authentic Europeanism was concerned, and in the end there seemed little left of Europe outside France, Italy, and what used to be the Central Powers, and we swept madly out of the illuminated whale's belly waving our arms about and leaving Jean to deal with enormous bill, and Maurice peering like an amused but slightly alarmed grey duckling over the edge of a spritely grey butterfly bow whispering *'Impayables, tu sais, ils sont impayables tous les trois.'* And then we surged up and down the Rue Bréa with Madame Davis sympathising with each of us in turn as we roared like lions and finally drove off in a gigantic car to a night club that was so exotic you couldn't see an inch in front of your nose, and everything was made of lapis-lazuli and violet brocade and was lighted solely by a single luminous glass orchid in the middle of each table, and Orson did a lot of Magic Tricks, and cheered up. Though even as he caused handkerchiefs to disappear and several thousand franc notes to take their place in the open palm of his hand, he continued to say that I could go on eating *paella* and talking French and German and smoking Gauloise cigarettes and wearing Borsolino hats until I was black in the face: I was a British Islander (have a good mind to report him to Dáil Éireann for this) to the tips of my fingers and would never be a European as long as I lived. So then I took refuge in the What does it Matter what any of us Are technique which is (of course) what I really believe and so (of course) does O., and I often find myself half wishing that, like him and other fundamentally sensible people, I had conducted my life on this principle, and not allowed a combination of atavistic instincts on the one hand and of theoretic abstractions on the other to narrow my life, even while they had given it whatever shape it has that distinguishes it from the life of any other treacle-voiced speaker of English with a talent for mummery. So I rather reproachfully reminded the party that we were flying home to-morrow—I'd forgotten to mention it, but we are—and Orson said how *awful* it was and how *sad*, to think of us flying away home to our wave-haunted islands, firmly convinced that we were still in *Europe*. However, soon, very soon, we would all be together again in that Great Big Aviary called Italy, and then we could get on with a little Shakespeare, and at the very name we all felt an extra heart-beat and decided that life, whether we were Europeans, Americans, or Islanders, was well worth living as long as we could go on reading, and listening to, and wondering about, and trying to interpret, through any medium the ingenuity of man may provide, the plays that Fate had chosen to pluck out of Warwickshire. So then we said goodbye in peace and happiness.

PART V

October 7th, 1949, to January 18th, 1950

IRELAND welcomed us with a show of sunshine as vividly golden as anything in Rome or Paris, and we're having all our meals in the garden. This has been allowed to go a little wild, so that one can pick blackberries from the bushes at the far end of it, and Rachel the Cat uses the long grass as a hunting jungle, and the pears fall off the trees into thickets of sorrel and dandelions.

Have seen Lennox and Dolly Robinson and Shelah Richards (looking about seventeen and full of fine new frenzies); also Adrian and Helen Holt, who are making plans for Irish films and hope to enlist as writers Seán Ô'Faoláin and Francis Stuart. The latter I haven't seen since about 1919, when he had a fringe of tortoiseshell-coloured hair and used to drink tea and talk about literature and theatre with R. N. D. Wilson and Arthur Shields and F. R. Higgins and me in a basement in Dawson Street which was called An Fód Móna, the Sod of Turf, and lived up to its name by having white-washed walls and potato cakes and Irish-speaking waitresses and a turf fire burning on an open country hearth, and nobody remembers it now and I wonder would Francis. Maybe Lennox would not have forgotten, though I cannot recall that I ever saw him there, but his memory is Irish as its length, and Irish in the old-fashioned way in that he remembers amusing things as vividly as cuts and bruises, and probably his gentle courtesy, as rare in this 'unmannerly town' as rain in Egypt, grows out of this. All this very retrospective and nothing to do with Adrian and Helen, who are courteous too as well as being gay and kind, and who never remember a thing and are so passionately of To-day.

OCTOBER 12TH

We went down to Connemara for three nights and I've returned in melancholy condition and filled with desire to found some sort of Society for the Preservation, not merely of the Irish language—still on the ebb in its last stronghold—but of all the things that accompanied it and are in slow but visible decay. I ponder on the withering of fine things that seems to me in full swing everywhere: on the destruction of the Claddagh in Galway, vanished now but for two or three houses and replaced by a maze of stucco bungalows that would be an eyesore in Bradford or Wigan; on the destruction of Lady Gregory's house at Coole; on the newly constructed wing of an historic house in Kerry which looks like an awfully go-ahead public convenience; on the falling into ruin, bristling with chromium-plated horror, of towns like Galway and Kinsale; on the replacing of Georgian Dublin with stream-line fantasies jerked up indiscriminately here, there, and everywhere; and I wonder is there anything that can stop this inane aping of all that is meanest and ugliest in Blackpool or Cincinnati?

Dined with Michael Scott, who is not only an architect of distinction but one of our best friends, and with us were his wife Patty and the Holts and Betty Brittain, and the dinner was at the Bailey in Duke Street. I was charmed to see that its re-decoration has been effected with an eye to the original character of the house and general feeling of the quarter, which is mid-Georgian, and they haven't tried to make it look like the Woolworth building or the Eiffel Tower but have done their work with insight and affection, so that one seems actually to be eating *where one is*, which is in a room in an eighteenth-century street in the small capital of a small country with an historic tradition and the elements of a living culture, not in a vague imitation of what the designers could remember of some unspeakable commercial

Exhibition; so I was emboldened to speak of what I'd been thinking about, and said wasn't it shameful about Lady Gregory and Kinsale and all the rest of it, and what about a society of architects and cranks to see what could be rescued from the destruction? Michael in passionate agreement, but doesn't see what we could *do*, and he is too involved with the row about his new bus-station, as we with our plans for a new theatre, to start things going, though I know that sooner or later I'll do something shameful like writing to the papers or getting up on a soap-box and saying: 'Save what we have in Ireland before the last house in the last street in the last town has been swept away to make room for a bad cheap imitation of a bad expensive style and the whole country has become a parody of Coney Island that will frighten all but holiday campers away and so not be even of commercial advantage to anyone.' And then, remembering Davis's verses about Ireland, having been so long a province, becoming a Nation Once Again, and Yeats's lines on Easter, 1916, I shall say:

> All changed, changed utterly,
> A terrible suburb is born,

and go on to demand how, in what architecturally is a poor period anyway, we hope to save anything at all except by the hoarding up of the bits that remain to us. And then I knew I was becoming A BORE, so we talked about his bus-station and our theatre and the film.

Have noticed a not unnatural tendency in Dublin to say 'When are we going to see this *Othello*?' or 'Isn't that picture finished Yet?' or 'Why are you being so Long about it?' and find it impossible to answer these questions except by saying 'Well, Orson is continually having to raise some more money, and when he has got what he wants in Italy we're going back there to finish it, but God knows when you'll see it because even the Moroccan sequences aren't done with yet and sooner or later we'll have to go back to Mogador and get down to it, and when we've finished with Italy and Morocco there'll be some dubbing to do in London, and then the music, and then the cutting, and by the time that's done there'll probably be another war and you'll never see it at all.'

My God! wouldn't it be ghastly if that were true? Seven months of work and travel without end amen, and nothing to show for it but a lot of rubber stamp-marks in a passport.

OCTOBER 16TH

Wire from Orson, and a second one *urgentissimo* from Giorgio Pappi: I have to go to Italy to-morrow. Hilton not wanted for about three weeks, so I travel alone. Endless appointments put off, Arthur has spent the day flying up and down with clothes, Rachel, who seems to have grasped the fact of my departure, is in a condition of outraged dignity at being once more abandoned and has already turned her attentions, with ostentatious parade of devotion, from me to Hilton, also to Winnie Menary, who lunched to-day and promises to take her (Rachel) back to Earlsfort Terrace when Hilton leaves.

My own nature, as cat-like in its easy settling into the rut of locality as Rachel's, is full of regret at being once again torn away, especially in this deep amber and blue of October, with the leaves burning in the garden and a wilderness of Michaelmas daisies under the chestnuts. We went to Howth to-day to say good-bye, ate several pounds of blackberries, and came back with bright purple mouths.

VITERBO. OCTOBER 17TH

Left Dublin at indescribable hour for Viterbo near Rome. Morning a haze of mellow October sunshine as I drove away with sorrow from partner, secretary, domestics, and Queen of Siam, accompanied by manager Raymond and Old Pal Tiger, to find even the airport looking festive in a glow of sunshine; Collinstown with its new washed air of innocent surprise, and Northolt at midday with sort of determined nonchalance. That well-trained English Can-I-help-you-sir routine is fascinating. There is no attempt to express a personal impulse, it is as abstract as Bovril and gives the same sense of well-being. Large car drove through a town called Hayes to London airport; the chauffeur, a gaunt blond with a cloven neck and ears like jug handles, remarked that it had been a record summer and that this driving business was a bit of a change from the R.A.F. and no mistake, adding that he wouldn't mind coming over to Dublin and getting his teeth into a Nice juicy Steak, ha-ha. After this, conversation languished.

Heartrending scene of tigerish Jewish mamma departing from daughter and son-in-law was outmatched by Restrained one of elderly English lady leaving with tears her gigantic and embarrassed offspring with cavalry moustaches, who said repeatedly: 'I say, do buck up, Mother, you'll be Bright as a Button once you're in Teheran'—which not unsurprisingly failed to convince her. Other passengers included minute Maharajah with British secretary, exotic-looking couple who quarrelled softly and unceasingly in four languages, one of which I couldn't place, probably Persian, and beaming Canadian lady who assured me I didn't know her (quite true) but that she lived in Toronto and knew me well *from the front*, to which I, naturally, had no answer ready, though several occurred to me during ensuing flight. Usual deafness descended as the Alps were skirted, accompanied by equally familiar homesickness, and I began to wonder (*a*) if there was any reason why elaborate Shakespeare film, once having started, should ever necessarily be finished; (*b*) why Orson had chosen Viterbo as next location (what was Viterbo to him or he to Viterbo?); (*c*) whether my Iago costume had been cleaned; and so on down to (*x*), which was whether I had gone deaf for life; (*y*) whether anyone would be at

Rome to meet me; and (z) whether, if I fell out of the plane, would anyone care? This conjured up wistful visions of (very short) appreciation appearing in *Irish Times* and other papers, and decided, after deep and distasteful reflections on their possibilities, I'd do better to write it myself (rather long). Thought a lot about this, and had got as far as 'And Ireland mourns the tragic end of this man of many parts who, in spite of certain faults in his life as in his work—' when, with usual sickening thud, we arrived.

Customs, although in traditional operatic confusion, most agreeable and Giorgio Pappi waiting for me with habitual smile as of lean and harassed young stag. Interminable drive through dark country roads came to an end at last in small ancient town at door of small newish hôtel; big bedroom with inevitable stone floor turning the feet to ice, and then the dining-room where the remnants of the company cheered my appearance with loud applause.

No sign of Orson or of Waschinsky (of Warsaw). I am told the former is in Rome and the latter in Tuscania, where shooting is to continue to-morrow and where he has found small but delightful villa in which he can be quiet. Miss both gentlemen badly but am enchanted to find Schnucks, looking very young and exhausted after long day's work, clad in a black dressing-gown and absent-mindedly eating octopus; also Brizzi, and two new American girls, Mary, the secretary, and Ruth, the script girl, both it seems charming. Also Gouzy of Berne, who still spends a lot of time agreeing with everybody with light but resonant jocularity in five languages. Eat a few octopuses in a dream, faintly distressed by recurrence of homesickness and also by incandescent Mauvish neon-strip Lighting so undeservedly popular in rural Italian interiors. Join in animated discussion on the gullibility of Othello, the fattening qualities of all the foodstuffs one enjoys most, the difficulty of obtaining hot water from the bathroom taps and the Arctic temperature of the little eleventh-century church at Tuscania where work is being carried on. Schnucks at this gives dolorous sniff and murmurs something about anti-grippine tablets (very subdued: what's wrong?) and the conversation turns on cosmic subjects such as Is Life Worth While? We resolve to leave decision on this till results of *Othello* are known to the world, and go to bed. Call for 10 a.m. in Tuscania, dressed and made-up. Delighted it's so late.

OCTOBER 18TH

Rose, in spite of late call, at seven, and at nine drove to Tuscania about 15 kilometres away, through gentle country haunted by cypress and olive and drenched in rain. Reflected sardonically on Ireland's brilliant sunshine (had breakfast in the garden at home yesterday) as compared with this Mediterranean gloom, and feeling of nausea, caused no doubt by drinking too much of the national liqueur known as Strega last night, swept over me. Location (eleventh-century church) superb: an enormous gloomy beauty falling, not very slowly, into decay. Schnucks (already on the spot and made up with deep salmon-coloured face, heliotrope lashes and elaborate Renaissance hair-do, but dressed in slacks and woollen cardigan) spoke feelingly of French-Canadian home, apparently of unsurpassed luxury, where at this very moment Maman would be regaling large family of adorable brothers and sisters with Lucullan dainties in atmosphere of central heating and crackling log fire.

Appearance of Orson (dragging forbearance about him like a cloak as he emerged wild-eyed from a car in heavy garments suggesting an Eskimo chief) put a stop to all this; and together we inspected the crypt below the church, which is like a forest of twenty-eight slender columns, supporting low arched and vaulted roof. Orson said I must rest to-day as he will be shooting with Schnucks and won't need me till nightfall, and why did I leave my bed in Viterbo to come to

Tuscania? Why indeed? I wonder, emerging with him into thick, fast-falling rain, and why, if I wasn't wanted to work at once, was Giorgio's wire for me so urgent? At this moment observed Waschinsky wading towards me in purple and green check shirt, leather jacket and corduroy trousers tucked into high suède boots, and the depths of a bad cold, which made his ponderous laughing face more like a benignant character in a Gogol story than ever.

'Why you no come and rest in my Villa, Micheál?' he asked in his booming Polish basso profundo, and went on to say in German that his room was untidy and probably reeking with the germs of *grippe* but that I was welcome to it. So the rest of the morning passed in slumber in the Villa, which turned out to be bright yellow maisonette with chickens and pigeons clucking and cooing among antique statues in the garden, and bedroom containing the most comfortable bed I have experienced. Read excellent short story by E. F. Benson called 'Pirates', realised that Orson was being more than considerate, wire or no wire, and slept for an hour. Woke at twelve-thirty and started to write this. Still raining.

Later. Lunch in the town in a small shuttered restaurant of lugubrious aspect separated by doorway and steel-beaded curtain from café full of workmen engaged on coffee, red wine, cards, and the national pastime of screaming at each other in melodious, wounded, heroic, light baritone voices. Good food but passionate refusal to supply any vegetable but chicory salad. We, being quality, are discreetly led through steel-beaded curtains to back room hung about with photographs of relations Obviously Deceased (cannot tell how one knows this but one does). Our table contained Orson, Waschinsky, Suzanne-Schnucks and myself. At the next Gouzy (of Berne) in terrifying form, and, on Orson's disappearance (for he regards fruit with aversion and has swift way with coffee), she began throwing bread pellets at Italian

echnicians, who responded with gusto. Room immediately
n uproar of Italian, German, English, and French. Gouzy,
ow petunia in the face but still unvanquished, disappeared
vaving *Othello* script like a flag, and we returned to the
:hurch in two cars followed by every child in the village all
elling 'Viva gli artisti!' to encourage us.

At six-thirty was made up by de Rossi, stouter and rosier
han ever and wearing the same beret, bewigged by Vasco
f Rimini, clothed and dressed by self as Iago (*hadn't* been
:leaned). Tunic and tights decidedly damp; set in an uproar;
ntire crew yelling, shouting to each other for help, cut-
ieces for shadow effects hammered into their places, lights
oing dazzlingly up and down. A brief scene of Iago watch-
ng Desdemona disconsolately sitting on enormous stone
taircase after being struck in the face by Othello, and of
tealing catlike away, was rehearsed about seven times in
letail by Orson. 'No lines in this, so you needn't tax that
oor old brain'—and at eight we shoot it nine times. After
ong interval of readjustment we do a close-up of same action;
he taking of stills occupies another half-hour, and at last
Orson says '*Buona sera*' and, still dressed in his Othello
:lothes (leather jerkin, black tights, long white burnous and
:hocolate-coloured make-up), disappears. I go to unsavoury,
ce-cold corner to change and am about to hunt for my
rousers when I realise that everyone has followed Orson's
example and I am completely alone. The lights all go out,
ι door bangs far away, and I am a prisoner. I yell in Italian
for lights, trousers, and a little companionship. After ten
ninutes of growing panic, during which trousers are dis-
:overed, glimmer of light is perceived and beaming electrician
:omes into view with torch, but assures me all the cars have
returned to Viterbo. Nobody, he says, would dream of dressing in damp, dangerous, and probably haunted church. As he
speaks large portions of the roof fall clattering on the marble
pavement. Outside the rain falls with soft hissing sound.

After what seemed an hour but was really only five minutes the car appears containing Gouzy (whose idea it was to return), Schnucks, and the two American beauties. All the boys, says Gouzy, are in the *other* car, except Walter of Parma, who is sympathetic about my plight. We return, I in that sort of rage that actors get in when nobody fusses over them, and are all soothed by dinner and an array of wine bottles.

Later. To my great surprise Orson had fled from haunted church not to go to Rome but to come back to Viterbo to dine. When it was over we sat together over coffee and a bottle of brandy and the others slowly disappeared. Alone, like Hilton, he is always at his best, and soon we were in the depths of one of those impractical and seemingly profitless talks that are among the best things friendship has to offer. Starting, as far as I can remember, with the universe as a whole, thus at once reversing usual order of such talks, we speedily dismissed it as unworthy of attention and, floating lightly over such themes as the Bible, the art of acting, the American language, black magic, the Church, cooking, women, hares, bad luck, bull-fighting, and clowns, came at last to now completely bemused speculation about existence of Golden Age, especially Golden Age of England. (Why England? Neither O. nor I, American and Irish spirit of independence in full swing in emancipated Latin atmosphere, cared one way or the other about England, but to-night she put up a sudden war-worn finger pointing for once to a forgotten past.) No such time as the Golden Age, we agreed earnestly, had ever *physically* existed, Merrie England being but a memory dreamed by the Forest People (Orson's title for Celts, Teutons, and all the wandering barbarians of the North), and this being but a portion of their answer, the answer of Northern Europe, to the Mediterranean leit-motif which dreamed of death in cypress and marble. A great dark Being like a bird, O. assured me, hung brooding over the

Mediterranean; she was Death, the Goddess, the malevolent womb; the mother of the caves, the vineyards, and the hills, a Medea, the Eumenides her messengers; Spain alone, I thought, preserving her spirit in the modern world. In the North, the Forest People searched for light: Ireland had found the Land of the Young, England her fabulous Merrie Self. (Cackles of regretful laughter from us both.) But it was always a memory, it had never been a pragmatical fact. Even in Chaucer's day it was imagined as a thing of the past; the oak trees and the flowering chestnut, the Maypole, the lambs, the lads and lasses, the garlands of flowers, formed one great Moment of mysterious gaiety in time, in space, and only the oak trees and the flowering chestnuts remembered truly. I saw for that great Day a slow wearing out into twilight—not a Celtic one, a gnarled, queer, Saxon affair— a brownish twilight haunted by monstrous haystacks, oast-houses, owls, rushlights in latticed windows, by nightcapped heads, whispering voices, drooping fogs, toadstools, growing under the deadly nightshade in the ditch, rank meadow-sweet, forgotten hay-cocks, drifts of dead leaves, gnarled hands that gathered sticks to light a fire—haunted, in short, by Witchcraft.

At this word O. grew suspicious, ruminating no doubt on some experience of his own, and remarked that witches to him weren't English things any more than olives were, and we started to talk of Italy and of Personal Matters, ending the (now deeply diminished) brandy bottle with a suggestion from him that if 'Our Islands' (he meant Ireland and Britain) *really* wanted to save gas and therefore money, a law should be passed by which no cook or housewife should be allowed to boil vegetables for more than five minutes, thus ensuring eatable food (for a change) and several million pounds worth of gas per annum. Was so staggered by brilliance of this that there seemed nothing more to say, and have come to bed.

OCTOBER 19TH

Call for eleven this morning: was grateful, as exhaustion followed conversation of last night. On the set at Tuscania at ten to be made up for shooting at eleven, but no need as there'll be no scenes for me till after lunch. Sun has come out with an almost audible rush and entire countryside transformed.

Spent morning walking all over large village of Tuscania, which, after the manner of all such things in Italy, is of incredible beauty and dates from Etruscan days to late Renaissance when it stopped, very wisely, dead. Only modern things are monument to last war: naked young man in dejected attitude in the middle of small piazza overhanging green ravine and river, and some ruins caused by bombardments of '45. Women saunter about the streets with straw bags, men huddle in groups and melodiously shout their views on life, the round autumn sun blazes down on balustrades, fountains, faded awnings, piles of fruit and vegetables, vine-shaded balconies carved in stone. I like it all so much I want to do something about it, and sympathise with those ladies, mainly aunts, who haunt such places with camp-stools and produce home-made water-colours.

Shooting for me begins at two: we resume the jealousy scene (begun last June on the battlements of Mogador) in small subterranean chamber furnished with unerring taste by Trauner, who moves calmly and with a gently cynical benevolence among a seething mass of Roman technicians adding last touches. Passage chosen is from 'I see this has a little dashed your spirits' down to 'My Lord, I see you're moved'. This is accompanied by much business of Iago's relieving Othello of steel armlets and gigantic cloak; Othello moves up small staircase to landing in order to stare at own black face in Carpaccio mirror for the line 'and yet how nature, erring from itself—'; camera gets view at this moment of back of Othello's head and reflection of face in mirror with Iago staring up at him from below stairs. We rehearsed perhaps a dozen times. Interval while lights are reset, make-ups (now in advanced state of decay) seen to by de Rossi, and wigs combed, patted, pulled and twitched by Vasco, who is like good-natured gadfly, has hawk's eyes, and is incapable of leaving anyone's hair or wig alone for more than forty seconds. Shooting pursues its habitual wild way. In shot one cloak refuses to part from Othello's shoulder—shot two, I stumble on hidden electric cable—shot three, I enter too slowly—shot four, the light goes wrong—shot five, O. feels pace too fast—shot six, I'm *acting* it, not *thinking* it—shot seven, O. thinks he was overplaying, didn't Waschinsky agree? No, Waschinsky thought '*Perfekt, aber* perhaps too much push down eyebrows—so—and Micheál—so——' (Polish chin and lips thrust forward in depressingly good imitation of my worst habits.) Didn't *I* think O. was overplaying? No. (The real Truth: was far too absorbed in own miseries, to notice) Shot eight, Fly walked across Othello's nose (*Flit per piacere, Flit, Dio mio, Flit!!!*). Flit is applied with a passion only known south of the Alps; we all choke and gasp; flies dart merrily out of sight. Shot thirteen, ironic-ally, was the lucky one. Test; still; reverse positions; change lights; new angles; de Rossi and Vasco resume their fell work on us, and the whole process is gone through again.

Schnucks is the next victim and is reported missing, but soon discovered fast asleep (ruining salmon and heliotrope face) on pile of mattresses in remote corner of church. She is hauled away for repairs and I take her place on lumpy mat-tress. Extreme difficulty of writing propped up on one elbow fills me with thoughts of long refreshing sleep.

Later. Long refreshing sleep was not encouraged by sudden determination of staff to hammer like blazes at walls, ceiling and scaffolding in crypt below. Or indeed by crowd of small local children who had stolen into church to observe me and called sweetly 'Carlo! Carlo! Carlo!' Deep disappointment on discovering that I was neither Chas. Boyer, Chas. Laughton, or Chas. Chaplin; seemingly many bets were lost. Work resumed on further fragment of jealousy scene: this lasted till ten-thirty, when I returned with Waschinsky in his car to dine in Viterbo. He recited favourite poems in Polish and I, not to be outdone in musical but incomprehensible sounds, took refuge in Love Songs of Connacht: both of us delighted with each other's suffering countries.

OCTOBER 20TH

Work all day in Tuscania. Disconcerting decision forms in my mind that while it is true that the camera can read the actor's thoughts, it frequently misinterprets them, and continues to do its relentless work out loud.

OCTOBER 21ST

Tuscania. Work all day. Mattress moved to still remoter corner of church, but found it out and slept. Informed Schnucks and Mischa Waschinsky. O. has no time for sleep and never seems to need any.

OCTOBER 22ND

Schnucks, looking rested and radiant, in terrific form at dinner in Tuscania last night. (She'd had the mattress most of the evening.) She was always a *strange* girl, she informed us—well perhaps not *strange*, but not like *other* girls. That was her trouble, she simply wasn't like *other* girls. She knew she had looks—heaven knew she had little else. . . . Long pause for contradiction, but we continued to eat our delicious veal. . . . Well, looks meant nothing to Schnucks. Or men. Or any of Those Things. She just wanted to find the Truth. That was all. The Truth about just Everything. It was so simple. She was not interested in trying to charm people, yet babies and dogs always formed the most *absurd* attachment to her. Wasn't it silly? What she *mostly* wanted, however, she went on, was, of course, a mother's love. As a matter of fact she prayed untiringly (in two languages) for Maman to abandon Ottawa and fly to her side. She also cabled, when she had any money to do so. (Close-up expression now directed towards Orson and Giorgio.) But Maman—dear, wonderful Maman—was entirely occupied with brothers and sisters, all of whom are models of beauty, intelligence and moral perfection. One sister is a nun. She, Schnucks, wished also to be a nun (here Waschinsky snorted and mixed a large salad smelling of garlic), but this was not to be; all the same she *knew*, she was certain, that Maman loved her. Didn't we feel it too? Well, didn't we?

This, not unnaturally, plunged us all into profound yet fidgety gloom, but Orson lifted large, taurine, slightly blood-shot eyes and began to inform her in almost caressing tones that she was too *big* a girl to say things like this any longer and that it was, indeed, high time for her to remember that she had Teeth in her mouth, and plenty of them, and could bite on life quite hard if she chose. What was more, con-tinued O., warming to his subject and pouring out tumblers of red wine all round the table, how dared she attempt to get away with that sort of baby stuff to grown-up people who had to work for their livings? 'Don't you realise, you great, big, cosmic mass of uncompromising egocentricity, that if you are foolish enough to wish to impress an adult audience with the assumption of an attitude that has nothing whatever to do with the facts about yourself, you could conceivably find better models for style than stories from the Girls' Own Library or their probably inferior French equivalents? And another thing,' he went on before she could answer, spearing a large piece of Gorgonzola and popping it into his mouth, 'if I were your Maman, I should be heartily glad to have you way over the other side of the Atlantic doing your proper work, which I now pay you the inestimable compliment of telling you is Movie-Acting, so shut up about your Maman and your everything else, for if you felt as you wish us to think you feel, you'd never talk about it so easily. What is more, you are conspicuously Failing to hold your Audience.'

This bracing speech, received by us all in silence, produced the astonishing answer from a totally unmoved Schnucks that such an attitude 'Suited her Appearance'. To this diamond of sophistication, unmistakable as the mumps, we gasped.

'Why that's terrible, Suzanne,' cried Ruth, who is of an earnest and judiciary nature, but O. lifted his glass.

'I'LL drink to that,' he said gravely, and we all did while Schnucks, looking prettier than ever, said with immense tolerance and a very slightly French accent: 'He can't understand, you see. I'm sure you and Monsieur Hilton would.' And had there been some Sweet Posies in a bowl on the table she would undoubtedly have bent over and kissed them.

Reflected silently that Monsieur H. would probably have had an even severer attitude to such echoes from the works of Florence Barclay and Mrs. Henry Wood than Monsieur O., but said aloud that we all had a Little Nell or Little Lord Fauntleroy (as the case might be) side to our nature and very pleasant it could be too; which sent Orson off to further eloquence about my 'fatal and misleading *Kindness*' which, if Schnucks allowed herself to take the smallest advantage of it by such activities as leaning, sheltering, cushioning, propping, refuging or drugging, would have a lastingly injurious effect on her career. As for Monsieur Hilton, well, perhaps Schnucks would change her mind about Monsieur Hilton (well-known as a Tyrant) when he arrived in Italy. Meanwhile the name was Edwards, and Schnucks should not expect to gain supporters by prefixing Monsieur to a Christian name, as that remark about her appearance stamped her indubitably for what she was, the Wolf Disguised as Red Riding Hood: no one who had heard it could swallow the

'Dear Little Suzanne' myth any longer; she was forever
Schnucks the Invincible, terrible as an army with (or even
without) banners.

This over, we returned to the crypt for a further three
hours' work on reverse shots and on the way home Suzanne
decided in my ear that 'ce pauvre Orson' was really 'trop
drôle' and that what he *really* wanted was 'l'amour d'une
brave femme'.

OCTOBER 23RD

The whole day free. Tuscania now a thing of the past, and
small thirteenth-century round church in Viterbo (disused)
being decorated for bedchamber where strangling of Desdemona takes place. (Hope, in view of last night, that all will
end happily in this direction.) Schnucks returned from Mass
in bouncing form to reset green button eyes in large black
rag doll which has been mauled by minute yapping dog
called Piccolino belonging to, and totally neglected by, Mary
Alcaide, Orson's secretary, who tells me she has kind of lost
her religion and is busily seeking a new one.

Went round before lunch to see setting for strangling of
Desdemona in disused chapel of Santa Maria della Salute.
Superb, with inlaid Carpaccio bed like the one in the vision
of St. Ursula, slender pillars supporting canopy in olive
green and dull crimson with gold tassels, Trauner at his best.

O., his hair being curled by Vasco, stopped shouting orders
to the staff in order to tell me story of idea for farcical comedy
about the Borgias with really wonderful business of poisoned
Banquet. Schnucks looking ravishing in shell pink nightdress
with minute smocking and embroidery. Agonising business
of making her cry included onions and salts of ammonia and
lasted for hours. She finally did it unaided.

Later. I'm on my way to Rome to dine with Waschinsky
and Countess de Fraso, whom I met at the Lido in the
summer. O. says don't hurry back as I'll not be needed until

Tuesday. Ample-bosomed landscape is dyed in saffron light
as the sun goes down to a bed of rose and cobalt cloud
behind olive trees and brown broken towers, but train too
bumpy to write.

Later still. Back in Viterbo . . . Waschinsky flung open the
door of his Roman apartment saying 'We go straight back.
I must *quite* annul Dorothy de Fraso' (he meant cancel) 'and
now we eat some liddle tiny ting and go back. Orson wants
me for conference, and you work early to-morrow. I am quite
disgusted, I svear you.'

We ate some liddle thing, which turned out to be superb
soup followed by Polish eggs with anchovies, Wodka, veal,
salad and cheese, then fruit, coffee and more Wodka. All
this consumed more in sorrow than in anger, and then were
driven across Rome, away over the river and down the long
black country roads marked with white stones, also white
aprons painted on tree trunks, through thick fog, by Angelo
the driver, who suffers from a delicate heart contracted in war
service in Russia, and who groans a good deal. To counteract
these heartrending sounds we turned on the radio and were
regaled through the fog with superb orchestra from Milan
playing *Don Giovanni*.

OCTOBER 24TH

Orson forgot appointment with Waschinsky, so our return
rush to Viterbo pointless. I, however, did work this morning: nine o'clock found me on steps of Palazzo Papale, half
ruined by time and bombs, but still imposing. (I refer to
Palazzo, not to self, though indeed parallel might be drawn.)
Scene was reverse of Othello's entrance from castle to stop
fight between Cassio and Roderigo—'How comes it, Michael,
you are thus forgot?' Original version (favouring Michael
Laurence as Cassio, Jean Davis as Montano and me as
Iago) was taken in Safi three months ago, so scene as
enjoyed, we hope, by Large International Public on screen,

will be one half Moorish July and the other half Italian
October.

Poor Gouzy, wrapped in scarves of divers colours that
made her look like a gay little haberdasher's window, had
mislaid one of her many reference books, and awful continuity problem arose: was I carrying short stick in Safi shot
or was I not? Final decision: I was. Shot prepared. Usual
pandemonium—Did I, accompanied by trusty pals, Cassio
and Montano, enter camera Right or Left? Gouzy, minus
reference, now completely demoralised and takes refuge in
Swiss dialect in which she mumbles curses, first to herself
and then to the universe at large, causing meanwhile violent
storm of papers to fly round her head as she ransacks large
attaché case. Orson, pacing up and down Renaissance steps
like stout black Puma in frilled shirt and military boots, stops
to ask her which *is* she, honey, a Continuity Girl or just a
Great Big Swiss Cow? 'Great Big Continuity Girl,' says
Gouzy, with a bright smile, hunting more madly than before.
Reference book finally discovered in other case on top of
sound machine: we entered camera *Left* and must now, therefore, be camera *Right*. Gouzy, protesting she knew this all
along, produces large sausage sandwich which she proceeds
to devour, saying '*Gott! meine arme Nerven!*' between mouthfuls and rearranges attaché case; shooting is about to begin
when sun disappears behind vast grey cloud. Hordes of
Viterbo natives grouped enthusiastically round Piazza (with
police to hold them back) give way to passionate wailing at
the sight, but cheer encouragingly on reappearance of golden
radiance.

Lunch not available until three-thirty.

OCTOBER 25TH

My birthday. Mischa Waschinsky, the only one who knew
it, appeared in my room during breakfast with a handsome
silk handkerchief and packet of cigarettes; many wires from

home. Broke a tooth on incredible piece of toast resembling Rock of Cashel; felt this must be an Evil Omen. Lisped and whistled my way through lunch. Painful afternoon at country dentist resulted in synthetic addition to buccal furnishings which I feel may (and probably will) fly out at any moment. Ruth and Mary, charming American girls, learning of birthday from Waschinsky, presented me with sweets and drinks and sang 'Happy Birthday, dear Micheál' at dinner to-night. Was genuinely touched, and confirmed in opinion (resented by O. as condescending, which it isn't) that Americans are far kinder and friendlier than Europeans.

OCTOBER 26TH

Hilton arrives to-night.

Was driven to Rome by Angelo, as Orson, always considerate, thought I'd like to meet him, and Waschinsky lent his car. Narrowly missed death several times as many Roman drivers (not Angelo) rank speed far higher than life. To pass time while waiting for plane I bought some ties and socks, then had Turkish bath, then tea alone at W.'s flat, which is kept in enviably perfect condition by pearl of a parlourmaid, and full of luxurious pieces, Polish, French, and Italian, that betray sumptuous and somewhat regal taste, and was finally driven to airport of Ciampino. This full of yelling international hordes including several Mongolian-looking officers in American uniform talking pure Brooklynese, who swarmed around the bar where I gave Angelo coffee and he enlarged in respectful and deprecating tones on nerve and heart troubles contracted in Russia, and on depressing reaction of these on his wife.

Sometimes, said Angelo, he was so nervous, and his heart fluttered so much, that things simply *flew* out of his hands on to the floor. And this always happened, Angelo added darkly, when he ate *spaghetti*. It simply flew Off the plate and On to the floor; and that was what depressed poor Maria, who cooked it superbly with mushrooms. (Could only hope the driver's wheel would not follow the example of the spaghetti, but said nothing about it.)

These gloomy reflections at last interrupted by announcement of arrival of the plane from Paris, and there was Hilton in brand-new overcoat with my tweed one (very old) over his arm; bottle of Jameson for Orson, French cigarettes for me, and presents for Waschinsky and Schnucks. He declared the lot and didn't have to pay, customs official declaring, after brief glance at passport, that he adored artists and that they *always* bought each other presents, this, he added, being part of their *charm*.

We dined at midnight (for customs procedure agreeable but interminable) in deserted Neapolitan restaurant illuminated and decorated as sad sea-grotto and inlaid with views of Capri and Amalfi. Sad fat gentleman played sad Neapolitan airs on piano while sad fat wife accompanied him on violin, which she played into our ears with throbbing passion and handfuls of wrong notes. Finally rejoined Angelo, still brooding over Russian experiences, and drove to Viterbo. Everyone had gone to bed and we crept thoughtfully up stone stairs to our rooms accompanied by entire hotel staff in night clothes carrying luggage and rendering our tiptoe technique negligible by vivid epithets hurled at each other in ringing dialect.

OCTOBER 27TH

Still in Viterbo. Murder scene (Othello *v.* Desdemona) continues in Santa Maria della Salute; my only work here being concerned with out-door shooting, and weather having decided on cloudy mood interspersed with brisk showers, I am more or less idle. Endeavour to get back to work on new comedy for Dublin: synopsis complete, or so I had imagined, but dissatisfied on re-reading and must change a lot; good situation but central theme cluttered and flimsy. Can surely do better than this at my age? (Or can I?)

Hilton and Orson, at every spare moment and in every available corner of set, street, café, or hotel, discourse with broad Roman gesticulations on forthcoming production of *Julius Caesar*: these discussions continue in dining-room after work is over till the small hours. When that is over H. always ready to discuss future Dublin plans with me. Energy of both H. and O. quite overwhelming, and capacity for cigars and red wine nothing short of scandalous. Am reminded of envoi to H.'s favourite joke in ancient edition of Punch: 'Collapse of Stout Party,' and predict this end for both Stout Parties if they don't curb themselves. H. enchanted with Viterbo but can talk of nothing but (*a*) camera angles on ancient Roman streets and (*b*) effect on Irish public of enormous apron-stage coupled with re-opening of Dublin season next year, with Orson as Othello or Emperor Jones or both.

OCTOBER 29TH

Stout Party No. 1, I mean Orson, has had partial collapse and warned by doctor not to smoke any more, as heart anything but satisfactory. (Red wine not mentioned, but coffee taboo.) I nobly resisted saying, not I told you so, but I told my diary so. Poor O. very dejected, and sinister rumour afloat that a rest of three weeks has been indicated. Schnucks also informed she has enlarged heart, and gave lurid descriptions at lunch of doctor's emotional reactions on beholding her X-ray, she, however, remaining aloof, fatalistic, and resigned.

Walked down with two Stout Parties to seat of action this afternoon. O. in better spirits and tells us what I find irresistible story, that Fascist salute was not, as is commonly believed, revived from old Roman custom by Mussolini or Hitler, but simply the invention of Mr. Cecil B. de Mille in super production of *Quo Vadis* to give ten thousand extras simple and effective business with Arm: this subsequently much admired by Muss. and Hit. (who presumably visited cinema together and decided to adopt it).

ROME. OCTOBER 30TH

Lightning-like and inexplicable decision last night to abandon Viterbo for Rome caused panic-stricken conversation at very late dinner. All methods for the unravelling of problems called into use through metres of spaghetti, from elementary Sherlock Holmes methods to elaborate psycho-analysis of the already absent Orson, who had wisely driven away from us all to Eternal City in full Othello make-up having finished shots of the settling of Schnucks's hash in round church at Viterbo. Schnucks again advanced theory of his Deep, Deep Restlessness of Soul; this scornfully discarded by other members of company, and cynical suggestion made that (a) he was fed up with country life and cooking and with so much running in and out of dazzling metropolis, and (b) that picture had really Collapsed and that Rome was a better centre in which to disperse us all than small country town. Hilton and I, during these impassioned scenes that took the form (and indeed the sound) of a satanic litany, preserved dignified silence as befitted our years, and all were ready this morning at eleven-thirty. Driven through simmering autumn sunshine—'Oh, honey, don't you just *adore* Fall?' screamed Mary, Ruth and Schnucks in intervals between discussion of Life, Love, and Art—and finally arrived in Rome. Installed after some difficulty in old haunt at Ambasciatori on Via Veneto.

Lunch over, H. decided on short but refreshing nap, and I on walk (similar adjectives) through Borghese Gardens. Was amazed on way through Via Veneto to see Orson and Giorgio (more like surprised and youthful stag than ever) taking coffee outside Rosati's. Was invited to join them and informed that we were going to Venice to-night (if by train, to-morrow if we preferred plane). Decided, in spite of terrors of deafness, dizziness, and ultimate probable destruction, on latter means of transport, and, after long healthy exhausting walk among pine trees in blazing sunshine, returned to tell Hilton. He had unpacked, even to the last sock, but received news stoically. Date for lunch with John O'Flynn of Co. Tipperary and Vatican City, already arranged, postponed with regrets, and am now retiring to bed amid a wilderness of quasi-unpacked luggage.

Meanwhile, Schnucks and other girls vanished in mid-air, though Mary Alcaide turned up to-night with American companion (male) for dinner: should she, she wonders, be Adventurous and stay with O., braving discomforts of Morocco and even worse, or should she, seeing what Kind of a Girl she Is (have no idea what that may be) follow her Hunch and quit Right Now? Finding Mary enchanting, I enlarge, accompanied by surprisingly passionate and admiring support from American male companion, on strange wild charms (though plumbing admittedly poor) of Morocco.

VENICE. OCTOBER 31ST

To-night is Hallow-e'en, and Venice a queer sort of place to spend it in. Hilton and I ordered a rum omelette *flambée* to celebrate and ate a few nuts, thinking fondly of home. I decided that, while Viterbo was full of hauntings and of witchcraft, Venice seemed to know nothing of such things, concerning herself always with elegantly diplomatic relations with the next world as with this, but I may of course be wrong here. Who knows what may have gone on in those twisted back-streets and dimly lighted water-fronts, where the shop-windows now are stacked with figs and cheese and chestnuts and bright novelties in wool and fur and silk and embroidered cloth and all the attractions of autumn?

Flight here uneventful, except that Schnucks felt ill and

decided during break at Padua to continue journey to Venice
in taxi. O. also left plane at Padua, murmuring something
about Verona ('Verona for a while I take my leave to see my
friends in Padua'), but turned up later here in Venice, looking very gay, saying there was no money for anyone anywhere, and ordering *fine champagne* and other delicacies all
round. He remembered suddenly it was the anniversary of
his famous Martian broadcast in New York and assured me
this was originally planned as Hallow-e'en joke.

Shooting begins to-morrow at seven-thirty—I wonder will
it be seven-thirty?—with Hilton as Brabantio in first take.
Schnucks to begin at eight—I wonder will it be eight? My
call not till nine—I wonder will it be nine?

Was sad to leave Rome looking so languorous and Roman
in apricot-coloured sunshine this morning, but glad to see
Venice again, cold, wave-ridden, echoing to the sound of
bells and distant footsteps and the lapping of water on
marble, inexorably beautiful in the mirrored autumn twilight.

NOVEMBER 1ST

I was right, and my call was not at relatively civilised
hour of nine. Was wrenched from fascinating dream about
Miss Margaret—Beauty Prize—Lawler (whom I have never
met) rehearsing for *Julius Caesar* with Hilton and Margaret
Burke-Sheridan (whom I certainly have met) by frenzied
waiter carrying rattling tray of *caffè completo*, and accompanied by Venetian boy of bird-like aspect and vocal equip-
ment called Sergio, whom I remember dressing me in
Venice last August, and being spoilt and screamed at equally
by self and Fay Compton, for whom he used to bring
coffee (invariably ice-cold and mainly in saucer by the time
it arrived). On asking the time, I was informed it was
six-forty-five and that Signor Welles had changed his mind
and that I was to shoot first. Had dismal shave and bath in
clouds of steaming self-pity, and descended dressed as Iago,

with modern trousers over tights and Renaissance boots, and heavy tweed coat (thank God H. brought it after all) over jerkin—to icy Palazzo Ducale to find Schnucks and Hilton sitting with chattering teeth on steps amid dire confusion. Orson greeted me by saying 'Good morning, dearest Micheál, and why are *you* here?' to which I could only reply 'Because you sent for me.'

'There is no need for you at the moment, nor will there be, probably, for hours,' said O. in a bright and disinfectant voice calculated rather to brace than to soothe, and I spent the rest of the morning jumping madly up and down among a crowd of extras, trying to keep warm while the sun crept slowly over incomparable fifteenth-century court and H. and Schnucks shot several scenes.

No break for lunch, and we were a God-send to hundreds of Venetians, deprived by autumnal weather of usual tourist diversions, and who had to be kept back by policemen and ropes. Was neither made up nor bewigged till four-thirty, when sudden inspiration of obviously Demoniac Origin caused O. to make us walk several times across large stretch of piazza on series of kitchen tables (for sake of angles) outside San Marco, accompanied by hundreds of pigeons, whose fluttering above our heads he encouraged by having handfuls of maize flung in the air. This combination of spectacular novelties moved Venetians to cheer softly—a mild and agreeable people who, I am informed by O., have never known revolution except for a couple of exciting nights during Risorgimento, and who, as I remember personally, were the only people in Italy in whose presence one was not frightened to talk English during Mussolini's heyday (Venetians, like sailors, apparently don't care). One woman in the front of the multitude begged me to shake hands with her baby son aged ten months, adding a tactful *Viva l'Irlanda!* as she did so. Delightful people: I tremble to think of reactions, cynical or bellicose, of inhabitants of many cities I could name at spectacle of foreign mummers wandering across kitchen tables and preventing them from taking favourite evening promenade.

These shots the only work I did to-day, but came back to hotel, accompanied by the bird-like Sergio, exhausted. Waschinsky dined with us and told us stories of Poland.

NOVEMBER 3RD

Working too hard to write. Freezing in the Palazzo Ducale and still more so in Ca' d'Oro. Long-distance shots in vogue with scores of male extras; teeth all clattering together with cold.

Hear that Michael Laurence has arrived to-night to make new shot of Cassio, also Nicholas Bruce to resume part of Lodovico, and am delighted. Hoping for news of Dublin from Michael and of his mother from Nicholas, as she is the immortal Karsavina whom I am promised I may meet some day. I'm hoping both these boys brought Antarctic clothes with them, as Venice, though the sun blazes down in great splendour, is more petrifying than anything I can remember except Switzerland and Canada.

Orson to-day gave me superb book of Canaletto Acquaforti, and Hilton history of Caesarian Rome. Dined succulently with dear Waschinsky to-night on *fritto misto*, *goulasch*, and fresh asparagus (where in God's name do they grow this?). W. gave inspired imitation of Pola Negri in villa near Paris ordering colour of bed of tulips (visible from window of her boudoir) to be changed from day to day, and accusing the gardeners, with the gestures of Phèdre, of plotting for her downfall—'Red tulips—this means blood! CHANGE! . . . White—this is for me a funeral, they want me die! CHANGE! . . . Mauve—they find now I growing old! CHANGE!' Mild Venetian waiters so overcome by this impassioned performance they cowered against the wall and one of them upset large dish of prawns over indignant French customer (elderly, male, and, like Victoria, not amused), who immediately left the building. Am now very tired, and must be up at six-thirty.

NOVEMBER 7TH

The work so hard these last days there has been no moment free from shooting in icy Doge's Palace and totally congealed Ca' d'Oro (or from ensuing total exhaustion) in which to write. As always on these days of intensive activity, most of the time is passed by the artists in sitting in full make-up and costume awaiting the sudden signal to shoot: much of this is passed by Hilton, Schnucks, and myself, our numbers now reinforced by Michael Laurence and Nicholas Bruce (both of them agreeably full of scandals from English and Irish capital cities), in small and dim, but relatively warm, offices of the guardians of civic monuments. The November Sun, having passed those muffled moments of the early morning which witnessed our shivering arrival from the motor-boat (the call being generally for seven-thirty), streams down over the Doge's Palace on to immemorial marble of great stairway with its two guardian statues (well over life size) and august arcaded court; beyond the carved walls rise up the domes of St. Mark's surmounted by spiked clusters of golden globes that gleam against a sky growing deeper, richer, azure as the day crawls past. At noon the cannon is fired and the pigeons rise in multitudinous grey and pearl flight, then return to their scattered meal of maize, provided chiefly by tourists. Orson has taken undying loathing to the pigeons, and when not using them for shots (which he frequently does, in spite of angry old Venetian gentleman who assures us that they didn't come to Venice till eighteenth century) abuses them and sometimes chases them up and down the piazza, hurling transatlantic insults after them. The extras, attired as soldiers, senators, and body-guards, leap, dance, skip, beat their chests with their clenched fists, or, when young enough, rush up and down to keep warm whenever there's a free moment, and we, having pursued the same sketchy exercises for an hour or two, retire to the lodge to read, or write letters, or talk abstractions. At one we eat hard-boiled eggs and pears and drink red wine; Sergio, who dresses me, is sent away for coffee; and work, with its attendant jumping and arm-waving, is resumed at two. At the Ca' d'Oro the same process: here, in the lodge, there is the added excitement of a small stove which must be fed with logs, also of a sun-drenched loggia overlooking Grand Canal and continually flooded by it. All through these days the indescribable beauty and grace of Italy makes life much more than bearable; things are helped too by extreme friendliness of everyone and by excellence of Italian coffee, but most of all by the sun. ('Give me the Sun, Mother, Give me the Sun.') To-day all is changed and the rain pours down, falling with a faint hissing sound into the water, turning the rose-coloured palaces with their black and olive shutters into grey silhouettes that melt sadly into the sky, and crowding the deserted tarpaulin-covered gondolas under the bridges. The streets bob darkly with umbrellas and the people pick their way over the uneven stone and marble in galoshes; these unusual conditions produce a queer form of despairing friendliness and everyone smiles with vague pitying expressions at everyone else as they splash in and out of puddles with ejaculations of '*Mama mia, che tempaccio! Fa attenzione alle pozzanghere, cara mia—Madonna! Sono annegato!*'

Hilton and I are free, which is lucky, as both of us in the throes of colds; H. much worse than I and spends entire day in bed reading Suetonius on life in Ancient Rome and Granville Barker on the art of the theatre. Admire this purposeful spirit, but after brief and excitable walk through town, bewitched by spectacle of Piazza San Marco under nearly two feet of water which mirrors shivering, sodden beauties of mosaics and gilded domes and incongruous El Greco sky in black and grey, and of plank bridge extended from Café dei Quaddri ˙on one arcaded side to the famous Florian's on the other; can think of nothing, in spite of wistful glance at New Comedy (on which I should indubitably be working), but warm dressing-gown and book of ghost stories.

NOVEMBER 8TH

Telephone call last night from Architect Michael Scott, who is in Milan. H. and I persuade him to come for a day to Venice, and I'm hoping he'll arrive to-day. How these fashionable Dublin architects get about. Am experiencing faint hopes that Venetian style will have strong influence on old and sensitive friend and that we may yet see O'Connell Street in noble Arcades. What more suitable to Irish needs than arcaded streets? Perfect for average weather for reasons too obvious to mention, and would also provide shade for more rare occasions when entire population is stricken by appearance of shy sunshine known to them as Desperate Heat. ('Janey Mac I'm boilin'! Looka, you know what it is, I'm gaspin'! Oh thanks be to God for them Scotty arcades!') Am agog, as they say, for news of Dublin (Michael Laurence's stock of this having been duly plucked, roasted, and eaten) and for tidings of our future theatre plans, and feel Michael S.'s visit, if he gets here, should be interesting.

No work to-day for anyone till after lunch, and even then not for H. or me. Hotel so empty that they're cutting off heating on the mezzanine where we now are and moving us to rooms on the second floor. H. not at all well and so full of theories as to cause of malaise (varying from incipient leprosy to softening of the brain—actually it is a bad cold) that I have phoned for doctor, though he was in bouncing form last night and conducted spirited conversation with Orson on the Inequality of the Sexes. According to H. and

O., women have invented Nothing—not even hats, the best designers being men—but I demur and point to Comedy. Am convinced that first laughter ever heard in the Cave Days was from a lady, and picture her stitching away at bearskin pants and laughing in surprised, naïve fashion at husband's absurdities with lady in adjoining cave. Merely, said O. with great bitterness, at moment when husband tripped on stone-age equivalent of banana skin. Women's humour was like that, insisted O., not merely rudimentary but rude. H. added further jibes and said that women may have invented belittlement but not much more. I stick to my comedy theory and go happily to bed. Trip on imitation marble floor as I take off my trousers, and am very glad no women are present to prove O.'s cynicism justified.

NOVEMBER 10TH

Arrival of Michael Scott last night, stepping (appropriately enough) from gondola straight into lounge bar where we are all recovering from day's work. Schnucks, curled up in a corner of the sofa and looking ravishing, regarded him over top of tall infantile lemon-squash and decided that his face was *gentil, mais bien triste. Une mélancholie de Celte*, she finished triumphantly, before sweeping off to bed and black rag doll. Regarded Michael's familiar Sanscrit hair, putty-coloured features and oyster-shell eyes in these unfamiliar surroundings and saw Schnucks had hit nail on head. He was breathless with admiration (as well he might have been) of journey in gondola from station to hotel; the back canals dimly luminous with starlight and lamplight and eight centuries of architectural masterpieces leaning over dark water. Took him for a walk to see St. Mark's, and found, in spite of his cries of astonishment and delight at seeing fantastic jewelled domes and frontage glimmering faintly across deserted square and flanked by lace-like casket of the Doge's Palace, that he was starving, so gave him *goulasch* and red wine in small restaurant in the Spadaria. Received enormous pleasure to observe staggering effect of Venetian genius on his architect's soul as we came home. (Have I soul of Cook's Guide? Probably.)

Michael Laurence and Nicholas Bruce still in the bar on our return, and beckoned us vivaciously to their gin-fizzy sides. I exercised commendable will power in refusing to drink with them all, as call this morning was eight o'clock on set (Doge's Palace) dressed and made up, and left M., who was weak and willing, to their mercies. My work this morning brief, and consisted of one short shot (seven takes) in the middle of the Piazza, balanced on fourteen-foot-high scaffold with overfed pigeons flying past my head, pursued by loud jibes from Orson. This shot taken from all angles, and then returned to hotel and long discussion of Dublin plans for the future with H. and M. Scott.

NOVEMBER 11TH

We for our part make brief shots in Doge's Palace. Confusion reigns owing to Hilton's deciding on lightning flight to London for business purposes; all bags packed and ticket as far as Milan in hand. Arrival of wire from London at very last minute fortunately rendered journey unnecessary, so he unpacked again. The two other Irish Michaels, Scott and Laurence, have departed, the Cassio shots having been at last completed. Orson, leaning over bridge in early morning mist, spied their gondola passing beneath him and shouted, 'Where are you two Harps going at this hour?' to which they yelled back the one word 'Ireland' and, waving their Rolled Up umbrellas, vanished from his sight. He, of course, not slow to appreciate almost Wagnerian effect of this simplicity of statement in Venetian dawn.

Rumours afoot that we may be shooting Senate scenes in Perugia as, oddly enough, nothing that is available in Venice is thought suitable either by Orson or Trauner. O., clothed from head to foot in deep black (shirt and all) which gives him air of Habima Hamlet, is leaving to-night.

Long walk through the town with Nicholas and Hilton. N. has been shopping with Schnucks and says how tiresome women (even the prettiest, in fact especially the prettiest) can be. They can never see any article of clothing they don't want to buy and they then spend hours making up their mind about it and further hours regretting purchase. We all agree, how *tiresome* and how *typical*, and, suddenly observing wonderful ties on stall near Rialto, we spend at least an hour choosing them, and buy six each. Mine all dazzlingly beautiful and totally unsuited to any single article of clothing in wardrobe, most of which is still in Dublin anyway. This trivial incident leads to dismal reflections on equality of the sexes which, as I have always suspected, is No ambitious feminine fancy but merest statement of Humiliating Fact, reflecting credit on no member of human race, male or female.

NOVEMBER 14TH

Orson has gone to Perugia to spy out possibilities for Senate. Bade farewell, leaving Waschinsky and Fanto, new cameraman, laden with instructions for work in his absence, on perfect night that might have been summer, followed by blue and gold day, during which we took counter shots round and about the Ca' d'Oro. Narrow street, which leads from large and busy thoroughfare to steamer and gondola stage, very difficult to work in, and shots constantly ruined by indignant citizens who not unnaturally wish to catch their steamers. Mishap succeeds mishap as scene, shot in bright midday sunshine, was supposed to be Misty Dawn, so smoke torches were lit and excitedly waved to and fro by Roman staff to give correct impression, and indignant citizens, convinced that their own or their friends' houses were on fire, became more indignant than ever and suggested phoning fire station. On learning their fears were unfounded, their Indignation passed into Fury. This feeling not assuaged by the sight of me in sinister dark-red wig with fringe, sulphur-coloured make-up, and high laced boots, charging out of Ca' d'Oro brandishing large sword; but on beholding Schnucks, who looked rhapsodic in ivory gossamer with golden tresses streaming down her back, they cheered up and murmured 'Bellissima'. (All this sort of thing very bad for Schnucks, though she ought to be, and probably is, used to Italian susceptibility by this time.) At end of gruelling morning—Waschinsky and Fanto grand—we were informed film itself was of imperfect quality and all would have to be re-done. Shrieks of dismay from Fanto in Hungarian, English, French, and German, neatly translated into Italian by Gouzy of Berne and Casablanca (busily devouring sausages and hot chestnuts shared by us all), to the effect that the light was no longer any good and further work to-day was impossible. Waschinsky made a call for some scenes on the morrow, and the rest of the afternoon passed in talking Russian Ballet with Nicholas; occasional ejaculations from Our Darling Schnucks of how she lóved Everything Russian except Communists and had read the Brothers Karamazov in secret at The Convent.

NOVEMBER 15TH

Venice once more shrouded in rain. No work possible. Nostalgia descends overwhelmingly as I remember the old days the Gate, Coralie and Meriel and Betty and the rest of them, and the Purcell music for *The Provok'd Wife* and the Grieg concerto for *Brand*. Confide these sentiments to Hilton, who replies by saying in bronchial voice (cold still on) 'Well, who wanted to make a film?' Decide that, what with *Othello* now and *Caesar* to come, filming will never be over, and that if we ever play on a real stage in Dublin again it will be a miracle.

Later. Have determined to accomplish miracle.

NOVEMBER 17TH

Two days of brilliant icy sunshine; shot bits and pieces with Waschinsky, in Orson's absence, still directing, at Ca' d'Oro (where we caught fresh colds) and Fish Market, where, amid reek of newly-caught and still twitching, wriggling crabs, eels, and other dainties, we attracted enormous crowds and achieved several set-ups, and, as Waschinsky assures me 'some wery nice vork—I *svear* you thees is something marvelloos, thees big head from you, Mike, und der Hilton in en gondola who looks like en picture from der Veronese'.

Actor friend from Milan, Giancarlo Galassi-Beria, turned up with company called Il Carrozzone (which means The Waggon), playing in Teatro del Ridotto, doing Shakespeare and Goldoni and other things. Saw them last night do Goldoni's *Accidente Curioso*, delicious comedy done with great simplicity and humour. Giancarlo dined with us; and he said my *Ill Met By Moonlight* to be produced (in translation) in Milan in early spring. Famous actress for Catherine, and can't remember her name.

Last night Lea Padovani turned up—radiant as ever after London triumph in new picture. Her English unbelievably improved, and she and Schnucks gave superb performance at dinner of two Great Artists who, in spite of whips and scorns of time, and oppressors' wrongs (to say nothing of proud men's contumely), had remained unembittered, dewily simple and full of awe, and who, notwithstanding the triumphs earned by their lovely April's prime, had preserved an astonishing girlishness of heart and a boundless admiration of each other's beauties, talents, and goodness. This followed by departure of Nicholas, whose work as Lodovico is over (though he can't understand how or why, as at least three important speeches, he says, remain untouched). We accompanied him in gondola to station; usual rhapsodies over silent gliding motion through still black waters with golden puddles of lamplight and dim shuddering palaces. Half an hour's wait at station where exquisite Tabby Cat was kind to me, and where we all drank a great deal of cognac while Schnucks and Lea continued Superb Performance, enjoyed mainly by me and Nicholas, H. being absorbed by imaginary camera angles of canal.

MARSEILLES. NOVEMBER 20TH

Arrived in Marseilles the night before last, which was Friday: am about as certain of this as of anything else the last few days. Are we *en route* for Morocco? If not, decision to send us here as inexplicable (also as swift) as all other decisions have been since *Othello* started. Nocturnal journey in gondola to station in Venice repeated; this time it was our own luggage that was piled in the rear, and Hilton, Schnucks and I who were saying good-bye to Italy. Conventional misery at leaving the only entirely perfect city in Europe dealt with as we glided once more through darkened canals. Schnucks very pensive on the journey and did a good deal of work with Black Rag Doll. Journey lasted all night—we had sleepers and slept till nine—changed at Genoa (whose name, in English at any rate, still reminds me irresistibly of unpleasant cake much sought after in old-fashioned bun shops throughout British Islands); then continued relentlessly and without restaurant all next day. Train stopped at every station, including Monte Carlo, which revived usual memories; finally arrived, at what seemed long past midnight but was in fact nine-thirty, in Marseilles, had baths in pleasant airy pea-green suites, and dined. Were then phoned from Paris by Jean Davis, and informed we should be in Bordeaux. Why were we *not* in Bordeaux? No answer to this at all, as none of us had the faintest idea why we were in Marseilles, or indeed anywhere else, and said so, but were assured that the idea was some starting point for Mogador, and that the managers, true to their national character, must have muddled things. Slight depression resulting from this news not assuaged by hearing torrential and apparently tropical rain beating on windows. This continued all next day, and Schnucks wisely departed for Paris with determined expression, saying she required clothes and wished to see to her apartment and have her hair *fixed*. Waved at us with rag doll out of taxi window and disappeared.

Lunched and later dined at great risk of drowning in cheerful and expensive restaurants; several stimulating entertainments, including Cortot, Jouvet, and Opera Season, advertised all over the town for immediate Past also distant Future, but nothing on at the moment except movies, most of them seen by us already and all featuring Barbara Stanwyck, or Orson, or Mickey Rooney, dubbed into French.

To-day sun burst out in Provençal splendour; H. and I ate bouillabaisse for lunch and decided to cap this gesture to the conventions by pleasant trip to Château d'If. Embarked on small and extremely unpleasant boat, regaling each other the while with reminiscences of the first time we had read *Monte Cristo* (was there a second?) and of charm of Robert Donat's performance. We were then steered over heaving waves to putty-coloured rock island crowned with towers and bastions, but brazenly informed weather too rough to land, though other boats visibly landing with greatest ease.

Suppressed sigh of relief and gave vent to idiomatic ejaculation of disappointment, and on return to the mainland felt strongly inclined to warn fresh batch of passengers waiting at quay-side in a piercing draught that excursion was obvious hoax, but refrained. Telephone message from Nice on return to hotel: Julien Derode had left word that Orson was going to the Auberge de la Colombe d'Or at St. Paul de Vence near

Nice and wouldn't we join him there to-morrow? Orson wanted us to have a Real Rest. Felt grateful, said yes, and realised after ringing off to-morrow impossible, as I have arranged for doctor to syringe H.'s sinus, also for me to recover cheques from American Express lost in Venice or on train, and several other things. Rest of evening spent in trying unsuccessfully to contact Julien. Dined pleasantly on Frogs and forgot our troubles. Am now filled with grim determination, seeing lateness of date, to get home for Christmas, but feel sure Orson has plans for large Christmas tree in market-place at Mogador, entertainment probably to include brief but startling personal appearance of O. himself as Santa Claus.

ST. PAUL. NOVEMBER 21ST

Left Marseilles by train the day before yesterday, having accomplished visit to famous specialist who told us H. hadn't sinusitis but something else (name now forgotten by us both, which is a nuisance and source of bitter reproach from H. to me). Doctor then submitted him to lengthy and probably unsuccessful treatment; saw Italian film of *Bicycle Thieves*, which is magnificent, and ate several luscious meals. This, in spite of cooking standards being lower in South than in North of France, is the chief entertainment of Marseilles, where weather is very wet and streets in usual state of semi-repair as well as being littered by large damp fragments of posters torn from hoardings by citizens presumably in throes of passionate aesthetic and political prejudice. Our train swept past vineyards of Provence in glowing autumn colours of crimson, russet, amber, and madder-brown under enormous Turquoise Cup of a sky, with pine-covered hills and distant sugar-white peaks, which lifted our hearts. Julien Derode met us at Nice, took one good look at us and immediately Left for Paris. We climbed into the waiting car and drove up here to St. Paul, arriving in downpour of rain, also in time for tremendous welcome by Mary Alcaide, Eva Vogel, new secretary, Czech, very pretty, astonishingly Anglicised; also Fanto and Orson, the latter still in black and weighed down by the world's miseries but also in flashing form, a sort of Neronic gaiety in the midst of burning Rome. In this mood, a frequent one, he is a *fête champêtre* in a haunted valley, a thunderstorm (probably arranged by himself) rumbling ominously overhead. Burning Rome and thunderstorm images suggest themselves, I suppose, because a new blow seems likely to fall on us. O. has heard rumours, growing in volume and certainty, that *Caesar* idea has been already started in America, which would render the idea of our doing it in Egypt in January out of the question. Also, *Ulysses* to be done it seems in England: this too was in his plans for next year. He and Hilton plunged in a delirium of gloom and talk vaguely of *Salomé*, O. as Herod, H. directing, me as Jokanaan. (Will have to take figure seriously in hand if this comes off: 'How wasted he is!' No more risotto.) Later on H. and I stole out in order to forget these troubles and to inspect astonishing beauty of mediaeval town, twisted stone streets and fountains plashing in black night air, series of antiquary shops and general atmosphere of discreetly arranged turning to account of native charms. H. suddenly found a kinship between St. Paul and Kinsale at home and we both grew melancholy, thinking of French wisdom in preservation and of inbred neglect and indifference to such things in Ireland.

We have rooms here in the annexe, and I am told with awe that mine is the one occupied by André Gide in summer months and has also been slept in by Winston Churchill. Try to imagine effect on both these illustrious men of large woolly painting of dubious influence and intention representing muscular Lady in Mercury hat flying from small Riviera town (manifestly St. Paul itself) and bearing bouquet of pale blue flowers to other Lady clad in abbreviated orange négligé and sitting in expectant attitude on top of moonlit Eiffel Tower and other well-known Parisian landmarks; this occupies a lot of space over mirror on right-hand wall. (Fail to visualise reactions of either Winston or André.) One looks from the window over a garden filled with orange trees, cypress, and olives to main part of house; behind it wooded hills, and dipping down from its flanks a wide ravine with cactus, wild fig, and willows, bamboos, olives, and running streams: beyond that more hills and a range of snow-capped Alps. The sea is behind the annexe: to-day is brilliant and warm as summer. This hitch in a film that should have been finished weeks ago is maddening, but Orson has wonderful talent for finding superb setting for hitches.

This morning met Jacques Prévert, the poet. All went for a walk: Prévert charming, stocky, green-eyed, radiant and communicative. He jumped about a good deal, ate a few flowers, and gave me an elaborately printed handbook of the Joyce exhibition now on in Paris; also told me of a fall he had from a window last year—Prévert not Joyce—assuring me that he had been stone dead for several weeks and that it had all been most interesting. This the second person I've met lately who claims to have been dead and to have come back to life, the first being Fay Compton. Both Fay and Prévert seem enlivened by the experience, which I find cheering.

NOVEMBER 26TH

This delay fills us all with unrest: weather reflects our mood and the rain pours down. Went this evening for solitary walk and met parish priest, a small, elderly, lonely figure, who invited me to his house to drink a glass of home-brewed wine and told me he was a disappointed man as nobody in St. Paul went to Mass. Promised to go myself on Sunday and bring some friends, which appeared to cheer him.

Orson has departed, with Fanto in attendance, to Paris.

NOVEMBER 28TH

Went to Mass with Hilton and Eva Vogel, the Anglicised Czech. Reasonably large attendance, which most unreasonably irritated me, though I hope my better self was pleased. Had pictured three of us distinguished foreigners sitting in isolation as we listened to rapturous discourse on St. Francis or similar topic, instead of which I was wedged in behind large population of school children led in responses by determined lady in Mackintosh. (Why? Sunshine reigns unthreatened by a single cloud.) Was not recognised by priest, who stared at me coldly as he delivered lengthy and very cross sermon about Communism.

DECEMBER 1ST

Orson still in Paris and no news except that Eva has been sent for and has vanished, complete with impeccable Chelsea accent and several suitcases, and Mary Alcaide (young, pretty, Italophil, restless, American, and in advanced state of reaction against her own country and century, to both of which she does credit), dear Gouzy (who has added to girl-guide qualities the radiant and steadfast good nature of a wayside shrine, though without its *wistful* appeal, her note being one of Do but never Die), Hilton, and I are now, all four of us, in isolation on our mountain top. Sun blazes down on to orange trees gaudy with fruit, pink and yellow houses, cypress, cactus, beech-woods only just going golden, and all the more popular characteristics of Southern charm, but we are still *disturbed*, and are living as it were through nightmare in Paradise. I am working fitfully on new play.

DECEMBER 2ND

Life flutters and crawls. No news from Paris, but rumours of disaster hinted at by Gouzy, who is in telephonic touch with Julien Derode. Galaxy of sunshine atones for much.

Drive nearly every evening to Nice, where last night we heard Beethoven-Wagner concert. Well-chosen programme played with passionate individualism by orchestra all apparently at daggers drawn with each other and led in fits and starts by conductor who seemed to have little if any control over them. Were saluted by pleasant young man and sister from Dublin who asked when are we opening and is it true we're *still* doing *Othello*? H. asked them to lunch; there was no bus and they turned up to tea bringing blond male Swedish friend. Walked them all madly over village and then played superb game introduced by Orson before departure for Paris. One player goes out of the room (so far admittedly not entirely unknown method of beginning a game) and the others decide on a person known to all, either as individual mutual friend or world-famous figure, and questions then asked by absent player (now returned) as to what colours, food, sports, muses, clothes, and so on most nearly suggest this individual. Here is where the game is a little *different*, as answers must be extremely intelligent and somewhat surrealist (perhaps expressionist the better word). I mean it is bad form, for example, to say that the food for Puccini is necessarily spaghetti or that for Churchill roast beef; no, it must be the food that comes into the *mind* as one broods on their personalities. Hilton brilliant at guessing, and after hearing that the colour of the chosen person was silver and gold, the food black bread and the music a trumpet, said 'Would you personally cast Ingrid Bergman to play her?' and sure enough it was Joan of Arc.

So we pass our days, and Mary draws pictures of our activities to send to friends in Italy: me at the piano, Gouzy feeding the pigeons, Hilton with a pipe in his mouth, and herself being kicked in the company of Eva Vogel out of the best room in the annexe by Orson's boot to make way for me, an incident which occurred on the night of our arrival and which she and Eva, not unnaturally, have vividly remembered. Find despairingly that I am stuck in the play: H. suggests I write it first as a novel. Begin to wonder shall I ever write or act again.

DECEMBER 4TH

Days deep-dyed in sunshine; a cloudless sky smiles over our bitterness of *far niente*, the lemon and orange trees are laden with fruit, and there is no news of the outside world at all. Money has run short, but we are still driven to Nice by Caesar (a chauffeur and brother of Pierrot, the waiter), where we see films and drink brandy. Impressive teas occasionally taken in Negresco, which is almost completely deserted but wears usual air of arch Edwardian coquetry and has small and quite unbelievable string orchestra which plays *Kiss Me, Kate* as though it were Chaminade every evening. Mary has turned out to be militant balletomane, and has worked with Danilova and Astafieva. This provides deep solace; we compare notes and she even goes so far as to envy me my age because it has enabled me to have seen Nijinsky, Karsavina, and Pavlova.

DECEMBER 5TH

A call from Paris informs Gouzy that we go to Morocco on the 7th. Mary in despair and says she knows she'll hate the Arabs. Long lecture on the foolishness of prejudice, especially about places and people unknown, combined with vivacious description of the virtues and charms of these children of the Prophet. Well, maybe, says Mary, but what about the *plumbing*? The diabolical pertinency of this plunges us all into silence. Gouzy, apart from her enlightened defence of the Moorish nation, is in raptures, as her home is in Casablanca and she is, it seems, looking forward to seeing her Bees again. (Never knew she kept any, but she does, and indeed makes a lot of money out of them.) Hilton and I ready for Anything.

Later. Further news from Paris: we're *not* going to

Morocco, says Gouzy, her face still scarlet from communication with J. Derode, but somewhere she couldn't quite *hear*. Mild conjecture mingled with abuse of poor Gouzy's hearing and intelligence ensue: how *could* she, we all ask, hang up the receiver without being *sure*? She didn't hang up, protests Gouzy, as if she could possibly Do such a thing: she was *coupée*. 'Is that cut off?' says Mary, in a flat, wintry voice, and I say, 'Yes.' The name she couldn't grasp *might* have been Parma, continues Gouzy, looking flustered. Positions now completely reversed: Mary in Seventh Heaven ('if it can only be somewhere in Italy!'), and Gouzy sits brooding over her Bees. H. and I still ready for anything.

Later. Derode rang again and this time all is clear. *Not* Parma: Paris; and *not* Gouzy or Mary: just Hilton and me. News received with mingled emotions, and we all pack our bags and prepare for temporary separation.

PARIS. DECEMBER 7TH

Departure from St. Paul, looking radiant in golden afternoon, with Prévert and the others waving us off. I by far the saddest to go: but for its uncertainty, I found it enchanting. Farewells from Mary and Gouzy sincerely regretful, though we'll obviously meet again when *Othello* continues, but regret embroiled in sudden discovery by me that I'd left passport, cheques, and wallet in shop in Nice. On return they'd been handed to police. Long interview ended by getting them back; police charming, but so deliberately methodical we nearly missed Blue Train. Slept all the way in *wagon-lit* and were met this morning by dear Trauner, surrounded by vast aerial vision of Paris in bluish morning mist, very northern and remote from orange-tree landscape that had almost become a part of our visual habit. Trauner in high spirits, though full of financial woes, and looking like blond beneficent gnome as he gave us some money and drove us to the Royal in Montparnasse. Too exhausted, in spite of sleep in *wagon-lit*, to do a thing, but we're lunching with Orson to-morrow.

We still don't know any news.

DECEMBER 9TH

Paris drenched in rainstorms, iron-black naked trees shuddering in dun-coloured mists that go blue at twilight with golden lamps shining through. Am forced, not for the first time, to conviction that Paris is like description of Cecily in *The Importance of Being Earnest*, 'the visible personification of absolute perfection', under any conditions at all.

Hilton and Orson scream at each other all day long to their own great enjoyment. Their new topic, the fact that *Othello* once more on financial rocks—how like recurring nightmare this situation has become—has spurred O. to grand new scheme for six weeks' tour of *Importance of Being Earnest* (slightly cut) and Marlow's *Dr. Faustus* (exceedingly cut) to be performed on same night in such centres as Brussels, Antwerp, Lille, and Amsterdam. Hilton to direct *Earnest* and play Chasuble and Prologue; Orson to direct *Faustus* and play Algernon and Faustus; me to play Ernest and Mephistopheles; Schnucks Cecily and Helen of Troy, poor child; and Fay, if we can get her back, to be Lady Bracknell. Dior is to be asked to do dresses and Orson is going to Derain about décor.

O. and I awfully worked up about this and longing to trumpet about on a stage again; H. we find a little *sardonic*. His attitude in fact savours strongly of the darker side of Existentialism, but he is enthusiastic about me cutting *Earnest*, an operation I dread. Both he and O. believe that the more you cut out of a play the better it is, and I suggest, not without bitterness, that they would be better employed in Atomic Bomb Factory than in the theatre. These discussions fill up most of the day, after which O., pounding up and down the room with a gin fizz and continually colliding with H., who is doing the same with a mixed vermouth, suddenly rings for Eva and her typewriter and disappears to cut the tripes out of Marlowe; H. and I depart for the Rue de Rivoli, and at Smith's buy neat volume of *Earnest* with intention of doing similar work on poor Old Oscar.

DECEMBER 11TH

Spent morning cutting *Earnest*, and after lunch Hilton and I experienced keenest disappointment of the year by seeing Jean-Louis Barrault's *Hamlet* at the Marigny. 'Twenty-ish production, all ingenuity and grey tabs and set-pieces pulled and pushed hither and thither to indicate changes of location, and J-L.B. in the same mood, a slick, vivacious Puck of a Prince. H. cheered me up after the shock of the first court scene by muttering in my ear 'Harlequin, Prince of Denmark'; but general impression one of disillusion too deep for jokes: so fine an artist brilliantly engaged on so palpable a misconception. He treated the ghost as a leprechaun, and the friendship with Horatio as a mild Alma Mater flirtation, and Ophelia as if she were pestering him for an autograph. Saw dear Tanya Moiseiwitsch for a few minutes in an interval, came away early and dined with Orson, wild-eyed and in hell's-a-poppin' form.

Hilton gradually warming up to tour idea but confesses that the thought of Lille at Christmas time with himself playing Chasuble does not unconditionally enrapture him.

Took Eva, who looked drooping, to Folies Bergères, where La Baker is still appearing as Eve, Mary Queen of Scots, and her namesake the Empress (not to-night, Josephine), also in her best number, 'Minuit'. She has got rid of her cold but I thought gained a gramme or two in weight.

H. and I asked for our autographs in interval by group of

Bulgarian boxers, which puzzled us; they, it seems, had seen us play in Sofia in '39.

DECEMBER 12TH

Schnucks to lunch, in new and exquisite grey tailor-made. Informed us she felt a Woman Every Inch in it, and added pensively that it wasn't paid for, but that if she was to take Brussels by storm she *had* to have clothes. She evinced pleasure at idea of playing Cecily and skipped happily away to Smith's to purchase Wilde's collected plays.

DECEMBER 13TH

Saw for the second time this year Jouvet in *Knock*. H. enchanted and thinks it would *adapt* for Ireland better than straight translation. Worked all afternoon with Orson on touring plans.

DECEMBER 14TH

Forgot touring plans and worked for hours on plot for play *Alike in Dignity*. Am filled with apprehension when I realise that H. is right: so far it's a novel, not a play.

DECEMBER 15TH

My back, burnt to the bone on unprotected hot-air pipe in vapour bath a few days ago, gave so little trouble that I forgot I'd done it. It is now racking me with pain and the doctor tells me that this often happens with burns, the nerves are numbed for a few days and then revive and tell one all about it. Orson also in trouble: an admirer, overcome by his charms, dug enamelled Spanish thumb-nail into his hand (which she happened to be holding at the time) and poisoned it. This took place at a party in a night club in Montmartre, so what could he do? He couldn't very well say, 'Hey, let go, you're hurting me,' or 'Keep your talons to yourself, señora,' as I would have done, for like all people filled with intellectual scorn for The Sex he is a born Quixotic and the answer to all their prayers until he gets to know them. So now I have a plastered back and he a swollen and blackened finger, and we are fractious and glare alternately at each other and at Hilton (whom we find insufficiently sympathetic) as we work at new plans and feel we are envenomed for ever.

Date of our journey home for Christmas is now definitely fixed for the eighteenth and the tickets for direct journey Paris–Dublin are bought: we are both happy.

Later. Hilton's new plan, in case of rumours about *Caesar* causing this to fall through, is to adapt what we both consider fine novel of Dublin slums (identity to be kept a dead secret for a time) as movie, directed next summer by H., Orson to write the story and me the dialogue (Will authoress consent?). O., his finger now bearing strong resemblance to large purple golf-ball, lies prone under bedclothes without any pyjamas on, throwing long, stout, shapely, and still slightly sunburnt arms about (very bad for purple golf-ball) and bristling and bursting with ideas which he exhales in booming tones, and to which it appears to be bad form to contribute until he arrives at inextricable knot, when smouldering glances are cast first at H. and then at me and he says 'Now: what happens Next?'

A sort of story has begun to emerge; H. and I descend to salon to get it down on paper with aid of Eva, who eagerly covers sheets of paper with shorthand notes at Hilton's dictation, and we are too excited to sleep.

DECEMBER 16TH

Orson, in dark mood, declared that we had altered several points in his story, and that he must have Expressed himself badly. This always merest formality of expression: what he really means is that he has been Grossly misunderstood. He and H. strode up and down shouting at each other, then settled down into chairs at opposite corners of the room and continued to shout louder than ever; myself, sitting on (imitation) Louis XVI sofa, unable to do anything but follow them with my eyes like cat following strenuous game of ping-pong.

Sort of all-in wrestling match followed during which enormous area covered, including knowledge of Catholic dogma, human nature, sense of truth, public taste, avoidance of straining at gnats while swallowing camels, child psychology, understanding of Irish Temperament (passionate appeals to me on this which left me with firm conviction that there was no such thing as I.T.), dangers of generalisation, still greater dangers of being afraid to generalise, and so on. Ping-pong match at moments so abandoned my eyes nearly fell out of my head. Finally all was peace, with usual post-war accompaniment of exhaustion and bitter self-reproach by both parties. (O. much better at this than H., who is inclined to *simmer*, though O.'s claims during hostilities admittedly enough to make anyone simmer, let alone H.)

Evening ended with riotous dinner given by O., who helped me to caviare five times and said again that he was thinking of spending Christmas either in Dublin or Stockholm. Both of us pressed him warmly to come to Dublin, and I have visions of him carving turkey (cooked by Arthur as our cook Luke has left us, tired out no doubt with constant absence caused by this *Othello* business) with my aunt Craven.

Remarked, on watching strange, broad, squashed yet towering physiognomy and trying—not for the first time—to track its racial sources, that in Sweden if he went there, he would probably discover the land of his fathers. Frightful result: how *could* I, who had been so cherished by him all these years (and had moreover been given five helpings of caviare with his own hand at that very table and on that very occasion), think that he was, or could possibly be, a Square-Head? Unperturbably mentioned Vikings, Strindberg, Garbo, Miss Lagerloff, and many more, but he said, 'No: he was Anglo-Welsh-Illinois-Virginian pure and simple, and proud of it too, and was, moreover, completely *Latin* in his sympathies; and that if H. had called him Square-Head, now, he could have understood, as the British notoriously lacking in racial discrimination, but that for me of all people . . . Goddammit, it was the Goddamdest thing he'd ever heard Ever.' *Simmered* in fact for at least ten minutes, but cheered himself and us up with *pêches flambées* and we all bade a rapturous good night. (Swedish indeed! He'd remember that.)

DUBLIN. DECEMBER 18TH

We're back in Dublin. Aer Lingus hostess all kindness: at Bourget large party of homing and God-speeding diplomatists, including Seán Murphy, our Minister in Paris, Frank Aiken, Tim O'Driscoll, and James Crosby. Hilarious party in the bar. Conversation almost exclusively in language of Shakespeare, Shaw, and Queen Victoria (native tongue in evidence at approach of plane and accompanying farewells). De Valera was waiting at Collinstown to greet Frank A., and with him Maud, Frank's wife, whom I haven't seen for years, Dev and Maud beaming and very friendly. Raymond also waiting with taxi: Hilton's car, smashed in summer at Brignolles, now completely repaired and on its way home to be, I hope, sold for new one. Drove home through peerless indigo and pale-green evening smelling of rain-clouds and turf with moist stars appearing at first between naked thorn trees and later among chimney-pots, to be greeted at doorway by Arthur (in impeccable white coat), also by tea with scrambled eggs and fire. Arthur's brother Vernon has now Dublin job, and his wife and baby have gone to England for Christmas. V. will help A. with turkey, I hope.

Hilton pleased with house (thank God, the English having such hawk's eyes for most microscopic specks of dust which can and frequently do ruin pleasant evening). Winnie Menary and her two boys came round to welcome us, also Cathleen Delany looking radiant, Old Barty (Miss Ellen Barton according to travel permit) looking fragile, Bob Collis, Johnny, Tiger, Jim O'Brien, and others. Tendency of everyone, especially newspaper men who ring up at intervals, to say incredulously, 'Not *still* doing *Othello*,' to which neither H. nor I have more sparkling reply than 'Yes, we are.'

Card from Orson waiting for Hilton saying—Miss you badly already and hope for wonderful things in New Year. Large drawing of three hearts, O.'s signet, as the three vertical rods and three drops of black blood were Aubrey Beardsley's. Undeniably sweet side exists in O.'s nature.

Have finally confirmed long-growing suspicion that though travelling is the breath of life to me I'd rather be at home than anywhere in the world.

DECEMBER 24TH

Almost unbroken succession of friends and parties. Had lunch with Kate O'Brien back from New York, where her new play *That Lady* with Cornell had filthy press and is doing good business. Kate handsomer and grander than ever.

We have acquired new car called Humber Hawk (pale green) and in it went to visit my aunt Craven, also Shelah Richards, Jack Dunne, and others, and to-night shopped. Sacred annual mission to Moore Street accomplished, leaving car in large patch of trampled cabbage leaves while we bought holly, Christmas candle, and some ferocious ornaments for the Tree, also large bottle of Rum, as this year intended, as usual, to be what Tallulah Bankhead described in brief chat on the subject to Orson as A Real Old Fashioned Christmas.

Went home to our Christmas Eve party, into and out of which everyone in Dublin seemed to drop; very successful. Also joined by nieces Sally and Mary Rose; the latter slipped out to Midnight Mass and returned, looking elevated, to sleep on sofa by drawing-room fire with reinstated Siamese cat Rachel. Denis Johnston and Betty most expert and severely surrealist at new game taught us by Orson in St. Paul and now spreading wildly through Dublin. Erskine Childers a trifle Pragmatical in approach, but *sound*. (You know my methods, Watson.)

All the gin disappeared. Hope some Tavern or other will be open to-morrow.

DECEMBER 25TH

All went well (though overwhelmingly oversized turkey also slightly overcooked round legs in excitement and rather heartlessly christened St. Joan by Hilton). Everyone pleased with presents, also with lighted Tree (microscopic and wrong shape), which caught fire but caused no damage, and dear Barty gave us beautiful books of her own childhood in the '80's, illustrated by Walter Crane, Jacob Hood, and Kate Greenaway. Howth in the evening: McMaster cottage shut up owing to absence in Australia. Missed Mac and my sister Mana badly. Telephone talks with Marjory Hawtrey (London) and Orson (Paris). Marjory in almost Dickensian Christmas mood and thinks Life Worth While; O. in pain with his (Spanish Lady) hand, God help him.

JANUARY 1ST, 1950

Century, like self, growing old. Party at Carl Bonn's, wild bells a-pealing, everyone bristling with resolutions and busily kissing everyone else. Hope this spirit will continue but doubt it.

JANUARY 3RD

Beatrice Glenavy, Haggie Knight, and Norah McGuiness to lunch. Discussed J-P. Sartre, J. O'Dea, and the life to come, also Beatrice's son Paddy Campbell, whose mind she said she was surprised to hear me say I cannot grasp. (Don't believe she can either. His mind the kind that only the Public could fathom.) All of them delightful.

JANUARY 12TH

Weekend at the Oranmores' at Luggala in Wicklow. Savage drive over Feather-bed Mountain instead of prescribed Roundwood road (Arthur's suggestion; can he be plotting our destruction?) with hurricane howling in complete blackness overhead, ended in enthusiastic welcome from darling Oonagh (in slacks). Small house-party (in trousers, slacks, and skirts alternatively) including Dr. Bob Collis (trousers). Tendency to say, 'Still playing in that film?', with inevitable rider of, 'And when do we see you play again in Dublin?' undiminished.

JANUARY 14TH

Another party at the Oranmores', large party, no feminine slacks visible. Drove back this morning over Sally Gap in galaxy of wild sunshine, with an enormous wind whipping the clouds across inky mountains and three gigantic rainbows arching out of the sea.

JANUARY 15TH

Lynn Doyle to lunch. Talks, I think, better than he writes, and radiates good humour. Like his generation infinitely more than my own or the present one. Message from Orson, mad as the sea and wind and celebrating Nordic rites in Stockholm. Wants us in Mogador by the 20th at latest.

JANUARY 18TH

Parties. My back, now at healing stage, irritates appallingly; I spend every moment of solitude using doors as very old Bullocks use gates. Am continually being caught at this by strangers and have not yet learned how not to appear to be engaged in hideous and obscure Vice. Attempts to laugh things off in Gay nonchalant fashion only arouse deeper suspicions.

Johnny Finnegan to lunch: he thinks we're going to have another war and promises to let me know if it happens.

Must bid many farewells to-night; Arthur, deathly pale, is wearing worried expression that accompanies packing.

Later. No farewells possible as John D. Sheridan (writer and journalist, not Old Pal Johnny) and Georg Fleischmann (camera man), hearing of our departure, called up to remind me I had promised to speak Yeats's verse for Government Film of Yeats commemoration. Four solid hours of recording at Peter Hunt's studio, Hilton directing me. Invaluable: I understand Yeats better than he, but his knowledge of verse-speaking infinitely greater. Did *Innisfree* and *Sally Gardens* and *Stolen Child*, then *Red Hanrahan's Song*, *Ireland in the Coming Times*, and the finest lines from the Easter Week cycle. Exhausting but grand.

Faintly surprised at astonishment of non-actors on discovering our work is hard, and that we require a lot of help and don't mind getting it. Had the impression that J.D.S. and Georg F. thought I'd sail through between a few whiskeys with no bother, and that they were aghast at the number of readings neither Hilton nor I would let past. Many things I have consented to now fill me with horror: feel I've used too much tone. All the boys more than kind, and we parted with mutual esteem. Saw some of the rushes of the film (silent) the other day: Glencar, Ben Bulben, Knocknarea, and Lisadell. Very moving if they won't overburden it with musical score, or indeed with my voice or that of commentator. (Who will this be? At present unknown.) Moments of silence or of inarticulate sound will help—they should see and see again *Farrebique*, a masterpiece, with music in exactly the right places.

PART VI

January 20th to March 7th, 1950

MOGADOR. JANUARY 20TH, 1950 (*but probably, in fact certainly, 21st by now*)

LEFT Ireland in glowing winter sunshine: fog in London, but things seemingly far more prosperous there and people looking happier. Difficult to judge by Airports, but even these leave impressions. Ate British lunch of the 1939 order (pickles offered with *hors d'œuvres* and an array of puddings with fanciful titles designed to follow the meat, large Stilton to *follow* the puddings, an arrangement I cannot fathom); fruits, while making sensational appearance in beribboned baskets on sideboard, consumed by nobody. All however plentiful, also elaborately and cheerfully served by rather skittish waiter, who grinned and made respectful Pickwickian jokes with subtle air of one who knew his place but didn't see why he should stay in it.

Nobody to meet us in Paris but agreeable friend of Julien Derode's (Julien, it seems, already in Mogador), who handed us air tickets for Casablanca, and disappeared. Dinner at the Lancaster, everyone, including M. Wolf and head waiter, charming. At Invalides, the interminable Invalides, behold Schnucks appearing triumphantly through vast white arched hall, a small, misleadingly perplexed figure in long, misleadingly meek coat, also slacks, Existentialist hair-do, small suitcase and Black Rag Doll.

Enthusiastic greetings on both sides augmented by Jean Davis, who accompanied her, wearing smart belted *imperméable* with fur collar and looking as if he had dined terribly well; gave us some money and then said goodbye with habitual air of slightly preoccupied affection. Schnucks full of the story of her Paris adventures, grave and gay. These filled bus journey to Orly (with suitable ejaculations from H. and me), also portion of flight. This proved dull: no babies slung in hammocks, no fainting ladies: merely H. feeling unwell though not, happily, being it, and me taking sleeping pill which didn't work.

Strange sense of Eternity in relation to film of *Othello* overcame me as we alighted yet again at Casablanca: same patchwork of half-finished box-like houses, same shuttered windows, same smell of Morocco, half incense, half pepper.

Much later. Driven by Jean Gigonzac to Mogador through unexpectedly emerald green country under clouds, as Charlotte Brontë would have said, low and livid. Schnucks, after delighted cries at camels (never before glimpsed by her outside Zoo) and veiled women (never before glimpsed outside exotic number entitled *La Voilée Nue chez Hadji Baba* at Casino de Paris), subsided and read *Paris-Match*. Chief objects of interest during journey undoubtedly *were* the camels, padding through endless mud with habitual expression of refined nausea among small groups of jovial, blanketed Arabs, and on one occasion statuesque mother-camel regarding us for brief instant with displeasure through window of car and closely attended by wiry little foal. (Is it foal? Can't be?) Also several red-legged storks I had not noticed in summer, fields of geranium, and usual villages of saffron-coloured mud houses with conical straw huts in *déclassés* groups on outskirts. All this passing us at rate of 130 kilometres p.h., with frequent heavy showers dimming the noble violence of Moorish landscape.

On arrival in Mogador (not a stone altered, not a face changed, frantic display of welcome on all sides) we found that Orson was still in Marrakesh attended by Mary Alcaide and Gouzy (of Berne and Casablanca), so Schnucks, Hilton, and I began dinner alone. Soon joined however by Vasco (who has resumed slogan of explanatory 'Siamo in Africa!' uttered in tones of hopeless resignation), also James Allen, who is art-directing in absence of Trauner, and Patrice Dally, who replaces dear Waschinsky whom we miss (not for the

same reasons Macbeth missed Banquo). Patrice Dally, however (surely Paddy Daly in disguise?), a heavily built and
personable Frenchman who enjoys his food, speaks English,
and seems agreeable and friendly.

Rooms as they always were. I have number 7 previously
occupied by Bob Coote, so ghosts might mingle with shrieking in the square below, but all back rooms booked. Schnucks,
after one glance at number 5, having been told it was occupied by previous Desdemona, betook herself to Beau Rivage
next door. Rain pours down.

JANUARY 21ST

Back still peony-coloured. Rain still pours down. Sight of
Arabs in off-white and dun-coloured burnouses wading
through puddles not calculated to encourage.

JANUARY 22ND

Rain. Feel, in spite of Hilton's presence, homesick, and
wish we could get to work. Yet why homesick? Ireland, outside incomparable landscape and the houses of a few friends,
not the most attractive place in the world, being essentially
country of extremes. Her only reason for eight centuries of
struggle against occupation is profound consciousness of
existence in her soul of genius different from English genius,
but in the struggle she has lost whatever *talents* she may have
once possessed. Life with untalented genius apt to be strewn
with thorns: imitative architecture, ugly houses, dull food,
shabby dress, stupid regulations, nothing that is not copied
from elsewhere, inevitable model being despised conqueror,
little that is performed with distinction: little, in short, but
a grave and beautiful countryside, and from the air some
remote signalling, an essence, a perfume, a tune—what is it?
—that says 'Stay with me. Die for me. Tell my story.'

RABAT. JANUARY 23RD

Our despondency increases with every drop of rain that falls, and Julien Derode says: Why don't we, Hilton and Schnucks and I, betake ourselves to some place of interest, less familiar than Mogador, until Orson appears and work begins? The world, says Julien, is before us, and where would we like to go?

So we all decided on Fez, and here we are on the way to it.

Seen through streaming rain after a journey over endless mountains and yellow mud villages (also seen through streaming rain, Gigonzac driving us and bursting frequently into impassioned singing), Rabat, where we sleep to-night, seems large, glistening, French, and smart. Schnucks, nursing Black Rag Doll, gazed out of the window and said she had expected sunshine. Dined in great splendour and retired (back agonising) to bed.

FEZ. JANUARY 25TH

This is a fantastic city: white skeleton or white withered orchid, I'm not sure which. We are staying among the mountains at an hotel called the Palais Arabe, which lives up to its name by being in a style which I had always understood was purest Andalusian; patios and gardens full of orange trees, pomegranates, and lilies, a dazzling wilderness of ceramics all over the walls, coloured marble floors, dark cedar-wood furniture.

Schnucks has disappeared to make a motoring trip with a French gentleman and his wife, and Hilton and I are alone. Would be enjoying it far more if only I were well and if only the rain would stop. But I'm not, and it doesn't, so we splash about through the mountainous streets of the Arab town, which is indescribably beautiful if one admires skeletons and white orchids, which I do, though I find them macabre in the extreme and feel as though I were living in a pallid, gigantic Casket full of very old ivory chessmen uncannily endowed with the power of speech and movement. And everyone has a pale yellow face and looks ill, and the air is laden with sad perfumes of mud and wet spices and camel-dung and the floating fumes of joss-sticks, and in order to make one's way to mosques and market-places one leaps from rut to rut and from stone to stone as if one were crossing a river (which most of the time one is), and one's neck is being continually nuzzled by donkeys, mules, and camels.

JANUARY 26TH

Strange day spent with French professor of Arabic and with the Caid and his sons. They took us to see the sights, chief of these being the University, which is impressive and has a library full of ancient manuscripts: Moorish and Algerian classics and endless works translated from the Greek. The usual banquet followed and was held in a superb house overlooking a valley full of heliotrope-coloured rocks and crevices full of cactus and fern and wild flowers straight out of a Persian miniature; effect somewhat dimmed by sheets of rain.

Amusing Frenchman arrived at the hotel last night accompanied by famous American beauty covered in chunks of bar-baric gold and looking extremely wideawake with enormous black eyes like a gypsy, and we talked about films and New York and the life to come. They, like Schnucks, have now disappeared into the mountains, and are replaced by pleasant English doctor called Hemans, a descendant of the Boy who Stood on the Burning Deck, or rather of the poetess who celebrated him. We visited together the local *closerie d'amour* and found it much the same as the one at Marrakesh but rougher; the ladies dancing about as they rolled their burning eyes, their tatterdemalion dresses fished out of a bran tub, their pale mustard-coloured complexions and their make-up consisting of kohl and cochineal daubed over a sprinkling of Moles, are just as given to hissing and horseplay as their sisters in the south and very soon drove us back to the hotel through sheets of driving rain, our Virtue unblemished.

We have seen Fez at a disadvantage: this palsied ivory spectre sprawling over the mountains is patently one of the masterpieces of Islam; it has a vast panorama of forest and ravine, the finest mosques I have seen, the most entrancing streets, markets and shops, and the usual seething magnificence of squalor, as well as fabulous castles and fortresses and enough treasures to dazzle forty thousand of Ali Baba's thieves, but in order to enjoy these things one must feel well and one must have the Sun.

JANUARY 27TH

We have again pranced round the town, soaked to the skin, and have eaten yet another banquet; also visited doctor in the Ville Nouvelle, who informs me I have 'un peu d'excéma'. (What does he mean, 'un peu'?) Am now on a diet which forbids eggs, fish, spices, *asparagus* (why?) and alcohol, also am to have continual injections which make me feel as if I were being set on fire, which I probably am. Hilton the soul of patience and endeavour, but I know that if we don't get away quite soon, we will both be borne off in strait jackets.

CASABLANCA. JANUARY 28TH

Sunshine streamed over Fez as we left it after lunch, in a rickety taxi which took us to airport and contained, apart from our bags and ourselves, young and fidgety French lady entrusted to our special care by older version of herself who, we were at once informed by F.F.L., was her *belle-sœur*, being married—most happily—to Brother (Sonnez la Matine?) Jacques. F.F.L. didn't stop prattling or rattling (latter activity carried on with endless series of very small suitcases) until we got to Bus office in dried-up square near doctor's house in the Ville Nouvelle, where she sank into unpleasant-looking steel and leather chair and flapped her way through several ancient copies of *Marie Claire*. Waited at Bus office nearly two hours, spending time hovering between arid square containing four dusty palm trees and five shops (all closed), and reading Air-Atlas pamphlets. Suddenly bus appeared (obviously oldest and tiredest on the road, one felt a callous brute to ride in it at all) and we rattled away accompanied by series of explosions to airport, F.F.L. still opening and closing suitcases.

Plane rather empty, and pleasant Biblical view of barren hills with scattered villages (seen from angle of omnipotence). Descended at Rabat, where shoals of baby's prams were boarded accompanied by groups of excited ladies. Purpose of prams unknown but destination presumably same as our own. Casablanca reached at dusk: Doctor, immediately summoned to attend to H. suffering from bad stomach, turned out to be a Russian (I mean the doctor), consequently visit extremely conversational and prolonged. H.'s stomach completely forgotten, and evening ended by us all dining together at the Reine Pédauque, delighted with each other's company and that of Schnucks, who arrived at eight looking like Dresden Shepherdess and behaving like Schnucks.

Schnucks had been having the most Wonderful Time, Mister Hilton, with the loveliest friends—French husband (très distingué, tu sais, and of enormous influence in Morocco), and French-Canadian wife, and they had taken Schnucks all over the country in large and expensive car, and all the more noteworthy Pashas, Caids, and Sheiks had been most attentive —why, Schnucks simply couldn't imagine (nor, I'm sure, could Orson). She had also been most popular in the Harems, which her sex had allowed her, most fortunately, to visit (My Darling Schnucks). The wives—Ah ces pauvres femmes! si gentilles, si peu intellectuelles—une vie complètement vide, tu sais—had welcomed her rapturously and had dressed her

up in silks, velvets, and jewels, until Schnucks just didn't
know whether she was on her head or her heels. (Bet it was
on her heels.) Russian doctor proposed visit to Arab town to
see a little dancing after dinner. Knowing this performance
by now only too well—large draughty café like forsaken
lavatory with small stage at one end containing semi-circle
of males in various stages of decay attacking, at odd moments,
musical instruments of whose nature and use they seem to
have the flimsiest notion, and Occasional appearance of
buxom female in hazy edition of European dress with sequins
and paper flowers pinned on, waggling hips slowly and later
a little faster—knowing all this, we said, quite truthfully, that
we had an early call in the morning—car leaves for Mogador
at eight—and went to bed.

MOGADOR. JANUARY 29TH

Car call postponed till 3 p.m., so we had the morning to
ourselves. Collected Schnucks, whom we love—although I
do represent her in light of Iron Butterfly, which is true but
only partly—and visited markets and wonderful fairground.
The usual snake-charmers, readers of the Koran, trained
monkeys, storytellers, acrobats and dancers, but they still
fascinate me. One wretched man, a gentle, handsome-featured
giant from the country, had a solo number which included
a long pipe hung with coloured beads through which, between telling funny stories at which nobody laughed, he
played sad little tunes. Number was unprecedented flop
except for us, who lingered because we were sorry for him;
he held no one longer than a few seconds and squatted there
in the dust, a well-meaning, solitary figure. At last he put
away the bead pipe, rolled up his mat and rose to his feet,
towering above us all. We gave him some money and he said
something about Allah, and when he saw we didn't understand explained: 'C'est la vie—c'est le bon Dieu.'

Came away feeling that both he and le bon Dieu were being a little hard on each other.

Later. Mogador now its old self in glowing violet dusk after long drive, and Orson appeared at dinner in almost equal mood, also Mary Alcaide and Gouzy, both looking precisely the same, though Gouzy has acquired voluminous fur coat and emerald green foulard which she winds round her face, making her look more like a benevolent apple than ever, though why it should I don't know. Great reunion of the St. Paul Quartet, and we all agreed there was a lot to be said for the experience. Orson looking well but eyes *bloodshot*, so he's been worrying. We start work on Tuesday. (O. must be unaware of this or else have forgotten unshakable resolution never to start anything on Tuesday, this being considered unlucky day in Spain.)

JANUARY 31ST

Find that acting, even for films, is better than not acting at all.

Resumed work on portions of jealousy and epileptic scenes not completed in the summer:

> Marry patience,
> Or shall I say you're all in all in spleen
> And nothing of a man.

This simple snippet soon rendered inconceivably complicated by Orson, shamelessly aided and abetted by Hilton, who shares passion for Steps and the acrobatic twists and turns they demand. Me in steel greaves too, as legs visible to camera. Shooting was carried out in teeth of gale on flight of malodorous steps by the harbour and took up most of the morning, with addition of counter shots and close-ups of same sequence. The whole place haunted by ghosts of Doris (Bianca) Dowling, Bob (Roderigo) Coote and most of all by Michael (Cassio) Laurence, and by memories of merry laughing sequence between self and Cassio last July with background of unresponsive seagulls and Orson shouting 'Fish, Goddammit!' to bevy of shrieking Arabs.

I'm finding the work more and more manageable, and average number of shots before desired result obtained has been reduced from fifteen to six.

Visited Dr. Jean Ritter at hospital and was injected for my Back, which shows no sign of improvement. Ritter charming as ever but takes, to my mind, callously light-hearted view of my sufferings. Swears I haven't eczema at all but some light infection of a similar but less serious nature, and says the man in Fez is a fusser but if I like being injected why not humour me?

FEBRUARY 1ST

Work all day: a good day. O. at his best and we got a lot done. No time to return to hotel for lunch, so we Picnic. I like it better: mood not so shattered and much easier to get back to scenes.

Schnucks acted beautifully to-day in series of difficult frag-ments chiefly concerned with the reassuring of Cassio (Michael Laurence's back-view doubled by pleasant young Italian of same build) that she will do her best with Othello on his behalf, but she is depressed at not getting A Letter she Expects from Paris. This subject fills most of the con-versation between shots and is viewed exclusively from angle, not of what catastrophe may have overcome neglectful correspondent, but of *what* is it about *Schnucks* that seems to doom her to total abandonment, isolation, loneliness and tragedy? Why should it be so? What had she done? She whose life had been devoted to nothing but her art (*vissi d'arte, vissi d'amore*), what crime had she committed to deserve these cruel blows of fate? Life, Schnucks felt, was passing her by. Misunderstood, alone, too feeble to fight any more, she couldn't eat, she couldn't sleep. But for her religion she could easily imagine herself taking to drugs.

Felt concerned for her till lunch-time (repeated performance of successful picnic, Gouzy extremely active), when she criticised vulgar size and peasant simplicity of the sandwiches. After eating three at a blow, drinking half a bottle of Chambertin, and finishing with Camembert, two gargantuan pears and several cups of coffee, she leaned back against ancient Portuguese cannon looking more like Princess who slept on a Pea than ever and said her *real* trouble was her *heart*.

She had too *much* heart of course, that was her secret. She meant psychically speaking in the main, because she was, in the main, a psychical person. Sometimes she didn't believe she was of this earth at all, especially when her heartbeats made her feel she was nothing more or less than a *Bird*. All that was purely spiritual. As for the physical side, well, her heart was the wonder and despair of every specialist in Paris, to say nothing of Ottawa, Hollywood and other centres of learning.

'How is it possible,' they cried, 'that you can go *on*? How do you *do* it?' Well, to that Schnucks had nothing to say but 'It is my *will*.' And it was true. Her will was so indomitable, so strong. Even the Mother Superior at the Convent had always remarked that——

Sudden appearance of Orson and Hilton both fortified by pig, cheese, and wine and in no mood to stand any nonsense put an end to these musings; Hilton put her through her lines, paying much attention to French intonations and Canadian diphthongs; Vasco was summoned to her side to arrange her face; and she floated away to be assured that Othello could deny her nothing. Personally feel the same.

Worked till after six; deep saffron-coloured sunshine with the battlements casting immense blue shadows and the sea boiling below.

MARRAKESH. FEBRUARY 2ND

Hilton's birthday, and he received smart pair of gauntlet driving gloves and book from Orson with wonderful illustrated inscriptions; also enormous birthday cake with 'Happy Birthday Hilton' in iced sugar was presented (also by Orson) in the middle of the Place du Chayla outside the hotel. Very festive scene cutting this in setting of pale mauve twilight crowned by full moon; Arab children in their scores waiting for their slice, which they got. Sudden decision of Orson to drive us both to Marrakesh, so after long Day's work we threw pyjamas into small bags and were whirled through bushy, sandy, and rocky landscape (called Bléd) almost as bright as day. Intensely pretty Swedish girl waiting at the Mamounia at Marrakesh; hilarious dinner with champagne and kouskous gave us totally new and delightful views on life, and after coffee we all visited the Souks. I still like the town better than Fez. Spotted ivory-pale orchid gives place to enormous glowing pomegranate flower, and signs of distress and sickness, though visible, are less frequent.

Pretty Swedish girl emitted soft squeaks of surprise and delight at seething life, colours and smells of the bazaars; guides successfully shaken off; we visited Moorish cabaret which offered usual display. Find brief description, written by me in these pages a few days ago, uncannily accurate, if marred by sarcasm, and to-night observed new detail hitherto unnoticed. The dancers (three of them and all female) were garbed according to individual tastes, one in black net with red paper roses, another in electric blue (most trying to deep curry-coloured complexion) and the third, a little spotty, cheeks made up to resemble English pillar-box, in white with several bunches of what looked like dead Watercress pinned on here and there. While dancing, however, each wore over her frock species of Roman kilt made of stripes of material pendant from waist and heavily Encrusted, as Dorian Gray

would say, with puce sequins. Kilt was the same all through
and passed on, in friendliest fashion, when individual number
had been dealt with, to next performer.

Back began to burn, ache, and itch all at once; realised I
had drunk brandy as well as champagne, also eaten over-
spiced kouskous and that this was the punishment. Am now
much worse and not enjoying luxury of hotel as I should be.

MOGADOR. FEBRUARY 3RD

Rose at five and drove back to Mogador with Orson, leaving H. and Barbara, the pretty Swedish girl, behind us.
(Both of them, however, to follow us later as O. has an eye
on future film for her.)

Journey an interplanetary experience, with the sun rising
triumphantly over undulating ashen-coloured plain carved
like a piece of sculpture in the mingled light, for the full
moon was still high in the sky; Orson says this is because
we're nearer the equator. Very ill indeed on arrival and made
three shots of epileptic sequence in deep misery, then went
off to Jean Ritter, who took one look at my back, said 'Oh
la-la-*aaa!*' several times and with varying modulations, injected me as though he enjoyed doing it, and gave me a long
lecture on diet. Have resolved to live on herb-teas and
bananas from this out, and indeed have little spirit for
anything more.

FEBRUARY 5TH

Work has been in progress at port for last two days: link-
ups with scenes shot last July and mainly concerned with
reactions of Orson and self to arrival of Lodovico. This in
complete absence of Nick Bruce calls for much imagination;
the eyes, sweeping over the sea, reflecting momentary surprise at beholding advent of entire Venetian fleet, when all
they actually see is collection of wooden sheds, decayed fishing smacks, Hilton (returned in great vigour from Mogador

and accompanied by Belle of Stockholm) rushing up and down, cigar in mouth, and shouting in English to extras, Gouzy translating, between mouthfuls of sausage sandwiches, and hordes of delighted Arabs.

Before each take Orson goes through now inevitable ritual largely concerning my Carpaccio hat, never quite big enough for outsize head, and in absence of proper mirror invariably ridden up to jaunty angle suggestive neither of super-subtle Italian conspirator or of thwarted impotence. 'Now let's have a look. No, your hat's terrible. I'll fix it again. *There*. Now. See if you can hit those—wait a moment, there's a speck on your nose, that's better—see if you can hit those marks. Ready? Don't forget now; momentary surprise at sight of fleet: calculated as to effect on Othello: not too long a pause —none of your hornpipes—and down the steps fast. O.K. Let's shoot. Fanto, if the camera waggles I swear to God I'll strangle you with my own hands, you argumentative Central European. *Vai? Silenzio per favore.* Shut up! Hilton, can't you keep those cretins quiet? *Partito?* 842—Take One. Action!'

Eleven shots (that include O. tripping thrice over train of burnous, camera uncontrollably bouncing as it pans round to follow us, and self falling headlong down steps) finally result in '*Stampiamo con entusiasmo*' and test, during which greaves collapse and have to be borne off to ironmongers to be mended. Then break for lunch, consumed in fierce sunlit gale now blowing in from raging Atlantic and rendering long-waited-for shot of 'I lay with Cassio lately' out of question.

FEBRUARY 6TH

Work.

FEBRUARY 7TH

Work.

FEBRUARY 8TH

Work. Schnucks has decided Barbara the Belle of Stockholm is her soul-mate, and the three of them, Schnucks, Belle, and Mary Alcaide, have formed club called Marbarsu, object of which is obscure but includes a lot of whispering, gurgling, and other manifestations of rose-white girlhood. Orson and Hilton react with nausea and quote Nietzsche on Women.

Later. Sudden decision to leave Mogador for Safi tonight.

SAFI. FEBRUARY 9TH

Driven yesterday to Safi by Gigonzac, who quoted unknown French poets among which, we learned later, with much bridling and twirling of short Colemanesque moustache, he figures himself. Some of these set to tunes (also by himself) which, without overplus of pressure, he sang in pleasant if throaty light baritone. All occupants of car, including Schnucks and Hilton, soon drenched in *Hearts which beat among Pale Perfumed Twilights where were evoked halfclosed and palpitating Her Lips so Sad so Sweet* and other familiar fancies: strong influence of the earlier Pierre Louÿs and of Chaminade detectable in apparently inexhaustible répertoire.

Enthusiastic greeting at Hotel Marhaba; atmosphere of bar and lounge powerfully reminiscent of dear Fay, also of Waschinsky, Bob Coote, Michael and general *Stimmung* of nerve-strained white trash in Somerset Maugham play, and bedrooms evoked memories of H.'s pneumonia; but slept well and had pleasing dream that Gouzy was engaged to be married to President Truman. (Can this mean that Swiss–American alliance is imminent?)

Work much pleasanter in the Château than it was last summer owing to absence of flies, though sun quite as hot as in July, also preference of entire Arab population for every spot chosen for location as public toilet as marked as ever and as apparent to more senses than one. Also many shots spoiled to-day by constant appearance in portion of sky required for composition of glittering silver Plane.

Scene: view from ramparts over sea, with self in Big Head of Pola pouring poisonous phrase into Othello's Ear. (O. still in open shirt, and toilet now augmented by inch-thick layer of cold cream on nose and lips inclined to chap, also by coal black goggles: Ear unavailable. His double, agreeable fleshy giant acquired, like Mistress Emilia, in Mogador, and like her with us here in Safi, was disconsolate at not being allowed to stand in for this shot and persuaded Vasco, still muttering 'Siamo in Africa', to blacken side of his face, neck and ear, also to curl at least one side of his hair, but all to no avail.) Shot taken: I give superb performance, and silver Plane darts across the sky. Take it again: sun finds small but pitch-black cloud, hitherto, we can all swear to it, not in any part of the firmament, and hides behind it. Again: I am discovered to be looking camera *left*; it should be camera *right*. Passionate scene with Gouzy ensues. She makes strenuous protest and says 'No, left, Mr. Velles.' Is proved wrong and takes pensive refuge in muttering to Fanto and me in German and in large bag of macaroons which Orson absentmindedly takes from her, eats the lot, sniffs at the bag and says 'Where did these godawful things come from?' Mutterings pass from Hochdeutsch to Schweizer, Hilton comforts her with an apple, and we proceed. Again: superb performance fails to materialise. Unpleasing comments by O. making what Mr. Darlington said about my Hamlet seem unstinted, almost hysterical praise. Again: I am better, but something is *lacking*. (What, pray? Am convinced it was the only good one.) Again: large brand-new and glistening French battleship appears on the horizon just as I arrive at end of poisonous line, and seems inclined to anchor there for the rest of the day. Wait of half an hour. Again: my hat has descended to angle like that favoured by Frieda Jackson in *No Room at the Inn*. Possibly, says O., I think I look my best with it that way? Again: film gives out half-way through speech. Another wait. Light now completely changed: all angles readjusted. Again: Ah! that was it. *Stampiamo con entusiasmo*, and let's make just one more for *luck*. Again: French battleship, having seemingly changed its mind, recrosses camera from opposite direction, and Plane returns, neatly looping the loop. So on we go.

FEBRUARY 11TH

Work. Reappearance of silver Plane. O. convinced it's an Italian one, which makes it all, he assures us, far worse.

Dinner with Frédéric van Varsveld, the doctor who paints, and his wife. Both charming as ever.

FEBRUARY 12TH

Schnucks announces that Frédéric van V. is aghast at her Heart.

Am reading *Kreutzer Sonata* (incredibly enough for first time) and am filled with horror. This emotion not diminished by reading it between shots outside ill-smelling back walls of Château between Atlantic Ocean and Railway line, the latter, since trains are scarce, littered with personnel of *Othello*, and all of us squatting on camp stools and wardrobe baskets in teeth of sun and wind and clad in various articles of Carpaccio costume mingled with twentieth-century oddments: Schnucks in pearl hair-net and slacks; Hilton as rather crumpled edition of English gent on fishing holiday; Fanto in remnants of smart Riviera kit; Gigonzac, doubling Montano for distance shots, in relentlessly complete early Renaissance finery; Gouzy and Alcaide (to-day referred to by Orson as America's Most Leaden Backside) in anything that catches their fancy; Orson in steel armour, white burnous, blue linen pants and what appear to be football boots; self in repellent leather tunic, wig, hat, and modern trousers tailored in Viterbo (Children dear, was it yesterday?). We all wander about between intervals of squatting and wonder when the technicians will be ready for us, and Gouzy offers us dainties from apparently inexhaustible tuck-box. The motley sight we make is watched with tireless interest by hundreds of Arabs lined up on far side of railway track, their respectful silence occasionally broken by guttural Screams owing to police action when one of them, at regular intervals of uncontrollable enthusiasm, tries to break through lines to join us. Cannot imagine what they find to watch or enthuse over.

Small Arab boy of some six summers engaged by Orson to play page to Desdemona: a minute dusky beauty in a peak-hooded burnous several sizes too large for him. His name is Abdullah Ben Mohamet and his foster parents seem only too anxious to sell him to us, as he was, at the age of two, discovered by them tied to the very railway track where we are now working, having been abandoned there by his real parents (untraceable) to hideous death of the Anna Karenina variety but without his wishing it. He has been ordered a suit of velvets, satins, and jewels, also vast pink silk turban with pearls and an aigrette, and will probably never settle down to his burnous and all it implies with any satisfaction again. Familiar background of tragedy coupled with radiantly confident smile and burning eyes make me feel squeamish and shocked: there is something profoundly and catastrophically sad about very small and very gay children.

FEBRUARY 13TH

Work all day.

Abdullah Ben M. attired in splendour: face not dark enough for photographic values so has to be painted by Vasco, who tut-tuts disapprovingly and repeats 'Siamo in Africa'. Abdullah Ben M. (beauty completely obliterated by paint) is unaffectedly delighted and gobbles up incredible amount of food at picnic lunch, including several hundred grammes of cooked Ham (surely forbidden by his religion?), also turns up his nose at erstwhile companions, who return the compliment with guttural epithets, probably of obscene nature, as he shrieks back with raging eloquence and vivacity and shows admirably white teeth.

Later. Work to-day was scrappy and haunted by series of busy French journalists and photographers, but enacted in place of incredible charm: high brown battlemented walls of the city cutting into the sky and single round hillside over the sea enamelled with mustard-flowers and marigolds and speckled with white-robed women, their faces veiled in Pea-cock Green. The high-pitching of all this so dazzled me with pleasure, I found it hard to concentrate, especially as O. spent entire day perching me on dizzy heights in sardonic contemplation of deeds below. (Can he be planning my destruction?)

Police very active dispersing admirers, and one splendid row between two Arabs and three Jews (the first I have witnessed in Morocco) as to which of the two nations pro-duced the finest cooks. Large emotional gamut employed in a sort of French for our benefit, but no physical violence offered by either side: felt myself pro-Arab from sentimental preference as I place laughter higher than business acumen, but was held back by the fact that I prefer, on the whole, Kosher to Kouskous. Lightning decision to travel to Mazagan almost at once. H. to leave to-night, and O. and self to-morrow.

MAZAGAN. FEBRUARY 14TH

Orson disappeared to unknown destination: may be the Moon but suspect Casablanca. So I drove here with Julien through brilliant morning over high grassy hills by the sea. Mazagan all that I suspected, and discovered Hilton and the others in indescribable hotel described, I believe correctly, as the best in the town. Everyone too depressed to get out of bed but Schnucks, who darted about with Black Rag Doll declaring that it reminds her of the dear old days on tour in small French towns (can well believe it), adding that with a few flowers and a simple (but well-cooked) meal she can make herself happy anywhere. Maybe she can: but judging by smell mounting from kitchen think it unlikely that her second stipulation will be granted. Staff, however, consisting of Jewish waiter and Arab *valet* and *femme de chambre*, turn out, as so often happens in dingy hostelries, charming, obliging, and solicitous for our comfort.

Back still under treatment, so hauled H., who looked dazed and said every bone in his body ached, from his bed and we went to dig out Dr. Jean Lauzié, armed with letter from Fred van V. Found Lauzié in surgery in the Mellah (though he's French not Jewish) in entrancing fifteenth-century house like a set for a Goldoni translated into Arabic, if you see what I mean. White twisted square of a courtyard with arches, staircases, a penthouse window with under-ceilings in carved cedar-wood, sly little balconies, bird-cages, crooked alcoves, pots of flowers and an enormous and very sinuous vine. Lauzié himself most likeable, very suitably impressed by sufferings and took intelligently lenient view of diet. Drove us back to hotel, said he felt himself *isolé* in *la vie bête et bornée de Mazagan* (have no doubt he does) and could he come and see us at work, and would we dine some evening at his flat in the new French town?

Later. Reappearance of Orson looking as if he had been pulled through several hedges in all sorts of directions. *What has he been up to?* Have explored town with him and Hilton and seen the cistern where we are to work. My God!

Its beauty, of undeniable and bewildering quality, only equalled by its enormous size, foetid, clinging air, and general aspect of nameless doom. It lies in the heart of the Mellah, a few yards distant from the doctor's surgery; it was built in the early half of the fifteenth century by Portuguese artists of satanic genius, less, one would say, for purposes of technicalities concerning water supply than for inspiring of deeds of horror by such families as the Borgia, of breeding of toads and armadillos, or of prenatal setting for unwritten masterpieces by Baudelaire or Poe. Ominous dark ceiling of stone is supported by scores of heavy pillared arches that soar into the dusk like the wings of bats; every sound causes faint echoes to reverberate from unexplored recesses; squat doorways lead the eyes (but not the feet, no, not the faltering feet!) to swiftly descending stairways; surrounding cloisters, half visible in the gloom, seem to be full of dull murmurings, yet a damp, dripping silence engulfs you as you step fearfully over the threshold. Familiar sight of dear Micky Khadásh and of Marc the master carpenter, both of them the soul of brawn and scepticism, cheerfully tapping and hammering at switches and rostrum and surrounded by well-known members of technical staff, cannot disperse the macabre sorcery of the place, which I suddenly realise would probably, in the hands of any modern director but Orson, be utilised as background for mystery-farce starring Abbot and Costello.

Such is our century. Especially suggestive to present-day mood of debunkment and caricature would be the activities of A. & C. with Messrs. Karloff and Lugosi somewhere about, as entire centre of floor—some hundred feet square or rather round—is flooded, causing arches to be reflected as in a wizard's mirror, and offering endless opportunities for horseplay of splash-bang variety, but Orson, again backed by Hilton, who is to direct these sequences, has decided on it for long-distance shots of Iago-engineered brawl between Cassio, Roderigo, and Montano. These, in absence of original cast, are still doubled respectively by Renzo, lean Italian boy, Paddy (my name for him has stuck) Dally, well-nourished French assistant director, and the poetic Gigonzac who, Schnucks tells me, has abandoned entire former life and knows his Destiny is to become a Star. Many days of work in Portuguese Cistern will probably result in his becoming a Rheumatic, but indeed that applies to us all.

Was hoping that my work as Iago could also be doubled and hear indeed that elegant Frenchman named Racine has been inspected already and is not only of same build as myself but fanatically eager to assist.

Small and unpleasing lap-dog also discovered to double the revolting Riquette of Mogador, at whose hands (or paws) I suffered last summer. It is said to be a male, but what to celluloid is sex?

Heaven knows what next few days' work will be like, especially as Orson tells me with demoniac glee (he's not of course in this sequence and H., as stated, will be directing) that colour value of water is too pale for film and must be dyed *black* with Aniline Dyes, so our tights and shoes as well as our feet, ankles and legs to mid-calf likely to be stained a sombre grey *in saecula saeculorum*.

FEBRUARY 15TH

O. again disappeared, this time with Belle of Stockholm, nobody can say where. Not even Schnucks, not even Gouzy. H. and I spend our time talking of future: this complicated by our having no idea of what it is likely to be for at least a year.

FEBRUARY 16TH

Work began this morning in Portugal's Answer to Poe, I mean the Cistern, for Orson has reappeared (looking as mysterious as his surroundings), and shouts directions about lighting for three hours without a single pause. Hilton, wearing immense pair of gum boots, is directing us, and splashes wildly to and fro across the dyed water as he arranges sword-fight between Renzo-Cassio, Dally-Roderigo, and Gigonzac-Montano. Involved and excessively wet work for us all, and the poor devils I have just mentioned get in for the worst of it as the business includes a lot of knocking of swords out of various hands into the water, and much punching and rolling and diving and kicking and plunging in order to regain them. Iago, wise man, contents himself with slipping cat-like behind various pillars, handing swords at odd moments to any of the gentlemen who find themselves with-out one, and with hissing or shouting such remarks as 'Hold ho!' or 'God's will, Gentlemen!' or even 'Diablo ho!' to anyone within reach. This didn't save me from getting my legs soaked or the rest of myself splashed from endless repetitions of the brawl, done in series of inconceivably short shots, each one of them taking what seemed to be hours and hours, and when the bits including me were finished I changed doublet and greaves with the enthusiastic Jeff, my French double (we have separate pairs of tights and shoes), who, while I am working, sits in a Singlet regardless of the freezing temperature and watches me with fanatical im-patience. So he works in all the long-distance shots, and both of us full of gratitude to Hilton, he for artistic and I for despicable reasons. Sensation of getting back into tights and shoes that are dank and stringy with the water, and into a doublet warm from Jeff's body, indescribable. The Mazagan dresser, an absent-minded adolescent of Spanish parentage with a passion for the films so great that he forgets everything I want and has to be yelled at, which causes pained expression, brings me coffee, hot towels, vapour rubs, and talcum, but nothing restores the circulation. Will probably develop rheumatic fever if this continues: the same fate doubtless in store for Dally and the others, to say nothing of the extras, of which there are scores and scores, all of them alternatively splashing and screaming all over the flooded floor and sub-sequently shivering in corners.

Orson and Hilton obsessed, when things are slack, by guessing games of enormous complication, and all of us are

roped in to play with them. Example: 'He is the most loved
and hated political figure of modern times and speaks the
language of his country with a strong foreign accent: who is
he?' and it turns out to be Stalin. ('Because he's a Georgian of
course, you silly cow,' says Hilton to Mary Alcaide, who
didn't know it.) One of my questions was, 'She sat, world-
famous and weary, on a property throne, and lunched at the
rest hour in Egypt or Rome or wherever the fancy took her,
but all within a few feet of the same stage,' and nobody
guessed it was Sarah Bernhardt because they hadn't read
Louis Vermeille's book and didn't know this was one of her
habits, but the popularity of this game, as of another one
called 'Five letters of the Alphabet', now frowned on by
Orson as Schnucks knows all the answers and wins every
time. She sits, dressed in her milk-white Desdemona gown
in the gloom and glare of the set, looking like the still un-
ravished bride of Tumult, eating Gouzy's grapes, drinking
Barbara's coffee, and complacently winning all the games,
and then, her mood changing, she gets into blue linen overalls and rushes all over the town to bring us tea and cakes;
and one day of life all herded together in that dripping subterranean vault has made us feel that we are prisoners in
an eternal night.

FEBRUARY 19TH

Worked for three days in the Vault but had a change to-day
and did the Cage Scene down at the harbour. This Orson's
invention and I've been dreading it for months. 'The time,
the place, the torture; O! enforce it' is to become in the film
a visual fact, so into a minute and excessively uncomfortable
cage I go, and am hauled up on a dangerously squeaking
chain to an immense height by a tower over the sea to have
my eyes plucked out by crows, yelling insults as I go. Felt
much more inclined to yell 'Help, help!' but refrained, and
went whirling up about a dozen times, to immense delight

of the Arab population who gathered in their hundreds to see the show, their favourite part of it being each descent when the cage with me in it was plumped slowly and unsteadily into the water. Faint applause every time this happened, but respectful silence on my upward flight. Profoundly unpleasant morning.

FEBRUARY 21ST

Back to the Underworld. Frightful series of scenes involving much rushing up and down of steps (in greaves) followed closely by hordes of extras, all of them apparently chosen for gruesome aspect and bird-brains and possessing inordinate passion for tripping me up, treading on my feet, and sticking swords in my backside. What the scenes were about I hadn't the faintest notion and didn't dare ask, as H. and O. both in Wagnerian rages, and in the intervals of screaming at me looked at each other with shaking heads and faint pitying smiles. So spent the day flying obediently up and down stairs brandishing a sword (am strongly convinced it was the wrong one and so is Gouzy, who assures me in panicky mixture of German, French, and English that nobody will notice), also opening and closing doors, gazing camera left with tense expression at nobody at all, turning, twisting, peering through windows, and getting myself kicked, prodded, slapped, pushed, and trodden on by extras till I was black and blue.

Sensation caused by sudden appearance of Abdullah Ben Mohamet, the Arab page-boy from Safi, now a complete movie star of slightly sinister aspect with huge pot belly, clothed in brand-new blue jersey, embroidered pants, hideous new canvas shoes, new djelabah, and shaven head. Made a bee-line for Gouzy and began devouring goodies out of her tuck basket: she, it seems, is responsible for shaven head. Found out later that he is officially under her care in Mazagan and is to resume work to-morrow, and can only say that, judging by his figure, they'll have to let out his clothes several inches or give him some sort of Maternity outfit.

FEBRUARY 22ND

Changes at the hotel: Orson has long since abandoned it and fled with Barbara to Casablanca, whither he sometimes drives us after the day's work for dinner, and Schnucks and Mary have betaken themselves to stay with my French double, Jeff What's-his-name, who lives in a very peculiar way on the edge of a green public park whence peacocks wander into his garden and sometimes into the house. So Schnucks does all the cooking and is transformed into a skilled if somewhat flushed *cuisinière*, and screams alternatively at the Arab *bonne* and the peacocks as she whisks up eggs and washes salad, and slices tomatoes and garlic, and grills *entrecôtes*—'so good for us, Mr. Micheál, because it doesn't add a single centimetre to the waistline'—and when she's not doing this she flies round the market with a straw basket haggling for cheese and chickens.

Hilton and I are alone now in the hotel and are regarded with great favour by Madame because we have remained so loyal, and the staff attends to our every want and bestows on us whatever is going in the way of comfort. This very essential as the work is desperate: we're still Underground and all the scenes we shoot there (usual movie atmosphere of an indeterminate first dress rehearsal) are inspired with violence and concerned with wrestling-matches, dagger-fights, and fisticuffs, and to-day Dally, looking on the verge of despair in Bob Coote's silks and velvets and picture hat, was ordered to jump down an extremely deep and unattractive well in the centre of the flood in order to rescue the lap-dog (double for Riquette). He, Renzo, and Gigonzac all dripping by 11 a.m. and remained in this condition and spattered with mud till twilight, when they were sent home to dine. Pondered, on hearing Gigonzac's heartrending sneezes, on Schnucks's account of his giving up All for a film career, and thought up sad little story à la Maupassant of handsome but headstrong *père de famille* who had staked his All on some artistic ambition and had, during his first week at it, caught pneumonia and died. These gloomy imaginings relieved for the moment by meeting him after dinner looking the picture of health, sneezing miraculously vanished, and in condition of scintillating enthusiasm ('ah, moi, vous savez, c'est pour la vie tumultueuse d'artiste!'), and proceeded myself to nightmarish scene of my rushing from justice after Emilia's death (taken in Rome some time last year) and being pursued by Montano's men. Worked till 3 a.m.

FEBRUARY 23RD

Finished work at five to-day—it's the end of our Underground Movement—and dined with Jean Lauzié, the doctor, and his wife and little boy. Jean played records to us afterwards of Chopin, Bach, and Debussy. Peaceful and perfect evening.

MOGADOR. FEBRUARY 25TH

Back to Mogador! (*Would the saga never end, he wondered, gazing up and down the old familiar Place du Chayla, and receiving vociferous welcomes from the faithful natives on all sides. For there were the same old square shuttered houses with their flat roofs and the brilliant Moorish sky above them, the same palms, gently rustling in the breeze, the same mosques and palaces, the same smiling Arabs in white and grave Jews in black, the same picturesque sights and smells as of yore, with the dear old Citadel breasting so bravely the Atlantic rollers, and all the ghosts of vanished playmates and comrades of his earliest days to whisper in his ears as dusk fell softly over the quiet streets.*) There, that's the sort of style I like, with perhaps a musical accompaniment from the works of Amy Woodford-Finden.

A row about Rooms when we arrived. We have now settled in the Beau Rivage, so that for first time in Mogador we eat and sleep under the same roof. A leaking pipe (from the bidet) had caused an otherwise perfect room to bear sinister resemblance to the Portuguese Cistern at Mazagan, which for all its beauty I hope never to lay eyes on again except in the complete film of the tragedy of *Othello*, so I ranged all my effects (that sounds very French, what is happening to my English?), I mean I placed all my belongings on high shelves and the tops of wardrobes and, having demanded a plumber, went disgustedly for a walk with Hilton. When I returned I found the floor mopped up and the pipes bandaged and all Schnucks's things in the room, and my own were in hers, which is on the same landing, and she wouldn't hear of changing back.

Feel ashamed of my acceptance and am bound to observe that Schnucks has not only a sweet but also a noble side to her nature, and when I remember the gibes I've made at her in my heart and probably in these pages I am all confusion. My only comfort is that she herself is all moods and changes—this indeed is for me a part of her endless and often infuriating interest—and her present incarnation as a gay and generous saint will probably be counteracted to-morrow by the reappearance of Demon Queen, Indestructible Fury, and Ivory and Gold Medusa. At present there is no signs of these as she sits with folded hands like Little Beth, Anne Brontë, Thérèse of Lisieux, or what you will, at the window, with Black Rag Louis on her lap, gazing out at the Mosque and thinking, she assures me (what are you dreaming of, *chérie*, with that Maeterlinck expression?), about Maman, far, far away in Canada. Darling Schnucks.

Work begins to-morrow at one of the Old Spots by the Harbour, with self dishevelled and mis-shaven on my way to be put in the cage (already done at Mazagan), with iron dog-collar studded with long spikes round my neck, and being dragged backwards through the dust by more Arab extras headed by Dally.

FEBRUARY 26TH

Emerged from Beau Rivage accompanied by Vasco, who hovered round me informing me that we were in Africa and must be prepared to face El Destino (he still speaks Spanish to me: my Italian gets hazier and hazier) in whatever guise it chose to present itself, and was made up with great skill to look haggard and unshaven (an unnecessary procedure as I already looked both) in the middle of the square between the public gardens and the sea. Fresh blue and yellow morning, with a stiff breeze and hundreds of Arabs garbed as soldiers and bossed about by Gouzy, who darted up and down in white slacks and an array of scarves munching a half-metre of *belegtes Butterbrod*. Observed in their midst the figure of Mohamet, who used to be porter at the Hôtel de Paris and has left his job for one reason or another and decided to be an actor, and who hovered near me saying from time to time '*Chic, quand même, n'est ce pas, Monsieur Mac, la vie de Vedette?*' till he was chased away by Micky the Electrician, an Algerian Turk who looks like a Boxer and reads Rimbaud and Prévert and is of great intelligence (whatever Orson, who calls him Turkish Delight, may say), as well as being my greatest champion, who thinks every one annoys me, which they don't, but I appreciate his sentiment. Orson and Hilton appeared together wearing withdrawn and pregnant expressions, dog-collar was fastened to my neck, clanking chain to dog-collar, and Dally and small band of ruffians to clanking chain, and work began. Was hauled six times forwards and seven times backwards (making thirteen in all) through mocking crowds; poor Dally, who is the soul of gentleness, being rated soundly for not tugging at the chain with sufficient ferocity, and by noon the entire thing pronounced a failure. So we do it all over again to-morrow.

Am worn to a shadow and feel amazingly well. Think this sort of commando training must really be very good for one's body even though the soul may starve for it. Spent the evening talking in glutinous mixture of Spanish, English, and Italian about Dante's *Inferno*, Milton's *Paradise Lost*, and the principles of Reincarnation with Troianni, who works the camera with Fanto and is a highly cultivated young man with a face like a Byzantine courtier, and with Mary Alcaide. Mary rose from the table at length and said Well, she always thought she wanted a new religion but she guessed it was simpler to stay right where she was (which was in a perfectly pleasant condition of giving everything the benefit of the doubt) or else to go right ahead and enter a monastery and substitute thinking for praying, and that now she felt she'd better go for a walk.

FEBRUARY 27TH

Repetition of agonising scene with Dog-collar. Dally more solicitous and more shouted at than ever, as he incites band of torturers to drag me up the same long slope where I made the 'Lechery, by this hand!' scene with Bob Coote and chased him over the tram tracks to his mark on the wall so many centuries ago. Poor Dally! his face a study of solicitous torment for fear a jerk too strong at the chain should break my neck. Meanwhile the extras behind him were tugging like mad and leaping with sadistic pleasure as they tugged, and being chased away by Micky (Turkish Delight) between the bouts of shooting. All a great success to-day, and scene added of Dally wrenching the dog-collar from my swollen and purple neck and hurling me into the cage, where I consoled myself by yelling, 'If she'd been blest she never could have loved the Moor' through the bars.

Afternoon spent on the beach with my discovery of Othello's body (it was the double's) lying prone and epileptic on pile of unspeakable rocks (place as popular for toilet purposes as ever) under tearing Atlantic gale.

Jewish dinner-party to-night at house of rich merchant; we ate strange delicacies and drank strange wines and were waited on by daughters of the house, a chorus of Dazzling Salomés. Citron-yellow walls, black hair, green eyes.

MARCH IST

These days have acquired the fly-away pace of a musical coda—not an awfully good composer—a sort of Orpheus in the Underworld gallop to end things up. Dally's wife has arrived from Paris, a tall, quiet, comely creature who, entering the scene at its latest and most abandoned phase, stands aghast at the whirling riot of it all and doubtless wonders what it is about. Orson, Hilton, and the rest of us fly from one location to another, frequently driven by Gouzy in her bumping little car, which is now tied together with string, or else perched on a jeep among gangs of Italian technicians and followed by hooting lorries and mobs of cheering Arabs and Jews (a good half of the male population is in armour and the rest still fighting for jobs), and on arrival at the various destinations a swarming, fluttering activity begins, punctuated by Orson's voice as, mounted on a pile of boxes with Hilton at his side waving his stick and hissing into his ears various diabolical observations, he yells, 'No no, not that way, Goddammit, pull that moron's helmet down! No, not down to his chin, you pronk! just over his eyes. Hey! stop waving your hands about, you in green. Hilton, look at that Great Big Piece in green. Oh my God! how did that one get here anyway? Gouzy, tell him in Siamese! Tell that great big Cissy in green to get his ass off the set. Out! Scram, Sister! Now all of you to the left, I said Left! To the Left, Goddammit! Stop that coal-black cretin holding his helmet on! Dally, stop him! Action! I said Action! Cut! Action, Goddammit!'

And all the while the sun beats down and the waves lash

up and Vasco says '*Mama mia! Siamo in Africa!*' and Turkish Delight shouts '*Fouttez-moi la paix, vous autres!*' and Schnucks murmurs 'I think it's my religion that gets me through, don't you think so too, Mr. Micheál?' and we whirl from quayside to ocean strand and from citadel to dungeon steps under the fish-market, and now at last the film is nearly done. It's nearly over. All that will remain in a few days' time will be the Senate scene, and that, Orson tells us, leaning back in a chair at the Club and drinking Pernod after the day's madness is checked by the sinking of the sun, will be achieved in a little over a week's work at Perugia at some not far-off date, and will not concern me as Iago, though I am to be invited there for a ten days' Rest.

Can only conclude that if Perugia turns out as the last few days have done in Mogador it might be more restful, though admittedly less exciting, to spend the time in Assisi, or even in Dublin.

MARCH 4TH

Superb setting near the harbour for scenes of the arrival of Lodovico, with tents and carpets and *pavillons* and little boats out on the water, and scores of soldiers with spears and fluttering pennons: the whole pageantry of it somehow suggestive, in its indescribable grace and gaiety and purity, of Monteverdi.

MARCH 7TH

Tricky bit of business in the pre-epileptic fit scene, at last achieved, of 'Lie with her, lie on her.' This taken in a long travelling-shot against a wall by the sea under a broken roof of slats and branches which cast their shadows on us as we walked and paused and walked again over most intricate network of tram-tracks, and when I stumbled on the second take Orson said 'Now now, Ireland's Answer to Nijinsky, let's do it again!' So we did, and all was well this time though he insisted on a few more takes and there were seven in all, and to-day is the seventh of March, and Hilton can say what he likes but there *is* something in it, for when it was all over and the sun had gone down once more into the sea, Orson went through the usual kissing ceremony, inevitable when he has got some load off his mind or his chest or wherever he keeps his loads, and said: 'Mr. Mac Liammóir, I am happy to tell you you are now an out-of-work actor. You have finished Iago.'

So after that we drank some champagne at the club and I felt a little sad and a little glad. Glad because it will be a good thing to get back to a week or two in Paris and make our plans for the next film, the Irish one, or the Carmilla one or whatever the hell it's going to be, and to hear of Orson's latest projects, which will probably include another world-tour or two and the squeezing of the last week's Senate scene in Perugia *en route*, and organising a festival in the Vatican if we should happen to pass through Rome. And it will be better still to get back to Ireland and the theatre and Arthur and Rachel, and the garden again, and one's own rhythm and one's own books, and all that goes to make up one's life. And it will be sad because we've emerged from another adventure, Hilton and I, and we both like adventures (within and often without reason, and this has been both). And besides, it's going to be a twisting, searing, wrenching sort of thing to say good-bye to Mogador, where, for me, the film began and ended. And most of all it's going to be sad to see them dwindle into the distance, these friends and fellow-adventurers that have remained to the last.

Already I see them in my mind's eye as if painted on a gauze, through which the back-stage lighting will presently shine, revealing other scenes and other characters, and I will feel that it has only been a painting on a gauze after all. But a very beautiful one, in the manner of a Primitive, I think, with the winged and bodiless cherub heads of Schnucks and

Mary and Barbara floating in jocund fashion over a hierarchy of stalwart mail-clad figures of Venetian nobles and soldiers. And Fay with her two angels trumpeting and fiddling. And all three of them cut out in blue and gold against a background of victorious armies and bright painted ships, with the Children of Jehovah and the Children of the Prophet rampant on a field of unravelled celluloid. And then Trauner and Dally and Brizzi and dear Fanto and the rest of them standing in serried ranks, the banners of their trades a-flutter stiffly above their heads. And behind and beyond them all is Orson, mysteriously grimacing as he lolls towards them with hands outstretched, waving Godspeed from his rolling banks of cumulus and thunder-cloud, the Painted Lightning forked ambiguously behind his head.